Information Tec

An Introduction

Information Technology
An Introduction

Fourth Edition

Peter Zorkoczy & Nicholas Heap
The Open University

PITMAN
PUBLISHING

PITMAN PUBLISHING
128 Long Acre, London WC2E 9AN

A Division of Longman Group Limited

First published in Great Britain 1982
Second edition 1985
Third edition 1990
Fourth edition 1995

© P. Zorkoczy & N. Heap 1995

British Library Cataloguing in Publication Data
A CIP catalogue record for this book can be obtained fom the British Library.

ISBN 0 273 60591 7

10 9 8 7 6 5 4 3 2 1

Printed in England by Clays Ltd, St Ives plc

The Publishers' policy is to use paper manufactured from sustainable forests.

Contents

Preface to the fourth edition

It is over a decade since the first edition was published and so much has changed that it has become a challenge to provide coverage in a text of introductory length. Perhaps the most significant characteristic of information technology though is the rate of change and adaptation. In 1981 personal computing was for a privileged few, electronic mail was only available to participants of military projects, and cellular phone systems were just ideas in a research laboratory. In fifteen years the cost-performance of the technology has reached the point where the majority of office workers start their day by turning on the computer, which is now networked for file-sharing and international electronic-mail services. Gone are the cryptic command-based dialogues that left so many users wondering what 'General read failure!' meant, to be replaced by graphic interfaces with menus, icons and multiple windows. Dictating to the computer is now a reality, as are video and audio conferences over the latest digital networks. Working away from the office is no longer synonymous with 'out of touch'. The mobile workforce can choose from a variety of notebook computers and personal digital assistants complete with fax-modems connected to cellular digital networks. Optical disc technology will soon provide the basic distribution medium for music, video and software and all can be combined into a single multimedia presentation or learning package.

The pervasion of information technology into work and family life has forced designers to reconsider the usability of their systems and user-centred design as now crucial to commercial success. This shift of focus prompted the authors to include an entirely new section on human-computer interaction, covering five major headings: designing for the user; interactions and dialogues; input devices; visual systems; speech systems; and health and safety.

Parts I and II have been substantially revised to reflect the changes in both the technology and the applications and new sections have been added to cover digital audio recording, multimedia and open systems.

Although a collaborative work, the responsibility for the final version rests squarely with NH, who has persisted with the intricacies of page layouts, embedded objects and encapsulated postscript. The printable version of the book represents almost 40 megabytes of data, with a further 55 megabytes of graphics and eps files.

Peter Zorkoczy and *Nick Heap*, July 1994

Part 1

1 About information technology

What's in a name? 'Information Technology' is a relatively recent and perhaps not particularly well-chosen addition to the English language. It has its counterparts in the French 'informatique' and the Russian 'informatika'. For many people, 'information technology' is synonymous with 'the new technology' – the use of microprocessor-based machines: microcomputers, automated equipment, word processors and the like. But the use of man-made tools for the collection, generation, communication, recording, re-arrangement and exploitation of information goes back in time much beyond the present 'micro-revolution'. For others, the significance of the introduction of a new term, information technology, is the belief that the principles, practice and terminology of information handling can be treated on a unified, systematic basis. Cynics may say that the words 'information technology' simply represent an attempt to make respectable some commercially motivated developments in electronics, and politically motivated moves to control the access to information.

Whatever is the truth behind these attitudes, to qualify as a 'technology', in the sense of being 'a practice of an applied science' (Oxford English Dictionary), there has to be a recognised science of information. Of course, the words 'information science' have been used, and are being used, to refer to a branch of librarianship dealing with the automatic retrieval of printed documents. But to rely purely on this aspect of information handling for parentage would be too restrictive for this infant field of technology. More properly, one must look towards the science of electronic systems and to computer science to legitimise the products of their convergence.

Even these sciences have their sceptics and it will be only when the science of information reaches a maturity of its own that one can use the name 'information technology' in any more than a loose way. We shall, therefore, not formulate a precise definition at this stage, but rather attempt to illustrate by examples, and describe in terms of constituent parts, the subject that is currently taking shape under the umbrella term of 'information technology'.

The motivating forces There are a number of reasons why information technology is becoming a subject of wide-ranging discussion and study. Each of these reasons is significant on its own, but by acting together, as they are doing at the present time, they are adding urgency to the need to understand the technical and social issues involved. From a *social* point of view, information technology promises changes in the way we communicate and reach decisions. Even in its era before the computer, progress in telecommunications – for example, telephone, radio and television – opened out horizons for individuals and society at large, and so placed at the disposal of people information about distant events and new ideas. This has helped us to understand some of the complexities of the surrounding world, but has in turn increased that complexity by making possible a greater degree of interaction among people.

The application of the computer to information handling has contributed a new tool and a new dimension of complexity, through its ability to store and process vast amounts of data at high speed. For many decades now, data gathering devices (e.g. measuring instruments) have increasingly extended the accessible portion of the physical world and added to the already vast stock of scientific and technical information. Improved technological tools for collecting data about people have encouraged administrative applications of information technology. However, the cost and complexity of these tools have made them the virtual monopoly of the state and of large commercial enterprises. This created a potentially threatening opportunity for highly centralised control and decision-making. Recent technology developments in microelectronics have somewhat changed this situation by reducing the price of some data handling tools and making them more widely available. But has the danger of information technology being used for increased control of peoples' lives been averted completely? The answer can be gained only through better understanding of the technology and its implications.

In parallel with the growth of information resources, there has been a significant social change: a shift in the profile of the working population towards service-related jobs and in particular information processing.

Fig. 1.1 Changes in the percentage of employees in various sectors of the economy of Great Britain.. (Source: Britain 1994: An official handbook. HMSO)

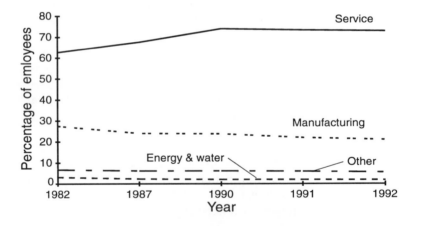

In Great Britain, for example, the proportion of the labour force employed in service-related sectors of the economy increased from about 46% to nearly 73% between 1961 and 1992. Fig. 1.1 above shows the underlying trends. Whilst general classifications of employment are readily available, it is much more difficult to determine how many employees might be regarded as 'information workers'; that is those whose daily tasks involves the processing of information. Table 1.1 does show a detailed breakdown of information workers for 1961, 1978 and 1987, but the classifications are continually changing, making comparison with later years more difficult. What is clear however, is that the trend toward greater use of information systems continues.

	Number employed (millions)		
	1961	1978	1987
Administrative, technical and clerical staff in manufacturing industry	2.00	2.06	1.34
Public administration	1.40	1.63	1.59
Insurance, banking, finance	0.68	1.15	2.30
Professional and scientific services (education, health care, communication, etc.)	2.12	3.68	4.25
Totals	**6.20**	**8.52**	**9.48**
Percentage of labour force (not including self-employed and the armed forces)	29.40	37.40	44.50

Table 1.1 Employment in information-related sectors in Great Britain 1961–1987. (Source: Department of Employment)

Note that these figures relate to employer classification, rather than employee, or occupational groups. There are no figures being issued for the latter in the United Kingdom.

In the United States the trends show a similar pattern, as indicated by Fig. 1.2 . Note that, by about 1960, more people were engaged in the handling of information than in producing food, manufacturing goods or providing services. The breakdown of the information-sector occupations indicates how the steady increase in the number of professional and technical workers, on the one hand, and managers and administrators on the other, was accompanied by an increase in the number of their support staff – the clerical workers.

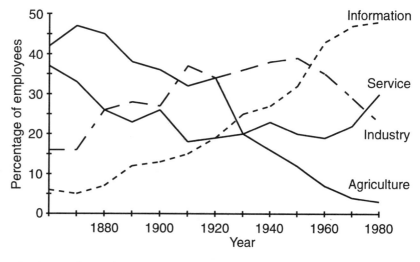

Fig. 1.2 Changes in the percentage of employees in various sectors of the United States economy. (Source: US Bureau of Labor Statistics)

Such social trends are not easily reversed, and there is no reason to believe that the information sector will lose its dominant position in the employment field. Information technology, then, will have a direct impact on the majority of the working population of developed countries.

From an *economic* viewpoint, the data in Table 1.1 and Figs. 1.1 and 1.2 indicate a growing imbalance between traditionally 'wealth-producing' and 'overhead' occupations. Information handling is highly labour-intensive, and information workers command substantial remuneration. Yet, the value of the output of such workers is difficult to measure. How does one compare the 'output' of a teacher or a researcher with that of, say, a production-line operative?

In the absence of reliable measures of relative productivities, the traditional response of employers is to attempt to balance the books in economic terms, by limiting overhead expenditures. As the most important component of this is labour costs, industry and government are turning towards information technology as a possible means of expenditure control. After all, it is argued, technology has a reasonable record in automating some production tasks; should it not be able to do the same in information handling?

What is the true cost of information? What is its market value? How does it fit into the present framework of economic decision-making? Attempts to provide answers to questions of this type furnish the second source of incentives to study information technology.

The third stimulus comes from the industries which have recently grown up around information-related products, in particular in microelectronics. Manufacturers already active in the computer and telecommunication fields – the corner-stones of information technology – have been joined by the silicon-chip industry in an attempt to open up new markets for their products: the office, the school, the publishing industry – the very places where information is in the forefront of interest. These manufacturers can be expected to turn out a vast range of products aimed at the population at large. But, to a large extent, the rapid progress in microelectronics caught the 'traditional' computer world unprepared for the greatly increased range of potential applications of its products. The engineering know-how is there, but it is still very much visible behind the thinly spread expertise on where and how to apply information technology, so that its *users* derive maximum benefit. In other words, at the present time, information technology is very much technology-led. Both the manufacturers and their customers require urgent answers to questions about the appropriateness and timeliness of various products. Such questions can be properly treated only by developing a better understanding of how the technology can complement human information handling.

Lastly, from the viewpoint of the *individual*, the possession and accessibility of information are becoming matters of personal importance. In societies made information-aware by computerisation, communication technology, and shifting job patterns, the possession of information is increasingly seen as a key to professional advancement. So the control of access to information could, even more than before, become an expression of power, a weapon to be used by, or against, the individual. The growth of information technology has already given rise to concern about diminished individual freedom (see, for example, Carlson in *Information Technology Serving Society*, Pergamon, 1979). At the same time, it is placing at the individual's disposal vast resources of information, and more accessible means of voicing an informed opinion.

So, will information technology be, and be seen to be, a means towards the greater, rather than the more restricted, freedom of the individual? No answer to this question is possible without a better understanding of the technical and social issues involved and without an informed public discussion of the alternative courses of progress.

Seen from these four viewpoints – those of society, economics, technology and the individual first – the common element of information technology is the concept of *information.*

What is information?

People have a surprising range of ideas on what information is. (Just try asking a few people to define it.) Even dictionaries cannot agree. The *Oxford English Dictionary* gives it as 'that of which one is apprised or told; intelligence, news'. Another dictionary simply equates it to knowledge: 'that which is known'. Yet other definitions emphasise the knowledge *transfer* aspect of information, calling it 'the communication of instructive knowledge', or 'the knowledge conveyed to the mind by a statement of fact'.

The cause of this diversity in the common usage of the term is that information is essentially intangible: we encounter it only operationally, through its subjective effects. We *derive* information from data – from observations from the world around us. We *convey* information by communication.

'Information is the *meaning* that a human expresses by, or extracts from, representations of facts and ideas, by means of the known conventions of the representations used' (*Guide to Concepts and Terms in Data Processing,* North Holland, 1971). This is in many ways an attractive definition, but it includes the word 'meaning', which is just as intangible and elusive as 'information'. (See, for example, Ogden and Richards, *The Meaning of Meaning,* Routledge & Kegan Paul, 1949.) An important point, to which the last definition calls our attention, is 'the known conventions of the representations used'. When the representation is a language, as it frequently is, the syntax and the semantics of the language form an assumed supporting structure for any information expressed through it.

For example, if we hear someone say, 'It is ninety-five in the shade', we can take this to mean that he is talking about temperature, that his numbers refer to degrees Fahrenheit, that the shade is not of any specific object, i.e. the temperature reading does not necessarily refer to only one place, etc. Consequently, by assuming that he employs the known conventions of the English language and culture, we can derive more information than was directly communicated by the original sentence.

The semantic and syntactic aspects of information occupy the attention of many linguists (see, for example, Bar-Hillel, *Language and Information,* Addison-Wesley, 1964), but have so far not led to a generally accepted definition of information. 'Information in most, if not all, of its connotations seems to rest upon the notion of *selection power*', Cherry tells us in his thought-provoking book *On Human Communication* (Science Editions, 1961). For example, we may think of a telephone directory as containing a great deal of information because each entry selects one person or organization, out of a very large number in the geographical area covered by the directory. It also links that person with a unique selection of digits (the telephone number) out of the millions of possible combinations of those digits. Moreover, the directory repeats this selection process for all the subscribers listed. The postal address given for a subscriber is also an example of the selective power of information. The address is located by a process of increasing refinement: area, town, street, house, etc.

Note that behind the selective aspect of information is the assumption of the existence of a finite, albeit large, number of alternatives which are known to *both* the originator and the user of that information. (Otherwise, the process is no longer that of selection.) Thus, in the case of names in a telephone directory, the possible alternatives are the various ways in which the letters of the alphabet can be combined. But the universe of knowables – concepts, ideas, facts, names, etc. – is practically *infinite*. This apparent impasse between what we may want to communicate and the way we communicate is resolved by separating the *content* of information from its *representation*.

The representation (symbols, signs, signals, etc.) can then indeed belong to a well-defined finite set (the alphabet, dots and dashes, etc.). The process of communication of information in that case becomes a process of communication of representations. New ideas will be communicated by new combinations of old signs. It is this totally objective way of looking at information transfer that is of interest to telecommunication engineers (and theoreticians), and lies at the basis of *information theory* (Hartley, 'The transmission of information', *Bell System Technical Journal*, 1928, p. 535; Shannon and Weaver, *The Mathematical Theory of Communication*, University of Illinois Press, 1949).

The quantity of information

Information theory quantifies information (more exactly, the signs carrying a message) as follows: it assumes that the more unpredictable the message (i.e. the sequence of signs) generated by a source, the more information is being transmitted. Information then is described in terms of the statistical rarity of signs, and their combinations, produced by a source. The recipient is assumed to be aware of the relative probability of occurrence of each sign, and of combinations of signs; the information simply directs the recipient to select one of these combinations – the selection process again. Note that by allowing for a prior knowledge of the probability of combinations, the theory includes an important characteristic of practical languages: redundancy. Redundancy, that is superfluousness, does not add to information, in this sense. It helps, however, in the detection and correction of errors which may occur during the transmission of the message.

Messages are transmitted by superimposing the signs on some form of physical medium – a carrier. The carrier may be paper, electromagnetic waves, magnetic tape, etc. Every carrier has associated with it a (theoretically) quantifiable limit of the amount of signs it can accommodate per unit space or unit time, and also of the amount of distortion it is likely to introduce into messages. Information theory tells us how to estimate these limits and, more importantly, how to represent (encode) messages so that when they are transmitted via a given carrier, the decoded message contains a minimum of errors.

By guiding telecommunication engineers towards achieving the accurate transmission of messages, information theory remains to this day a cornerstone of engineering practice. But, of course, accurate transmission of inaccurate information does not make that information any 'better'. The communication engineer does not, as a rule, concern himself with the content, or 'quality', of the information. The words 'better' and 'quality' reintroduce the element of subjective judgement into our notion of information, which we again consider to be the *combination of content and representation*. So let us look at some of the factors which may affect the quality of information in this wider sense.

The quality of information

We all expect information to be *reliable* and *accurate*. In other words, information should be in agreement with reality. The trustworthiness of information is increased if it can be *verified*, that is, corroborated by independent means. Information must be sufficiently *up-to-date* for the purpose that it is to be used. It must be *complete* and *precise*, allowing the recipient to select specific details according to need. If incomplete, the degree of uncertainty must be indicated, or else it should follow some well-recognised convention. For example, the statement 'It is sunny' is conventionally taken to mean that it is sunny at the time and the place where the statement is being made. Information must be *intelligible*, that is, comprehensible by the recipient. Again, there are rules, conventions and assumptions (of language, or symbols, etc.) which when obeyed ensure this aspect of the quality of information. These general characteristics of high-quality information may not be present in practical instances.

Low-quality information can be downright *misleading* or *distorted* (as a result of the deliberate action of the source or of the transmission process). It may be *inconsistent* with other information. It may be poorly presented, or even *incomprehensible* to the recipient. A noteworthy point here is that many products of information technology are aimed at detecting and, if possible, improving low-quality information before it reaches the recipient.

In addition to the general characteristics of high-quality information (such as one would expect from a public broadcasting or news service), there are certain desirable features associated with specific uses of information. For example, when a response is given to a well-specified inquiry, it should be *relevant* and *timely*; it should be in a form which is *conveniently handled* (interpreted, classified, stored, retrieved, updated, etc.) by the recipient; it should be of the appropriate *level of detail* and, if necessary, adequately *protected* (e.g. coded or the access to it controlled). People also appreciate if information is presented in an interesting and friendly way.

The above list is not intended to be comprehensive or uncontroversial. Its role is to encourage the reader to reconsider his or her views on what requirements to impose on existing and future products of information technology. If the quality of information is a controversial subject, a discussion of the value of information can lead into even more uncharted territory. However, this should not deter us from trying to identify some of the landmarks.

The value of information

In a reported study, branch managers of a bank were asked to rank four features affecting the quality of information made available to them (Neumann and Segev, 'A case study of user evaluation of information characteristics for systems improvement', *Information and Management*, 1979, p. 271). The four were: accuracy, content (the breadth or scope), recency (up-to-dateness) and frequency of presentation. The clear winner was content, with accuracy second.

On a more general level it has been stated (Gabor, *Lectures on Communication Theory*, MIT Press, 1951) that what people are prepared to pay money for is *exclusive* information and/or *predictive* information, the first being information tailored to the needs of the recipient, and the second enabling the recipient to select a particular action out of a whole range of possible actions. We can add to this that the perceived value of predictive information relates to the subjective value of the outcome of the selected action. For example, information on train departure times becomes the more 'valuable' the more crucial the purpose of the journey. Thus, the value of information is not an inherent or constant quality. It depends on the needs of the recipient and on the use to which it is put.

In the most general sense, information is valued for its *organising power*. High-quality information enables the recipient to make sense of the environment and to take action necessary to cope with changing circumstances. This power of information is rooted in the way it can represent physical and mental constructs, and is reflected by the dictionary definitions of the verb 'to inform': 'to arrange, to shape, to compose,' and also 'to form (the mind, character, etc.) especially by imparting learning or instruction' (*Oxford English Dictionary*).

A possibly helpful analogy here is to think of information as the building material for a personal or a collective model of the world. Any new piece of information contributes either to the overall structure of the model, or to its utilisation and testing. If, in addition, this new piece of information provides an important missing piece of the mental 'jigsaw' or helps to restructure it, we tend to attach greater value to it. To the extent that the model of the environment is internal to a person, the value of information is subjective. But for organisations, where the collective model involves transactions, data, rules, procedures, etc., it may be possible to make an objective comparison between the value of acquiring some piece of information and the cost associated with the acquisition process.

The cost of information

The cost of information is attributed to two main components: the intellectual labour involved in originating and handling it, and the non-human element made up by processing and storage equipment, distribution media, etc. The non-human costs are usually easier to quantify: it takes a certain amount of *energy* to form and transmit a representation of information, be it the spoken or written word, broadcast transmission, etc. If some physical record of the information is required, it also takes a certain amount of *material* to act as the carrier. Thus, a book, a magnetic tape or a filing card, for example, would have some inherent cost, quite apart from the production cost of the information which it carries. The equipment used in these tasks is priced on the open market.

When information is replicated in large volumes and is recorded on some physical medium, as would be the case with newspapers, books, records etc., the cost of the medium may well dominate the unit cost of the information-plus-medium. In such a case, the total product becomes a commodity, in the economic sense of that word. Thus, it can be bought and sold, and when exchanging hands, its ownership is clearly attributable.

The same is not true for 'pure' information. The originator of the information retains it, often together with legal rights to it, while also making it available to others. This fact, as well as the subjective nature of information, make it very difficult to treat it as a product or commodity. As a result, laws which attempt to treat information as an economic good – patent, trade secret, copyright or privacy laws, for instance – run into continuing problems of interpretation and enforcement. Partly to avoid these problems, 'pure' information is often given away virtually free irrespective of its cost (public information). At the other extreme, when the information has 'exclusivity value', the supplier is prepared to incur extra costs in protecting it for some time in the expectation of a high selling price (specialist reports, conferences, personalised advisory services, etc.).

Summary

Information technology has its origins in the technologies related to a restricted view of information: the generation, processing and distribution of *representations* of information. Examples are telecommunication and computer engineering, the data processing and office machinery industries. The products of these industries still form the bulk of information technology products. Progress in recent years has been towards the extension of this 'data engineering', or *telematics* to an increasing range of areas of application. This has brought with it an active interest in the human aspects of information (its quality, value, utilisation, etc.) or *informatics*. The new emphasis is reflected in, for example, a definition of information technology put forward in one US report.

> Information technology means the collection, storage, processing, dissemination and use of information. It is not confined to hardware and software, but acknowledges the importance of man and the goals he sets for this technology, the values employed in making these choices, the assessment criteria used to decide whether he is controlling the technology and is being enriched by it.

(Quoted in *Information Technology Serving Society*, edited by Chartrand and Morentz, Pergamon, 1979, p. 121).

A similar definition is favoured by the British Advisory Council for Applied Research and Development (*Report on Information Technology*, HM Stationery Office, 1980):

> The scientific, technological and engineering disciplines and the management techniques used in information handling and processing; their applications; computers and their interaction with men and machines; and associated social, economic and cultural matters.

With these views of information technology in mind, summarised in Fig. 1.3, let us look next at its uses and applications in various fields of human endeavour.

Fig. 1.3 The main
constituents of
information technology
and their inter-relation

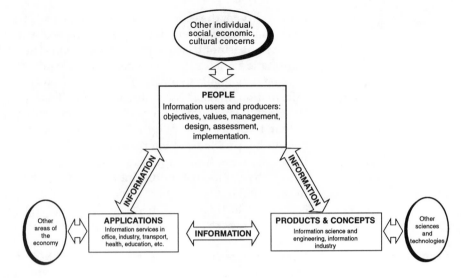

2 Information technology in action

Introduction

Information technology is advancing in two main directions: first, in the development of *products* (devices, systems) and *concepts* (ideas, procedures) which have a wide range of applicability wherever people deal with information; second, in the *application* of these products and concepts to specific areas of human activity. This chapter is about the second direction: it outlines information technology developments in the context of occupational and marketing areas, such as the office or the home. The emphasis here is on how the products and concepts appear to the users and what sort of changes they imply to existing ways of dealing with information. In the process, some of the emerging products and concepts believed to be of particular significance will be identified. A more detailed description of the products and of the concepts behind them will be taken up in subsequent chapters. One word of warning before starting: products, concepts, applications of information technology are currently in a state of rapid evolution. Sometimes it is very difficult to determine the stage of development of a particular product or idea from the published details. But for would-be users it is vital to know whether some new offering is

(a) what is already in routine use;
(b) what has just been introduced, or
(c) what is about to be introduced;
(d) what is currently in the research and development stage, and
(e) what someone thinks is technically possible.

In the descriptions that follow, distinctions will be made between what exists and what is possible, in terms of the state-of-the-art at the middle of the 1990s.

The range of applications of information technology is as wide as the range of activities where information is used. However, in terms of the number of jobs affected by it and the amount of effort, publicity and capital invested, one field stands out as the most significant area of work: the office. For example, in 1982 over 40 per cent of the US work force were office employees. By 1985, the figure had risen to over 50 per cent. So this is where we start our look at information technology in action. Following that, we shall turn to some other occupational areas listed in Table 1.1: the manufacturing industries, commercial, financial and communication services, health care, education and training, and finally to where we are all involved – the home.

The office

Information technology made itself felt in the office much before the present push towards an 'electronic office'. The 'mechanised office' started in the second half of the 19th century, with the introduction of the typewriter and the telegraph. During the first half of the 20th century additional office technologies appeared: automatically switched telephones, the ticker tape, the electric typewriter, telex, duplicating machines, adding machines, tabulators and other data processing equipment using punched cards, etc.

The rise of electronics during and after the Second World War brought about a gradual replacement of the mechanical equipment by the smaller, more reliable and more versatile electronic equivalents: private branch telephone exchanges, electronic typewriters, visual display terminals, dictating machines, copiers, computers and so on.

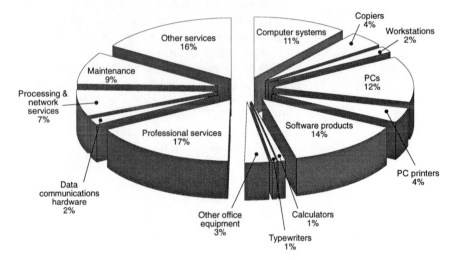

Fig. 2.1 Information and Communication Technology products and services breakdown for the EU and EFTA block in 1994. The world market value is currently estimated at over $430 billion.

The main role of office technology is to support the various information-handling activities that take place in the office. (There are also other justifications for the introduction of electronic office equipment. We shall return to them shortly.)

Table 2.1 gives a breakdown of these activities in a typical office of the late 1980s. A 1993 survey of US organisations suggests that time for meetings has increased and now accounts for between 7 and 15 per cent of all employees time. Managers also spend more time in meetings with typical values in the range 30 to 80 per cent. The result is an estimated 11 million meetings every day, totalling over 3000 million annually.

Although it is possible to group these activities in different ways, the above grouping shows, first, two of the main currencies of office work – the written and the spoken word. These two activities have so far been the main targets of office technology. There is also a third group, concerned specifically with aiding management tasks: planning, scheduling, decision-making, etc. More and more effort is being put into providing effective tools for this aspect of office work as well.

We shall now briefly look at each of these groups of activities in turn, and then toward some possibilities for an 'office of the future'.

Document preparation
Documents may include a text and a graphical (diagrammatic) component. Historically, documents were usually produced by several people:

Activity	Managers etc.	Others	All office
Written			
Writing	26	15	17
Taking dictation	-	1	-
Reading	13	6	8
Proof reading	3	2	2
Searching	4	2	2
Filing	1	2	2
Copying	1	4	4
Distribution	4	8	7
Operating equipment	4	18	15
Spoken			
Phone	5	9	8
Meetings	18	9	11
Management			
Calculating	6	1	2
Scheduling	3	-	1
Instructing	4	-	1
Travel	2	1	1
Other	6	22	19
Total	100	100	100

someone, say an administrator or manager, who originated and checked it, a typist, who prepared the text, and a draughtsman or artist who prepared the diagrams. The most highly mechanised stage of the document preparation process was text preparation, aided by the typewriter. The completely mechanical typewriter, invented about 1714, first gave way to its electric (strictly speaking, electromechanical) and electronic counterparts, and more recently to the *word processor*. The electric typewriter appeared circa 1940, the electronic one around 1955, and the word processor in 1969.

The major step in the transition from the office typewriter to the text processor was the conversion of the keyboard mechanism to the generation of not only printed images of characters but also of a *standard digital character code* uniquely corresponding to each character. With the text in computer-compatible form, it becomes possible to store and manipulate it in various ways before reconverting it to printed form, using established computer methods. It is worth noting here that the digitally coded form of characters making up text can also be generated by means other than keyboards. One method is the conversion of already printed text and of hand-written text directly into digital form by means of *character recognition equipment*. Such equipment currently does not offer a 100 per cent success rate, with handwriting posing the greater problems for the equipment designer. Even further down the development scale is equipment for the direct conversion of spoken words into digitally represented text (see p. 228).

Text preparation in the 'electronic office' is aided by an electronic keyboard linked to a computer (processor and memory), a video screen and a printer. The typist does not handle paper, instead the text appears on the screen. As far as the typist is concerned, the text is created and manipulated there and, when completed, sent away for storage, printing or even photo-typesetting. When creating the screen-image of text, the computer usually presents a set of pre-programmed formats as options (e.g. A4 blank or letterhead, memo blank or letterhead, etc.). The margins and tab positions are set automatically according to the option chosen. A cursor is used to indicate on the screen where the next keyed character will be positioned. Cursor-control keys or a pointing device (mouse, trackerball or stylus) allow this position to be changed at will, and, of course, the cursor moves on after each key stroke.

Automatic formatting facilities usually available on such equipment include justification, hyphenation, headings, footnotes, tabulation and change of typeface by a few key-strokes. Text manipulation facilities include the insertion, deletion or replacement of a single letter or passages of text, the replacement of a specific word in all its occurrences by another word, the pulling in of prepared passages, the ability to locate specific words or reference numbers anywhere in the text, and, in most cases, even spelling correction, automatic hyphenation and a thesaurus.

Diagrams and other graphical material can be incorporated into digitally manipulated text either as a separate operation at the final printing stage, or by creating the images directly in digital form and manipulating them as part of the total representation. In the former case, the layout of the text is adjusted to leave room for the graphics, but the lettering, captions, signs, etc., may be produced at the same time as the rest of the text. In the latter case, special *graphical input devices* or direct computer commands are used to create and modify (edit) images on the display screen.

Document-processing machines can either be stand-alone or shared-logic. In the UK in 1982 there were about 20,000 stand-alone word processors compared with 1500 shared-logic word processors (not including electronic typewriters). The annual growth rate for both was about 20 per cent. As shown in Fig. 2.2, a stand-alone machine has built into it all the facilities needed to key in, store or modify text. The printing of the final document may be either part of these local facilities, or it may be done with a shared-resource machine, on a more expensive centralised printer which accepts some electronically stored version of text to produce a high-quality printed document. Communicating machines are able to shunt around electronically coded text and graphics from one machine to another, along in-house telecommunication lines (so-called *local area networks* – see p.111). In addition, shared-logic machines can also link to a central (usually in-house) computer installation which may be much better at processing, storing and printing than stand-alone machines.

Due to the higher cost, however, of the central installation, its power is shared among the several work-stations which link to it (hence the name shared-logic or shared-processor). Text processing, combined with communication at a distance, can be used when office personnel are not located at the same site. For example, voice-mail enables an executive to leave dictation for his secretary from any telephone in the country. The secretary, who may work from home, retrieves the voice mail and prepares

Fig. 2.2 Stand-alone text processor configurations:

(a) A stand-alone text processor consists of a terminal containing a processor, keyboard and display unit, and is linked to a memory device and printer.

(b) Communicating text processors can gain access to common memory and printing devices via a switching unit or server. If they do not share the processor power, they are still classified as stand-alone

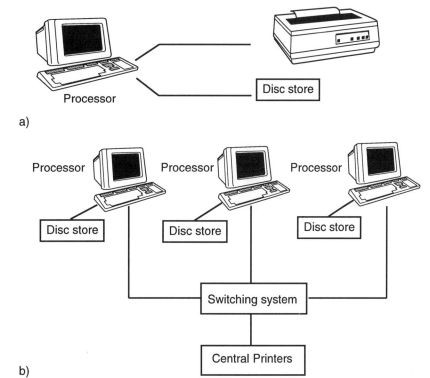

the documentation using a text processor and transmits it in digital form, again over the telephone, to the company's headquarters. There the document is printed on headed paper and posted.

Since 1981, a lower-cost option for text processing has been available: the personal computer with text-processing software. Word processors may be viewed as computer installations dedicated to the task of text processing, often with specially adapted keyboards and high-quality visual displays. Alternatively, personal computers with good printers are more than just text processors, they have become multi-purpose administrative and managerial aids. For this reason it is difficult to determine the precise number of PC-based text processing systems, since any PC with appropriate software is capable of undertaking such tasks. In 1994 the number of PCs installed in the UK "professional" market was approximately 5.3 million units, with a further 1.8 million units in the "home" market. By comparison there were 2.2 million typewriters.

The preparation of one particular type of document, the internal memo, is by implication not a cost-effective use of a text processor. Instead, memos can be sent through *computer-based message systems*, also called *electronic mail* systems. The input to such systems is usually of the same form as that for text processors (keyboard or character-recognition equipment). What is more unusual is the way the messages are distributed and presented to the addressee. So let us look at them, and at some other new office facilities, as means of document distribution.

Document distribution

Documents in the electronic office may be distributed either as electronically coded images presented on a display device (with the options of recording them as data for future reference and re-display), or as computer print-outs for filing in a conventional filing system, or as computer-produced *document images*. The distribution of documents on paper is aided by the recent generation of fast, high-quality printers. These include laser printers and photo-typesetters, as well as refinements of the more conventional printing methods such as ink-jet printers, electrostatic and xerographic printers. A common characteristic of the new generation of printing devices is that they can reproduce text faster than the typist's typing speed, so they offer the opportunity of separating the text production process from copy production, both in space and time.

Paradoxically, the introduction of information technology into the office has not led to a reduction in the amount of paper-based documentation. Most documents are still distributed in paper form: the United Nations and European Commission still print and distribute hundreds of millions of pages annually. Even electronically transmitted documents, such as *facsimile*, or fax (see p. 132), are printed at the receiver.

Historically more recent than telex and facsimile are computer-based document transmission methods, often referred to as *e-mail* (electronic-mail). These enable people to send and receive messages, such as memos, reports, reminders, via a network of interconnected computer terminals. The terminals, or PCs, may be linked via an in-house wired or wireless *local area network* (e.g. telephone lines, coaxial cables or microwave links – see p. 111), or the national and international telecommunication networks. According to a 1993 survey by the Electronic Messaging Association, the number of e-mail sites at head and branch offices of the top 2000 US companies grew from 94,000 in 1991 to over 180,000 by 1993. The number of users is increasing at approximately 17 per cent per year.

Electronic data interchange (EDI) aims to remove the need for handling business documents, such as orders or delivery notes in paper form. Documents in agreed computerised format move directly (along telephone lines, or other telecommunication lines) between the computers of companies which participate in this scheme of 'paperless trading'.

In addition to document transmission, a computer-based message network offers the possibility of *computer conferencing*. In a computer conference, a discussion document (or a nominated topic) is commented upon by participants at various locations, over a period of time. The contributions are usually stored in the sequence of their entry into the system, and can be seen by all participants.

In a computer-based system, messages are created in just the same way as in a text processor. But being based on larger, more powerful computers, the systems usually allow data held in the computer's memory (e.g. standard paragraphs, tables of figures) to be incorporated into the text of the message. A message can be addressed to an individual or to a group. The system incorporates safeguards to preserve the necessary confidentiality of messages, their integrity (accuracy) during storage, transmission and reproduction. The recipient is informed by the computer of a waiting message as soon as he or she contacts the system. The messages can then be read, either in their entirety or just to identify the sender and possibly the first line of the message. The computer can arrange messages in a stated order of priority. The message then can be deleted, read again on the screen, filed electronically, printed out as a hard copy, or sent to a third party without the need to re-enter it.

A very interesting feature of some such systems is that messages can be initiated by the computer itself, in response to some earlier stated requirement. For example, the computer may contain the dates of meetings in its memory, or a list of new documents or books, etc. circulating in the office, and notify individuals about items of particular interest to them.

Document storage and retrieval

It has been estimated (Haider, in *Office Automation*, Infotech, 1980) that there is the equivalent of 20 million million pages of A4 paper stored in offices in the USA, and this is growing at a rate of 1 million pages every minute of every day. Apart from the physical problem of storage, this presents an increasingly difficult organisational problem in locating documents relevant to specific topics.

It has been estimated that, in the USA, an office professional spends about 20–30 per cent of his or her time just looking for information. The computer-based distribution systems, with the added facility of storage of computer-coded text, offer one approach to reducing the physical size of records, and to mechanising their retrieval. The records, unfortunately, first have to be converted into computer-compatible form, and can be consulted only after re-conversion via some printing or display device.

There is also another important disadvantage to current methods of computer-held documentation: diagrams are profligate in the use of computer memory. So documents with graphical content are best adapted to the 'electronic office' by alternative means: *document imaging*. This involves the creation of a photographic or electronic image of a document. The photographic method results in physically reduced images recorded on film, called *microforms* (microfilm or microfiche).

Microforms are estimated to reduce the storage space requirements, in comparison with paper, by 98 per cent. They can be generated either by photographic reduction of documents or by direct output from computers. In the latter case, text created on the video screen can be recorded on film by means of a computer-output microform recorder. Microforms can be read by means of optically magnifying reading devices, or by equipment which presents the magnified image on a video display.

Recently, microform technology has been combined with computerised indexing and retrieval techniques. The result is a device able to hold several million frames, and locate and present any one of these, in response to a keyword request, in a matter of seconds. On the screen, the microfilmed information can be combined with up-to-date text or graphics, and, the resulting image re-recorded for future reference.

Electronic methods convert the document to a video image by a process of scanning. Before storage and/or transmission, the information contained in the image is electronically compressed (typically by the same factor as microforms). For example, in the United States and Britain, many insurance companies now handle forms in this electronic imaged version.

The storage of electronic versions of documents has been greatly advanced in recent years by the availability of *optical storage systems* (see p. 86). Electronic and optical methods of handling images of documents offer the advantage of ease of handling – even a relatively small organization may need to handle about 1000 documents a day – and reduce the need for copying – a paper business document is typically copied over 10 times in its 'lifetime'.

Another growth area of electronic retrieval is that of on-line literary services, providing access to libraries and information data-bases. Searches are conducted on-line and the relevant documents retrieved instantaneously or faxed to the user. A number of such commercial services exist, providing access to several tens of thousands of journals, each adding thousands of new articles daily.

Visual presentations

We have already noted the central position of the video screen in the 'electronic office'. It is used in the preparation and presentation of textual material and, in some systems, of pictures stored in computer memory or as microforms. It also gives access to visual information held in data sources outside the organization itself. The preparation of graphical material is aided by computer programs and also by special-purpose computer graphic devices. These enable people to set up bar-charts, line drawings, block diagrams and other standard office presentations with only a few instructions, and without special training. They also accept hand-drawn images, handwriting or already existing photographic or television images, convert them to computer-compatible form and store or transmit them.

Again, the key operation here is the conversion of information (pictorial information in this case) to a coded form which can be manipulated by digital methods. A recent trend is the simultaneous handling of text and images by the same system, treating them both as data representations.

An interesting by-product of this approach is that the code so generated can be transmitted to remote locations by a variety of means. If the picture is steady or slowly changing it can be transmitted along telephone lines or by broadcast links for their transmission. Such links may be internal to an organization or can utilise public telecommunication facilities (e.g. satellites or cables). The US company AT&T first demonstrated video over the phone as early as the 1933 Chicago World Fair, but a public service was not introduced until 1964. This service used a 1 MHz video signal transmitted over several pairs of local-loops.

Modern video telephones use digital transmission techniques. BT's Relate 2000 videophone employs a 14,400 bit per second modem shared between video and audio signals. The AT&T service uses a 19,200 bits per second modem. Both services offer colour images over standard telephone lines so can be operated from domestic premises.

More recently, it has become possible to apply the electronic methods just described to the organization of meetings where the participants are separated by large distances. Such *videoconferences* rely on the transmission of images of people and documents as well as voice via *telecommunication* and *data communication* networks. Two distinct videoconferencing services are now available. The first utilises full bandwidth video signals and hence participants are required to attend special videoconferencing centres. The second service is built around personal computers and ISDN. The BT service is marketed as PC Videophone and employs an interface card in the PC to handle the video, audio and ISDN signals. The software operates under either Windows or OS/2 and permits the user to transfer multimedia data to a remote PC. A special 'whiteboard' window permits sharing of notes and sketches, but any data file can be transferred between users. A conferencing facility can also be established between six concurrent users. Costs of the system are currently £3000 per station (1994 prices), but are expected to fall with increasing demand.

Spoken words

The telephone is, and will remain for the foreseeable future, the main office technology for dealing with spoken words. There are many advances and improvements to the basic telephone service. Most of these stem from the application of computer technology in the telephone itself, in the exchanges (private and public) and in the representation of speech by computer-compatible signals. For example, one form of local area network is based on the in-house telephone exchange. Some of these advances are aimed at overcoming the problems that have led, in the past, to the failure of an estimated two calls in three when the called party was engaged or away from the telephone. These problems are also being addressed by other, computer-based equipment. This can store speech until it is ready to be received. For example, 'vocal memos' can be sent to any extension on an internal telephone network; or, in combination with electronic mail, a written report, annotated with a spoken commentary, can be prepared.

From an office point of view, for example, it is becoming possible to interlink a number of telephones into a *telephone conference* (see p. 78). The participants in the conference can be reached by telephone. Prior to the meeting they may have already received, by electronic mail, the documentation to be used during the meeting. By using a graphical input device connected to the telephone line, they can draw diagrams which are seen instantaneously by all the participants on video display units, also connected to the telephone.

Dictating machines and automatic answering machines are also widely used aids in offices. They, and the people who use them, are unlikely to be displaced in the near future by automated speech typewriters or speech input-output computers, since the automatic recognition of speech is still at an early stage of commercialisation (see Chapter 24).

Management aids

It has been said that the main function of the office is not to multiply information but to make it more manageable – to filter the facts into a form useful for decision-making. Computer aids to decision-making range from the personal computer-based financial planning ('spreadsheet') and cash management packages to large-scale decision support systems.

Spreadsheet programs allow the manager to set up, in a simple way, mathematical models of various aspects of the organization (e.g. cash flow, production rates) and then investigate the effect of particular decisions or strategies (the 'what if?' approach). Cash management software enables the manager to obtain instantaneous information about the budgets and bank balances under his control. He can also initiate financial transactions using electronic funds transfer.

Decision support systems are a further development of management information systems (MIS). The latter, in turn, evolved from a backward-looking (historical) periodic reporting and accounting facility, to real-time operation. Information becomes available for inspection as soon as it comes into being. Management information systems are primarily aimed at lower and middle management, by providing data to help with day-to-day organising, controlling and directing activities.

Decision support systems are aimed to extend computerised assistance to the strategic planning tasks of senior managers. They do this by drawing attention to underlying trends and enabling managers to construct projections and to examine the outcome of hypothetical courses of action. All this is performed by interacting with a data-base of past and current information. Some decision support systems even come up with recommended courses of action, for consideration by the decision maker.

In between these two extremes of low-cost, personal computer-based aids and large-scale decision support systems lie a variety of other electronic management aids: electronic diary, notebook, message and remote conference facilities, mobile telephone and telex, selective presentation of news-agency and financial reports, etc. – an ever-increasing list whose usefulness and usability are not always immediately apparent.

Claims for the electronic office include increased efficiency and productivity through

(a) better use of executive resources requiring judgement, by automating the routine functions;
(b) better communication;
(c) increased ability to make sound decisions involving complex combinations of factors and doing so more rapidly;
(d) better use of time by making facilities available for 24 hours per day rather than 8 hours;
(e) 'extension of the walls of the office' to wherever the office worker happens to be.

But perhaps even more important than all these factors is the fresh, questioning approach to office organization, measures of success and human relations brought about by the challenge of automation.

Working in the electronic office
Before moving on to look at what may be in store for the 'office of the future' in the longer term, let us pause to consider some of the effects of the 'electronic office' on people who work with the new equipment. Perhaps the most striking point about the 'electronic office' is that it is not significantly different from the conventional office. The emphasis of the new technology so far has been on enhancing existing equipment or on offering an alternative medium to paper. It is not, so far, aimed at

automating complete jobs, rather at making them faster and more convenient to perform.

Whether this aim has been achieved, and whether it has contributed significantly to the overall efficiency of the office, are difficult to gauge. It has been estimated that in document preparation up to 70 per cent savings can be made if the author changes from the long-hand method of composition to the dictating machine and if the typist can make up the document from pre-stored passages. The electronic filing and retrieving of documents combined with an efficient indexing and keywording facility are also claimed to save secretarial and executive time (once people become familiar with the equipment, and once the equipment is functioning reliably). What is clear is that in offices where the new electronic equipment has been introduced people had to get used to new machines and new work patterns. For example, text processors are more cost-effective if they are used virtually continuously. Organisationally, this often means the creation of a 'word-processing centre', akin to a typing pool. For the typists, the change meant having to undergo a period of training (in some cases, all too short and inadequate training), then having to operate a machine which has no need for traditional layout skills but requires continuous concentration. As a result, some text-processor operators feel socially isolated (*Office Automation*, Infotech, Series 8, No. 3, 1980). A study by the Cambridge-based Applied Psychology Unit of the Medical Research Council has reported that some users of computerised office equipment are intimidated by the machines, feel inadequate in understanding what goes on ' behind the screen', and perceive such systems as 'unnecessary alien intruders' in the office. There has also been much concern about the health and safety aspects, particularly of TV-tube based and microwave equipment. The need for adequate training and for a gradual, well-justified introduction of new equipment is evident from all reports published on the impact of the 'electronic office'.

Research in the United States has indicated that it is the manager and the executive who are the most enthusiastic about office technology – but for the use of their clerical and secretarial staff. Yet it is with management and professional information workers that the greatest potential of the technology lies. Their numbers are increasing more rapidly – at the compound annual rate of 2.9 per cent and 4.4 per cent, respectively, while for secretarial staff the corresponding figure was 0.4 per cent. Their salaries increased, over the same time, by 7.5 per cent and 12 per cent per annum, as compared with 7.5 per cent for secretaries.

It is no wonder that the attention of both top management and office equipment manufacturers is now turning towards managers and information professionals as the targets for the next stage in the introduction of office technology.

The integrated office

A paradox of the rise of the 'electronic office' is that it has led to a compartmentalised structure of office organization. The data processing department, the telecommunications section, the word-processing pool and other services got separated from mainstream office activities.

Protagonists of office automation see this as an undesirable development

– it has allowed the manager to keep technology at an arm's length, not letting it have a major impact on his style of working. To make future office technology all-pervasive, it is therefore necessary to bring together, to integrate, the electronic systems of today.

However, most of today's systems are incompatible with one another. Text, graphic and voice-processing machines are not standardised, and output from one cannot be easily utilised as input to another.

Standardisation is one answer to this problem, and it is happening on an increasing scale. Its opponents claim, however, that the technology is evolving so rapidly that standards would stifle the innovator. The other approach is the introduction of local (in-house) communication networks which allow the inter-linking of all kinds of electronic equipment. An example of such a network is shown in Fig. 8.5 (p. 112).

Inside a building, the network takes the form of cables. Between offices the connection may be based on telephone lines, or microwave or light links. The idea of a local network is similar to the electrical outlets in a house, to which different individually incompatible pieces of equipment may be connected. The difference, though, is in the purpose of the connection: for the local network it is the interchange of data. The transmission rates in the network are high – up to a million characters a second (at these rates it would take about 20 s to transmit the Bible).

Once installed, the local office network has the potential for substituting the flow of computer-coded information for the flow of paper. It can interconnect text processors, personal computers and terminals to high-quality printers, computer-based file stores, facsimile machines, digital voice, video and other electronic office equipment.

An important feature of the local network concept is the possibility of interconnection with other company-wide, national or international data networks through a computer 'gateway' also linked to the ring.

A recent development, not yet widespread, has been the construction of new office buildings with the local area network, or 'information ring-main', and other computing and communication facilities already installed. Such so-called *intelligent buildings* typically also offer features like computer-controlled heating and ventilation control ('energy management'), safety and security systems. Groups of intelligent buildings have been constructed on selected sites in various countries to serve as working show-cases of information technology – these have been nicknamed *tele-ports*.

It is usually envisaged that in the integrated office the currently separate pieces of office equipment will be replaced by a 'multifunction work station'. Although this concept is in its early stages of development, it appears to aim at the complete replacement of the desk, the telephone, the office typewriter and the filing cabinet by a single electronic box having visual and voice links with the user. The visual display initially shows representations of the various items of office equipment, such as the filing cabinet. The user 'opens the cabinet' by means of an electronic pointing device, and has its contents displayed as a catalogue. A particular document can then be selected, its contents electronically modified, if necessary, and printed by simply pointing to the representation of the printer on the screen.

However, these are early days for the 'office of the future'. For one thing, it is by no means clear that the office, in the sense of a centralised administrative organization, will survive in the long term. But even in the nearer term, the cost-effective use of the 'new technology' requires the re-thinking of the entire pattern of flow of information within the office and the re-training of staff. This, in turn, is likely to demand organisational changes whose effects are bound to be even more far-reaching than the piece-meal introduction of the 'electronic office'.

Industry

Manufacturing industries are among the earliest and most well-established fields of application of information technology. As we have just seen, office automation helps to keep management informed about the state of production, orders, stocks, finances, personnel and so on, as part of *management information systems*. It has also provided tools for production planning, product design and industrial research. And, just as importantly, computers have assumed an increasingly pervasive role in the control of production processes and manufacturing equipment, in other words, in industrial automation.

As examples of these developments, we shall look briefly at two industries: manufacturing industry, and publishing and printing.

Manufacturing industry

Probably the earliest application of information technology to the manufacturing industry was the *Jacquard* loom, where the weaving pattern was controlled by a sequence of punched cards. The same principle was resurrected in 1952 with the introduction of numerical control (NC) of machine tools. In a system devised at the Massachusetts Institute of Technology, the cutting tool was guided through a succession of points by feeding their co-ordinates from a punched paper tape.

Numerically controlled machine tools started to appear commercially in the early 1960s, and took another 10 years before the paper tape was replaced by programs stored in the memory of computers. In such computer numerical control (CNC) machines various aspects of the machining process (cutting angle and speed, tool selection, etc.) are under pre-programmed computer control.

A further decade elapsed before, in 1980, the first flexible machining systems (FMS) or manufacturing cells were introduced. In these, a series of CNC machines carry out a number of operations on different work-pieces without routine human intervention. More recently, the initials FMS came to signify the broader concept of flexible *manufacturing* systems. These are not restricted to metal cutting but include a variety of production equipment. As shown in Fig. 2.3, the production machinery is interlinked by automatic handling devices (such as robots), automatic transfer systems (such as guided pallets) and communication lines. A computer, or a set of computers, is in overall control, being informed at all times where any particular work-piece is, and what is happening to it. From this information the computer can work out the optimum progress of each work-piece through the manufacturing system.

The main benefit claimed for FMS is that it allows automated production processes to be applied to small batches of products, whereas in the past expensive automated machinery could be justified for only very large production runs. With FMS it is possible to re-set the machines to cope with a variety of shapes, sizes and even materials. This also results in shorter lead-time in satisfying customers' orders, as it is no longer necessary to wait until a large production run is finished or to install new equipment. It also leads to better utilisation of machinery; for example, night shifts can be operated with minimum personnel.

FMS may provide flexibility of production and better, more consistent product quality. However, the financial case for it is not straightforward. In the case of a Japanese company, introduction of FMS resulted in the number of separate machines being reduced from 68 to 16, the number of operatives from 215 to 12, and the processing time from 35 days to one and a half days. But the financial return was only $6.9 million on an investment of $18 million.

This example illustrates a point that applies to a broad range of information technology developments: initial investments can be large and returns slow to materialise, in conventional accounting terms. These considerations have to be put against factors like the loss of market share caused by untimely or unsuitable products, or to more efficient competitors already employing advanced technology. There are also more intangible gains like the improved quality, consistency and reliability of products.

Other 'islands' of current application of information technology to manufacturing industry include activities on either side of computer-aided

Fig. 2.3 The raw component is loaded automatically on to a pallet and is carried on a conveyor belt past a bank of various machine tools (drilling, cutting, chamfering etc.). The robot picks up the component and presents it to the appropriate machine tool for machining. After machining, the robot releases the component and it passes along the conveyor for the next machining operation. Sensor devices monitor progress; a technician checks on visual display terminals. When one batch of components is finished, the technician resets the program for the next batch

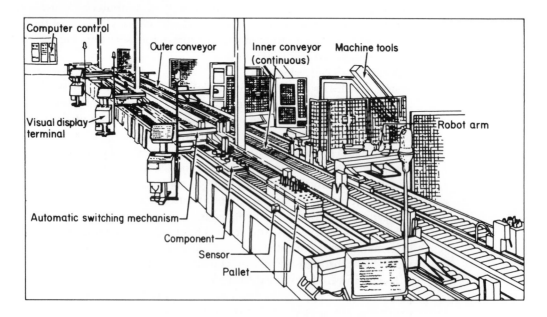

manufacturing (CAM), i.e. the initial design and the final testing and warehousing of products. In computer-aided design (CAD), designers work at computer-based work stations to draft, visualise and, in some cases, simulate the eventual performance of new products. For example, a 3-D solid-colour model of an aircraft wing can be 'opened-up' on the screen to examine the buckling effects of the simulated loading on the wing's internal structure. Any design faults can be rectified before the wing is built.

Computer-aided design has been successfully applied in many fields, not just manufacturing (as, for example, of computers themselves), but also in architecture and building design (e.g. for wiring layout, heating and ventilation ducting); in the textile and clothing industry (e.g. for experimenting with various lay-outs, patterns, overall designs). In some cases, the output of the CAD stage is linked directly to the CAM, or manufacturing stage. Such combined systems are referred to by another acronym: *computer-aided engineering* (CAE).

In other words, CAD + CAM = CAE.

Early examples of CAE came from the electronics industry, where integrated circuit lay-outs were created by CAD techniques and then transferred, via computer links, to the chip manufacturing stage. Similarly, various components, like integrated circuits, were automatically assembled on CAD-CAM prepared printed-circuit boards, and automatically tested before becoming parts of new computers or other electronic equipment.

The main benefits of computer-aided design seen by British manufacturers are the improved accuracy and legibility of engineering drawings and the ease of making alterations to designs, resulting in improved designer productivity.

Rolls-Royce, the aero-engine manufacturer, and Team Lotus, Formula One racing cars, have both invested heavily in CAD systems. Rolls-Royce have designed, built and tested their latest Trent engine entirely on a computer screen and Lotus routinely design and test new components with their CAD system prior to modifying the actual car. In both cases the time to introduce design modifications has been reduced from weeks to days.

For computer-aided manufacturing the advantages are seen to be: a shorter production time per part; direct links with CNC equipment; reduced lead-time and lower production costs, but in many cases these advantages have not been achieved consistently.

It can be claimed that CAE only does what people would do – after all, it was created by people. The counter-argument refers to: speed, accuracy and repeatability, leading to consistent quality; a better capability for the co-ordination of complex operations; and the possibility of examining various alternatives (at reasonable cost and with absolute safety) before final commitment to manufacture is made.

As with office applications, the future is envisaged by many to lie with the further linking up of the various 'islands' of activity. Perhaps not surprisingly, a name and acronym have already been devised for the next stage: *computer-integrated manufacturing*, or CIM.

Table 2.2 CIM
functions

Business Planning and Support	Manufacturing Control
Economic Simulation	Purchasing/Receiving
Long-Term Forecasting	Shop Routing
Customer Order Servicing	Methods & Standards
Finished Goods Inventory Mgmt	In-process Inventory Management
	Short-term Scheduling
	Shop Order Follow System
Engineering Design	**Shop Floor Monitoring**
Computer-Aided Drafting	Machine Load Monitoring
Computer-Aided Tool Design	Machine Performance Monitoring
Group Technology	Man-time Monitoring
CAD	Material Stores Monitoring
	Preventive Maintenance
	In-process Quality Testing
Manufacturing Planning	**Process Automation**
Process Planning Systems	NC, DNC, CNC
Parts Programming	Adaptive Control
NC Graphics	Automatic Assembly
Tool & Materials Catalogue	Automatic Inspection
Material Requirements Planning	Computerised Testing
Production Line Planning Simulation	
Bill of Materials Processors	
Machinability Data Systems	
Computerised Cutter, Die Selection	
Materials/Parts Inventory Mgmt	

Table 2.2 shows one possible view of how integration may take place. The already familiar components of CAM, CAD, monitoring and testing, and automated materials handling are combined with business planning and support, and manufacturing planning and control functions. The common element to all of these is envisaged to be a computer complete with data-base and data network. The computer optimises production flow and scheduling to satisfy the production plan. All machinery is in constant communication with the computer so that their operation is closely controlled. This should result in improved product quality through automated testing, simple access to test data and rapid action if the tests indicate a quality problem.

As shown in Fig. 2.4, in the ultimate CIM system in go raw materials, power, product specifications and orders at one end, and out come finished products at the other. Whether such systems will be commonplace in our lifetime is unclear. What is more certain, however, is that the technologies which are needed for computer-integrated manufacturing are already available, though far from perfect.

'Intelligent' robots

Robots are machines designed to replace human labour. Their development, particularly for replacing human muscle power, has been in parallel with that of information technology, but largely independent of it. The main manufacturing application of robots has been in the transfer and accurate positioning of parts within and between manufacturing cells. As of 1992 the UK industrial robot population reached some 7600, with the

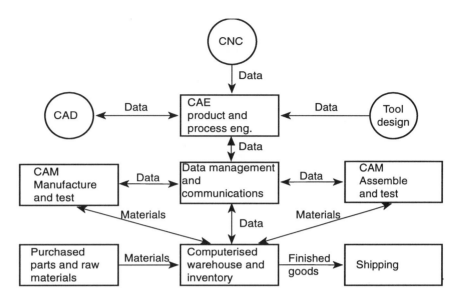

Fig. 2.4 Component processes and their interaction in a computer-integrated manufacturing system of the future

majority of applications within the motor manufacturing industry (2900 robots). By comparison Japanese industry had more than 325,000 robots, 60 per cent of the global total.

It is only in the previous decade that 'intelligent' robots started to appear, when robots became linked to other components of CIM, that the two developments started to converge.

'Intelligence' in robots is the result of building into them one or more micro-computers. These store data about the environment in which the robot operates, and guide its actions through continuous monitoring, via 'tactile' and/or 'visual' sensors, and closed-loop (feedback) control.

Intelligent robots are still largely under development and cover a wide range of applications. Of these perhaps the simplest are automated delivery systems that follow predefined tracks laid into the floor of a building, but smart enough to avoid obstacles in their path. More sophisticated applications include security devices for warehouses and museums, capable of detecting smoke, fire and intruders. The Frait 80 is the result of collaboration between Oxford University, the Devon company Firefly and the Dutch company Terberg, and provides a driverless trailer for moving containers at shipping ports. A central computer holds a map of the port with details of fixed obstructions and using this information instructs the Frait 80 which container to collect and where to deposit it. Radar enables the Frait 80 to detect new obstructions along its route and to update the centrally stored map, which in turn determines a new route. Sensors in the bumpers of the vehicle provide a fail-safe mechanism and should any object be nudged, the emergency brakes are applied. A complete Frait 80 is expected to cost around £150,000 (1994 prices). A conventional tractor-trailer unit costs about £70,000, but also requires a driver at some £25,000 a year.

Robots are also being developed to support the physically disabled and elderly within their own home. Operating in such unstructured environments poses numerous design problems associated with the safety of the human occupant.

As will be discussed in greater detail in later chapters, the main research directions lie, on the one hand, in the recognition and interpretation of images, and, on the other, in the capturing of human expertise in tackling problems.

On the third hand, as befits robots, we have on-going work on the appropriate use of 'intelligent' machines in relation to the human work-force they are supposed to replace. Considerations of health, safety, and quality of working life for people must all be taken into account when deciding on the introduction of robots.

Publishing and printing

The traditional business of the publishing and printing industries is the mass production and distribution of information, in the form of books, periodicals, newspapers and other printed matter. Their production cycle involves the entire range of operations which are of concern to information technology: the generation (authoring), processing (editing), storage (printing and warehousing), dissemination (marketing) and use (management) of information. As a direct consequence, their activities are among the first to be directly affected by advances in information technology. In publishing, the main innovation is *electronic publishing.* The essence of this is the replacement of the traditional means of printing, storage and dissemination of paper by the equivalent operations on electronic messages.

In electronic publishing, the text may be prepared on a computer-based text processor. Some publishers already work with text processors and so reduce the time taken for editing the manuscript. Many authors acquire their own word processors to save time on re-structuring, revision, correction, re-typing, spelling and consistency checking, indexing and other 'non-creative' tasks. Advanced text processors incorporate various authoring aids.

One system, developed at the Bell Laboratories, in the USA, includes a feature for simplifying an author's convoluted prose. For example, the following extract from Lincoln's Gettysburg address was typed into the text processor: 'Four score and seven years ago our fathers brought forth on this continent a new nation conceived in Liberty, and dedicated to the proposition that all men are created equal.' The processor converted this into: 'Eighty-seven years ago our grandfathers created a free nation here. They based it on the idea that everybody is created equal.' The author, of course, is not bound to accept the processor's recommendation, but it might serve as a welcome 'second opinion'.

Electronic publishing is having a significant effect on the traditional printing and publishing industries. Many companies now realise that they can produce publications in-house rather than employing specialist firms. In-house publications include technical manuals, sales literature, internal reports, newsletters, etc. It is claimed that companies producing, say, 10,000 pages of print per year can recover their investment in electronic publishing in about 2 years, and have greater control over the final product. Considerations like this are making electronic publishing into an important IT equipment market, worth about $4.5 billion in 1994.

An alternative to printing the text so prepared is to use a form of 'electronic mail', since the text is now held and distributed as computerised data. Would-be users must have at their disposal a *visual display terminal* (also called a VDU – visual display unit), which informs them about the range of available 'publications' and allows them to select specific items, either for viewing on the screen, or storing for later reference in electronic form or printing on a local printing device.

There are some major problems at the present time which probably prevent publishers from considering authors' word processors as a preferred medium for the presentation of manuscripts. These are cost, the incompatibility of various systems on the market (in terms of storage and transfer standards), and the necessary organisational changes, such as the role of authors *vis-à-vis* editors, printers etc.

However, when these factors are completely 'in-house' they can be more easily controlled. For example, Oxford University Press produced the latest edition of the Oxford English Dictionary (previously running to 12 volumes and 4 supplements) with the aid of a computer. All the text, over 60 million words, was converted to computer-compatible form. After that, it can be edited, up-dated and searched electronically. Up-to-date versions can be produced in conventional form more rapidly than hitherto or distributed in electronic form at less cost. The computerised version can be incorporated into 'intelligent' computer systems as an aid to natural language communication.

In addition to the electronic publishing media (the combination of computer, telecommunication and display technologies), progress is being made with the use of two other media for publishing: *microforms* and *optical media* (e.g. CD-ROM).

Microform technology currently enables the publisher to reproduce 200 pages on a *micro-fiche,* and optical discs can hold over 50,000 still frames (text or pictures or both). Of particular interest is the combination of these two media with computer technology: the computer can be used to prepare and edit the material; it can produce a direct output on microfilm; it can aid the user to find a specific item on a library of microfilms; it can control the replay of optical discs so that a particular frame is found and displayed, wherever it is on the disc, in less than a second. Electronic libraries based on optical disc are now a technical feasibility.

A combination of electronic publishing techniques and *data networks* (see p. 110) makes it possible for authors and/or publishers to distribute text and graphics in purely electronic form. Such 'electronic books' and 'electronic journals' need at no stage appear in printed form, unless of course the reader prefers to use printing facilities to create a paper copy. Numerous 'electronic journals' are now available over the various electronic networks. Authors articles are submitted and reviewed electronically and then distributed nationally via JANET or world-wide over the Internet.

A combination of electronic aids to authoring and distribution can significantly speed up the publication process but its economic aspects (in particular, the collection of revenue from readers) has so far restricted its large-scale commercial exploitation.

Another growth area is that of *multimedia* publishing employing CD-ROM or distributed over ISDN. Text, graphics, photographs, audio and video material are combined into an interactive *hypermedia* presentation.

Electronic libraries based on optical discs (CD-ROMs) are now commercially available. Readers can subscribe to national newspapers, such as *The Times* and *Guardian*, and receive discs quarterly covering the previous three months of daily papers. *The Times* has also produced a compilation disc spanning 200 years of publication, with themes linked to the new National Curriculum of the UK.

Other CD-ROM publications include BT's entire set of national telephone directories and a complete set of British Standards. In Washington DC Bell Atlantic is providing CD-I players to subscribers to replace paper directories. The CD-I contains 1.2 million residential numbers, 0.4 million business numbers and over 100 electronic adverts. The cost of the discs is less than half that of the paper directories.

These new publishing media offer some significant advantages over the conventional methods: the production time is reduced, changes and 'new editions' are more conveniently made, the distributed medium (electronic signal, microfilm, disc) may be cheaper than a bound volume of print. Against this, however, the cost to the end user is currently a great deal higher, because special display devices are needed in each case. These 'reading devices' are also less convenient to handle and read than print on paper. But these are exactly the same problems which are being experienced in the office and other applications of information technology and we can expect a concentrated research effort to solve them. In the meanwhile, electronic information technology is making inroads into the conventional printing side of book and newspaper publication.

The first major challenge to the established techniques of letterpress and lithography came in the late 1960s: it was *photo-typesetting*. Figure 2.5 compares the stages of preparing a printed page by the three methods. The computer helps in the editing of the manuscript and eliminates the need for molten-lead typesetting machines. More recently, the computer has also been employed to assemble ('make-up') a printed page from its various components – the galleys of text, graphics, advertisements, etc. It allows experimentation with the layout, choice of typeface, etc., on a video display before finalising each page. Today the entire contents of a publication are held and manipulated as computer data which can be electronically transmitted as made-up pages for printing at a remote location (see p. 132).

The international edition of the *Herald Tribune*, for example, is now published simultaneously in London, Paris, Zurich and Hong Kong by transmitting *facsimiles* of each page. The Hong Kong copy is sent via a satellite, the process taking a few minutes per page. If the text and graphics are handled as computer data, the facsimile stage can be by-passed and transmission speeded up. Compression techniques are commonly used to reduce the total amount of data to be transmitted, thereby reducing time and costs even further.

The range of new technologies available to the printing and publishing industries keeps increasing rapidly. However, the cost is high, the implications of change for publishers, printers and the public are great. In an industry where some publishers are yet to make the change from letterpress to lithography, any radical moves will be motivated only by the economic unviability of existing methods. With the increasing cost of

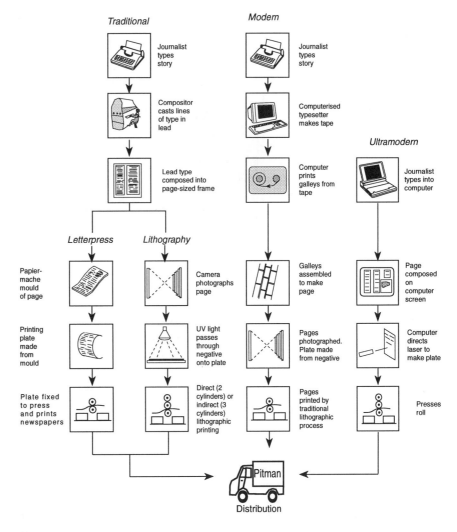

Fig. 2.5 The three ages of printing technology. (After the *Economist*, 19 July 1980, p. 99)

paper and printing ink, of sophisticated printing machines, of distribution and marketing, the replacement of many centrally-produced paper publications by electronically distributed, stored and displayed data, with an optional, locally produced printed version, looks a definite possibility.

Finance and commerce

If the office and manufacturing industry are good testing grounds for the potential of information technology, the field of financial transactions has been using it for some time out of sheer necessity. The reason for such expenditure is that every money transaction is also an information transaction: a record needs to be made (formally or informally) about the amount, the purpose, the parties involved, the data, etc.

The number of transactions has been rapidly increasing over the last few years: it has been estimated that in Europe there are currently about 1000 financial transactions per person per year; and in the USA about 1500, the figures increasing at the rate of several per cent a year. Of these the majority are in cash – historic trends for non-cash payments are as shown in Fig. 2.6.

Fig. 2.6 Trends in the growth of various forms of non-cash payments in Britain.

a) trends in non-cash payments from 1975 to 1983

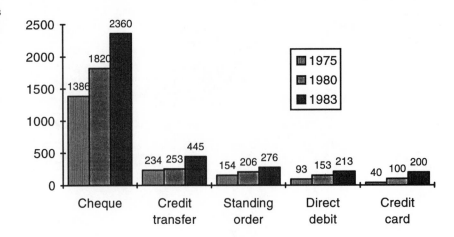

b) non-cash payments during 1992

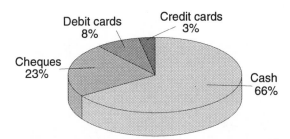

Data for 1992 (see Fig. 2.6b) indicates that 66 per cent of all payment transactions were cash, 23 per cent were by cheque, 8 per cent by debit cards (SWITCH and DELTA), and 3 per cent by credit cards (including store cards).

Until relatively recently, all such transactions were recorded on paper and processed by hand or by means of slow electromechanical equipment. This has proved woefully inadequate in the face of the explosive growth of transactions, accompanied by acute shortages of clerical workers in the large cities and pressure for shorter working hours by bank staff. The technological response to this need for a faster, more efficient, less labour-intensive method of handling financial transactions has been given the name of *electronic payment services* in the UK. In the United States, it is known as *electronic funds transfer* (EFT).

Electronic funds transfer
There are several distinct historical stages in the progress to electronic money transactions. The first stage involved the processing by computer of accounts and payments, within and between banks. The major banks have installed their own computer networks, with terminals in the branches. Since about 1960, the use of a standardised commercial code for identifying banks on cheques, etc., in conjunction with a standardised set of stylised symbols suitable for *optical and magnetic character recognition* (electronic shape identification), has helped to convert data about transactions to computer-compatible form. Later, it became possible to

transfer such data from one bank's computer to that of another, by means of a network of leased, high-quality telephone lines. Such clearing house operations were at first done on a national basis, but by the late seventies an international banking *data network*, Swift (Society for World-wide Interbank Financial Transactions), came into operation, subsequently updated to Swift II.

The second stage brought into this network the computers of some of the organisations, companies, etc., who conduct a large volume of business with the banks. Transactions like payments of salaries, share dividends, tax deductions, etc., could now be handled by the transfer of data, rather than of slips of paper. Standing orders (pre-authorised payments) and the preparation of statements could also be computerised. An electronic system, based on data networks, was introduced in the UK in 1984. It is called 'Clearing House Automated Payments System' or CHAPS. The US equivalent is the 'Clearing House Interbank Payments System' or CHIPS.

The third stage in this process extends the range of electronic financial transactions even further, by installing banking terminals for public use. Initially, such automated terminals ('teller machines' or ATMs) were installed in the banks themselves, enabling people to draw cash by means of a cash card. Cash cards carry a magnetic stripe to identify the account to the terminal by means of a digital code. The user of the card has also to key in a personal identity number at the terminal's keyboard. The computer authorises payment only if the two codes correspond and if the account will not be overdrawn as a result of the transaction.

The banks are now investigating the possibilities for providing other services through their installed network of ATMs. In 1994 the TSB launched trials of an interactive service through multimedia ATMs, capable of supporting audio and video. Users can obtain mortgage and life-assurance quotes electronically with the results displayed on the ATM screen, or they can initiate a live video link with an investment specialist at TSB's head office.

In principle, the terminals can be installed anywhere people spend money. They can even circumvent the need to withdraw cash, if it is to be spent again directly at the same location. Instead, the buyer presents a *debit card* from which details of the bank and account can be read electronically. The buyer's account is debited and the seller's account credited by the banking network. (A behind-the-scenes transaction is involved here between the buyer's and the seller's banks.)

Indeed, it is not even necessary for the transaction to be handled by a terminal connected to the banking computer network. It is technically possible to use the magnetic stripe (or some other form of electronic data storage) on the card to hold the details of the transactions for which it has been used, so that the amounts being spent are deducted from the card's nominal starting value, until that value is exhausted. At that stage, a new card could be issued. (Note the contrast with the function of the cheque, and the extra security for the seller.)

Visa International are about to launch such a service called the 'electronic purse', based on smart-card technology. The purse will store a cash equivalent and each transaction will automatically reduce the amount of cash available on the card.

Tele-banking

Although EFT is the major growth area of the banking sector, the banks have also been investigating ways of reducing other costs, especially those associated with branch offices, and providing services for customers who can't get to a bank. The number of bank and building society branch offices has fallen by 15 percent over the last 10 years.

One solution has been the introduction of tele-banking, customers arranging payments and transfers over the telephone network, rather than at the counter. The Bank of Scotland operates a computer terminal system called HOBS (Home and Office Banking Service), accessible from a PC or dedicated terminal. The service operates 18 hours per day, every day and customers can transfer funds between current and savings accounts, or arrange to pay bills on specific days.

Most of the other high-street banks have experimented with telephone-based services. Midland Bank's First Direct subsidiary was the first free-standing telephone banking operation. It has no branch offices, instead customers telephone the bank and discuss their requirements with a member of the bank's staff. Calls are charged to the user at local rates through BT's 0345 service, with the bank paying the additional costs of long distance calls. As of the beginning of 1994, First Direct was opening 10,000 new accounts every month.

The Nationwide and Halifax building societies and the TSB offer tele-banking via a computerised voice service operated in conjunction with a push-button, tone dialling phone. After dialling, the user is prompted through a menu of services by the computerised voice. Selection from the menu is made by pressing the appropriate telephone push-button key. The system reduces all user entries to numbers (e.g. account numbers and security codes) which can be handled via the tones of the phone. Balances and confirmation of transactions are spoken by the computer. Quality of speech production was an important issue for the banks, hence they avoided synthesised speech. Instead, they have opted for digitised segments of a real human voice which are combined by the computer to create complete phrases and sentences (see p.223).

Retailing

The introduction of public banking terminals is coincident with another application of information technology, this time in retailing. The late 1970s saw the introduction of computer terminals at supermarket check-outs, department store counters, and other points where the sale of goods takes place. In the jargon of computer marketing, these are known as 'point-of-sale' or *POS terminals*. There are two main types of such terminal – interconnected and free-standing. Interconnected POS terminals are part of a network, linked via communication lines to the retail organisation's computer system. They transmit data relating to each sale as it takes place. A free-standing terminal is a computer in its own right, which processes and stores data about the transactions. It may also exchange data with a central computer at pre-determined intervals, say at the end of the day.

In each case, the terminals are equipped with some means of supplying data about the details of a purchase in computer-coded form, and a printer to produce a receipt for the customer. The items purchased are identified

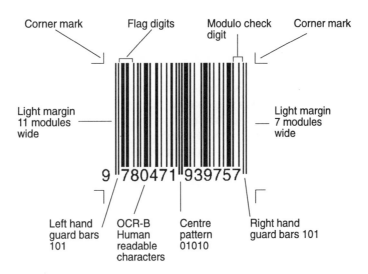

Fig. 2.7 Components of the EAN (European Article Numbering) system of bar-codes. Items for sale in a supermarket are identified by printed bar-codes which can be scanned by a laser at the check-out

Corner mark — Flag digits — Modulo check digit — Corner mark

Light margin 11 modules wide — Light margin 7 modules wide

9 780471 939757

Left hand guard bars 101 — OCR-B Human readable characters — Centre pattern 01010 — Right hand guard bars 101

by means of a bar-code, similar to the one shown in Fig. 2.7.

Each type of merchandise sold in a store is allocated a unique code, printed on its wrapping. At the point of sale, the code is read by a laser scanning device linked to the terminal. The computer cross-references this code with a price table stored in its memory and prints out the details on the receipt. At the same time, it records or transmits these details for updating the stock-list of the firm, held in the central computer. Management can then be supplied with necessary information about the current trading position, so that stock-holding can be finely controlled, and popular sales lines can be quickly spotted. An obvious possibility, not yet realised on a wide basis, is to use the same terminal to connect also to the banking network. A customer then would use a debit card to settle the bill, as noted earlier. The advantages claimed for the introduction of information technology into retailing include: reduced clerical workload, improved stock control, rapidly available sales information, better credit control, more accurate and consistent pricing – all leading to a more efficient and better service to the customer.

Future developments
What of the future? Electronic funds transfer has grown in recent years at a rate exceeding 30 per cent per annum, whilst cash and cheque usage is falling. The growth differential is expected to continue in favour of EFT as electronic payments terminals are installed in small shops, garages, etc. A further move in this direction is heralded by the increasing use of debit cards (34 per cent growth in 1993), of which the French 'smart card' is an example. This contains a microchip which can store and calculate the details of the transactions for which it is used. Apart from serving as 'electronic money', smart cards are already being used as identification and access control passes, bearers of personal and medical records, encryption devices and so on.

As with office technology and industrial automation, the trend here is towards the integration of computer-based and telecommunication-based services. There are several reasons why such integration is slow to materialise in practice. The obvious one is expense. It has been estimated that European banks will spend in excess of £2100 million on information technology in 1994, and this figure has been growing at a rate of over 10% per annum.

Electronic point-of-sale systems cost hundreds of millions of pounds to install. It is not clear who is going to benefit most from installing the terminals and the telecommunication lines. Also, the technology is not yet sufficiently robust to cater for the secure and reliable interconnection of different large-scale networks. If difficulties of this type are overcome in the longer run, the way will be open to link the payments-sales system to the information network of manufacturing industry on the one hand, and to the home-shopping mail-order networks on the other. The benefits, and costs, of such a large-scale trading network can only be contemplated at this stage. Whether such a network will ever come into existence depends, of course, not only on its technical feasibility, but also on its public acceptance, economic viability (coloured by factors like the availability of raw materials, energy and the general economic climate) and the willingness of the various interests involved in such an arrangement to co-operate. There are also genuine concerns about its threats to people's privacy and consumer rights, the possibilities of fraud and theft (discussed later in Chapter 14) and problems caused by incorrect design or malfunctioning of the system. In 1989, for instance, the computer of a London bank 'gave away' £2 billion in half an hour because of a computer programming error. A design problem of a different kind surfaced during the stock market crash of 19 October 1987: it is widely believed that the use of information technology in the buying and selling of shares greatly magnified the fall. The ability to transact business at a keystroke, if necessary in all major markets of the world simultaneously, can lead to very rapid swings in prices, which can be compounded by the 'automatic' selling of stocks by computers which are activated when prices drop to a pre-determined threshold level. ('Chaos theory' is being applied to try to prevent similar occurrences in the future.)

On a somewhat smaller scale, information technology can already provide some of the components of an electronic retail information system, for purposes of evaluation. In advertising, retailers and manufacturers can produce their catalogues in *video* form. Provided that would-be customers have at their disposal appropriate cassette or disc-replay equipment, these media add the possibility of motion and sound to existing forms of mail-order catalogues, at a comparable or lower cost.

Two-way telecommunication-based systems, such as *videotex* or *cable television*, can be used not only to advertise goods for sale but also to accept and acknowledge orders. Users of videotex are able to order certain lines by authorising the computer to supply their names and addresses to the retailer, together with other details of the order, which are keyed in by means of a numerical keyboard. In some cases, this facility is linked to the use of a credit card, with the keyboard again being used to enter the credit card number. A future development would allow the inclusion of detailed coloured photographs in the videotex frame and so approximate the current form of pages of a mail-order catalogue.

With video cassettes, discs and videotex, the customer can look at the advertisements and respond to them (or not) at his or her leisure. With two-way cable television, the advertisement goes out 'live', just like any other TV commercial, and the customers are equipped with a keyboard, linked to the cable, with which they can indicate their interest in the item which is being broadcast.

Computer and telephone-based information systems are also being used to give specialised services to the financial and commercial worlds. These systems carry up-to-the-minute information on stock prices, currency rates, world and national events, etc. Two of the largest of such systems are operated by international news agencies. Information appears as text on TV-style display screens. Users are provided with full keyboards which enable them to originate information, as well as to select items of special interest to themselves. Both these systems are international, in the sense that the service is available in many countries.

Finance and commerce also have available to them all the information technology which is being developed for the 'electronic office'. Document preparation and distribution are just as much of concern to business as they are to administration. Electronic office aids such as telex, facsimile, text processing, computerised telephone exchanges, graphical input and output devices, voice input and output devices, conferencing via telephone, television or computer links have just as much potential in the business environment as in government offices. The impact of the 'microelectronic revolution' on finance and commerce has been most noticeable in making these products, as well as self-contained microcomputer systems, available to a wider range of businesses than before.

A new industry has also developed around the production of *computer programs* for the business user. Such *software packages* will increase in sophistication and reliability and form the basis of many information technology applications in this area (see p. 98).

The reliable and secure operation of computer and telecommunication-based systems is of particular importance in financial transactions. Errors in the processing and transmission of data can be expected to become less frequent as the technical quality of equipment improves, the reliability of software increases, and the equipment is designed with greater attention to the requirements and failings of people.

New information technology products will also have to contend with the problem of criminal misuse, such as wire-tapping or computer fraud. Methods and standards for dealing with this problem are currently under development in research laboratories. Some of these methods, and appropriate legislation, will also have a role in protecting the privacy of business transactions. They are discussed in the chapter on data protection (see p. 149).

Military applications   Computer and telecommunication technologies have been employed in the military field ever since their beginnings. Calculation of the ballistics of artillery shells and the transmission and decoding of messages are among the first recorded uses of these technologies. The continuing quest for more powerful, smaller, lighter and more reliable equipment for military purposes, as well as for the space programme, has given rise, among others, to the micro-electronic technology of today. The current military interest in the 'automated battlefield' and 'strategic computing' also provides a strong motivation, and substantial resources, for the development of 'intelligent' weapons systems.

The 'automated battlefield' concept includes 'ultra-smart' missiles which find their pre-programmed targets with very high accuracy, as well as automated command, control and communication systems which allow commanders to keep close control over remote battle positions. Satellite-based communication systems are being used for surveillance and navigation purposes.

The acquisition, interpretation and display of the vast amounts of data, consisting mainly of images, from remote-sensing devices is an evident military application area of information technology, as is the ever-increasing complexity of encypherment and decoding of messages.

Military applications of information technology often pave the way for its introduction into other spheres of activity. For example, the use of simulators, including highly realistic computer-generated dynamic colour images, was first developed for military training. Although initially applied in pilot training, the technique has been developed to such an extent that, combined with *video, audio- and computer-conferencing* techniques, a complete European 'battle' has been fought on linked computer screens of NATO forces. Advanced simulation techniques are now also employed in many civilian training applications.

The military market has been one of the largest purchasers of electronic and information technology systems, but the political changes in Eastern Europe have seen major cutbacks in western defence spending. Fewer systems are being purchased and research and development has been cut back. Since 1986 NATO's expenditure on equipment and systems (including telecommunications and computing) has fallen by over 30%, as shown in Fig 2.8.

Fig. 2.8 NATO equipment expenditure 1986 - 1993. Totals are billions of US$.

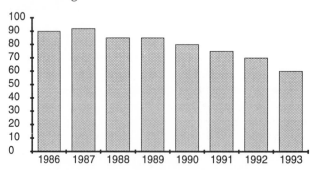

The present defence strategy would appear to one of developing rapid response units that can be deployed as required, rather than the large standing armies associated with the cold-war era. It is not yet clear how these changes will affect the spin-offs into commercial and domestic information technologies. Another common feature is the rationalisation of equipment manufacturers, both in the USA and Europe. The internal market within the USA is sufficient to support a rationalised, indigenous arms industry, whereas European production remains fragmented. The few exceptions are the cross-border developments, such as Eurofighter

(UK, Germany, Italy, Spain), Future Large Aircraft (France, Germany, Italy, Spain), and the NH-90 helicopter (France, Germany, Netherlands, Italy).

Communication and transport services

Under this rather broad heading is included the application of information technology in the telephone service, in specialist information services, and in road and air transport.

Telephone service

The telephone service is a vital component of many new systems and applications of information technology. Its quality, reliability, cost, and the range of facilities it offers are of major importance not only in its traditional role of providing a means of holding conversations at a distance, but also in the transmission of computer-compatible signals for whatever application. The latter services require use of a modulator-demodulator (*modem*) to convert the computer's digital signals to the telephone network's analogue signals (see p. 70).

At the present time the telephone systems of most countries are undergoing fundamental technical changes. At the heart of these changes lies the introduction of computers into telephone exchanges and into the telephones themselves.

The intention behind the computerisation is to improve the performance of the national and international telephone networks (see p. 71). When the change-over is complete, towards the end of this century, the users are promised a faster, more reliable telephone service. There are also new facilities becoming available as a direct result of the computerisation. These include:

(a) Abbreviated dialling – long telephone numbers, frequently called by a subscriber, can be obtained by dialling one or two digits.

(b) Repeat last call – a short code dialled after getting an engaged-tone automatically attempts again the last number called.

(c) Repeat last stored call – the number last dialled is put in a computer store (memory) so that other numbers can be dialled before attempting again the stored number.

(d) Divert calls – all incoming calls can be diverted automatically to a specified number; *or* this is done only after the original number does not answer after a given time; *or* only when the original number is engaged.

(e) Call waiting – incoming calls are acknowledged and asked to wait when the called number is engaged.

(f) Call barring – all incoming or all outgoing calls can be barred.

(g) Reminder calls – automatic call by the exchange at a requested time (as an alarm or reminder).

(h) Three-way connection – these can be set up from an ordinary phone.

(i) Remote control – all these facilities can be set up for the customer's own number from any other telephone.

The call-diversion facility is of particular interest since it will make possible a long-distance call for the price (to the caller) of a local call – the difference will be paid by the called party. The 'toll-free' or '800' calls already provide such a facility, to the advantage, for example, of commercial organisations which do not have to maintain a branch office in every city in order to answer inquiries or accept bookings. Many of these developments are being consolidated into *Intelligent Networks*, a phrase first coined at Bell Laboratories in the US. The Department of Trade and Industry launched its first consultative document on Intelligent Networks in December 1992, with service provider responses published the following year.

During the period of introduction of these new facilities, there is likely to be a need for explanation and guidance about their use. The *computerised exchange* caters for this by offering an automatic 'talking guide' to help the user through a sequence of actions step-by-step.

During the 1980s the telephone service was extended from fixed installations, that is telephones connected by wire to exchanges, to mobile ones. Users of mobile services are able to link to the telephone network via a portable telephone. One of the early means of liberating users from the fixed installation was the *pager* which alerts its mobile user that another person is trying to get in touch. The pager displays the number of the caller who can then be called back, from either a fixed or a mobile installation.

The next development was the mobile two-way telephone, or *cellular telephone*, which could be carried around in a briefcase or pocket. In the UK Vodafone and Cellnet operate national analogue cellular networks that support 1.6 million customers (early 1994). The tariff structure combines a monthly fixed charge together with timed call charges. Lower fixed charges have been introduced for infrequent users (as little as £10 per month) but actual call rates are much higher.

In the autumn of 1993 Mercury launched the first UK digital service, One-2-One, initially operational within the boundary of the M25 London orbital motorway. Full UK coverage is not expected until the year 2000. A comparable service operated by Hutchison Telecom will provide coverage for 50 per cent of the UK population during 1994. Both these services conform to the Personal Communications Network (PCN) standard.

Current developments in this area are aimed at providing a global mobile communications system. A pan-Europe standard has been agreed, the *Groupe Speciale Mobile* or GSM, operating in the 900 Mhz band. The main advantages claimed for the digital system are more comprehensive services, better utilisation of the frequency resources and greater security through encryption. Users will be supplied with a personalised smart card which locks into the GSM handset to provide user access codes and accounting information. A user travelling within Europe rents a handset within the destination country and plugs in their personal smart card, alerting the GSM system of their location and so permitting automatic redirection of all calls.

Several other digital mobile systems are being developed, commonly referred to as CT3 (cordless telephones), DECT (digital European cordless telecommunication), PCN (personal communication network) and ERMES (European radio messaging system). The basic differences between these systems relate to the frequency band allocated to the service, the size of the cell, and the control signalling protocol employed.

In the UK Hutchison Telecom did offer a CT2 service known as Rabbit, but it closed down shortly after its launch due to a lack of take-up. The service utilised base-stations in shops, garages, etc., but the roaming range was limited to about 100 metres from these stations. A user could dial any number on the national telephone network, via a base-station, but could not receive incoming calls. It has been suggested that lack of this facility was the primary cause of failure of the service.

Cellular technology is also being developed for satellite systems. Motorola has proposed a multi-satellite system, code named Iridium, employing 66 low earth orbit (LEO)[1] satellites in 11 polar orbits. Total costs of the system are likely to be in excess of $6000 million and the first test satellites have been licensed for launch in 1994. Inmarsat is also considering the development of a satellite-based mobile system, but utilising either 10-12 satellites in intermediate circular orbits (ICO)[2], or 4-6 geostationary stationary (GEO)[3] satellites. The first satellite of the Inmarsat P service is due for launch in 1998.

The main effects of computerisation of the telephone service can be seen in the exchanges and trunk network, with the replacement of analogue switching and transmission systems by digital switching and optical fibre cables. The introduction of the *integrated services digital network* (ISDN) has extended digital services to commercial and domestic subscribers, offering combined audio, data and video transmission services (see p 120).

Transport

The availability of telephones in cars is already providing a means of communication for people held up in traffic jams. Some other applications of information technology are aimed at preventing or at least reducing the occurrence of traffic jams.

One such development is the *radio data system*. This uses adapted car radios which give priority to transmissions of traffic information. Whether the driver has the radio in mute mode, or listening to recorded or live sound, a digitally transmitted code will override these to give the latest traffic information on the nearest local station. A modified form of the service can also produce a readable display of such information.

Information technology has also been applied to speed up the payment of tolls. Some of the tolls booths operating at the Dartford tunnel and bridge crossings over the Thames utilise special prepaid transponder units attached to the car windscreen. As the driver approaches the booth a signal activates the transponder, requesting the account details of the vehicle. If the account is in credit the barrier is raised, otherwise the driver must pay the toll in cash.

An alternative approach to IT-aided road traffic management, still under development, is the control of access to notoriously congested roads, such as in centres of cities. Induction loops buried in the road pick up movement of traffic and feed the information to a set of computer-controlled traffic-lights and re-routing signs. One version of such a system,

---

[1] low earth orbit corresponds to an altitude of approximately 750 km
[2] intermediate circular orbit corresponds to an altitude of about 10,000 km
[3] geostationary orbit corresponds to an altitude of 36,000 km

which also identified each car through 'electronic number plates' for charging purposes, was trialled in Hong Kong. The trial was abandoned when it became clear that the collected information could be used to track movements of individuals.

The UK Government's Green Paper on a 'pay as you drive' system for motorways is currently working its way through Parliament (1994). The scheme is intended to raise funds for expansion and repair to the motorway system and to limit access. It is envisaged that radio transponders within the car would be used to monitor motorway usage and payment would be by pre-paid smart cards. Users trying to avoid payment would be captured on camera.

Access control systems are under consideration by a number of provincial cities, including Cambridge, as a means of reducing congestion. The Cambridge system proposes charging drivers for the amount of time they spend within the city limits, rather than the distance travelled.

A further development in the pipeline is the visual and, if desired, speaking 'navigator' which guides the driver to his or her destination via the least congested route, on the basis of information keyed in by the driver relating to the destination, and information transmitted by control stations about the overall state of traffic in the area.

The safe control of traffic and the avoidance of congestion is also a major application of IT in air transport. Indeed, air transportation has been one of the earliest and most significant users of information technology. Complex information systems for pilots and air traffic controllers have been followed by automatic landing systems, computerised on-line seat reservation systems, and more recently by bar-coded baggage handling systems. Future developments include the use of 'smart' cards for ticketing, along the lines of similar applications already in use in the railway and telephone networks of various countries.

Specialist information services

Information services which are devoted to specialist fields and professional interests are one of the fastest growing areas of information technology. Their expansion mirrors the growth in the amount of published items – books, periodicals, journals, reports, catalogues, manuals, audio and visual (film, television, photographic etc.) materials, patents, designs, computer programs – the records of human intellectual activity. Indeed, it has been estimated that the sum total of human knowledge is currently doubling every five years (Martin, J., *The Wired Society*, Prentice-Hall, 1978).

Such an exponential increase in potentially useful information would be impossible to handle without some new tools for its storage and retrieval. Conventional 'store-houses of knowledge', the libraries, are running out of space and financial resources in trying to keep up with the output of recorded information. It is becoming virtually impossible for any particular library to possess every published item of information. Instead, libraries and entrepreneurial information services increasingly specialise on particular topics. Moreover, more and more of the information is being placed in *computerised data-bases* and/or recorded on microfilm.

Specialist computerised data-bases are now available in many countries.

Access to them may be gained through computer terminals which either display the required information on their screen, or can be used to request a printed version. The terminals may be located anywhere that has a telecommunication link with the computer. For example, a world-wide data-base on educational publications is held in a computer system in California. It can be used, day or night, by account holders in any country via the international telephone network. Telecommunication costs tend to make the use of such computer-based information systems rather expensive for 'browsing', but, again, technological changes are on the way. A form of data transmission, called *packet switching*, can reduce the cost of using specialist data-bases at long distance (see p. 115). For example, a European service, Euronet-Diane, employs packet switching to link together a large number of hitherto separate data-bases in various western European countries. An authorised user in any of the EEC countries can link to any one of over 20 specialist data-bases, ranging from Italian judicial case law to the European Space Agency's reports. The information on tap covers a wide range of socio-economic, scientific and technical topics. In this way, the concept of a universal, world-wide store-house of knowledge is again becoming a possibility, this time dispersed geographically but accessible through *data networks* (see p. 110) and the application of information science.

Health care

Health care is an area where the applications of information technology have so far been on a rather small scale. The obvious uses of computers, in the administrative side of the operation of health services, have kept step with similar applications in other areas. Thus, personal records of hospital patients and of recipients of national health assistance are being maintained in data-banks in many western industrialised countries. However, the detailed medical, as opposed to personal, information held about people in such data-banks varies between countries.

A more recent development, which also overcomes the problem of centralised storage of confidential medical records, is to provide people with 'smart cards', capable of storing computerised data. These are similar, in principle, to the cards already mentioned in connection with financial transactions. An optical-memory card capable of holding 800 pages of text or 8 digitally recorded TV pictures has been tested by a London hospital for the individualised storage of the medical progress of 100 expectant mothers. In another experiment 8500 inhabitants of Exmouth were given 'chip cards' capable of storing 12 A4 pages of text, updated each time they attend a hospital, a dentist, a pharmacy or a general practitioner. Passwords and personal identity numbers (PINs) were used to control access to different portions of the card and patients were given access to all information recorded about them. General practitioners can now use microcomputer-based filing systems and text-processing equipment for the day-to-day administration of their practice. The systems deal with the financial accounts, lists and 'profiles' of patients, and print reminders of appointments, repeat prescriptions, etc. These systems would be restricted to the practice itself, and the control of the data would remain with the general practitioner. In Britain, there have been several plans for linking up the country's 26,000 general practitioners by a nationwide computer network. The latest plan involves placing terminals into doctors' surgeries where they will be used, in the first instance, to report on observed side-effects of prescription drugs.

The National Health Service has also started to exploit the benefits of electronic data exchange with its suppliers of drugs, clothing, dressings, etc. A closed user-group network has been established, known as Pharamnet. A hospital needing to purchase any of these items simply completes an electronic order for each supplier and then posts the orders into Pharmanet. Next time the supplier logs onto the network the order is read and acknowledged. After completing and dispatching the order the supplier notifies the hospital and sends an electronic invoice. The system is claimed to be saving thousands of pounds a year in data entry costs and reducing the clerical errors that used to arise from transcribing lists between paper copies. Many small suppliers who were initially reluctant to join the service now find themselves benefiting from the cost savings.

Another, well-publicised, application of computers in health care is computer tomography – the visualisation of internal structures in the human body from data provided by an array of detectors (Fig. 2.9). Recent developments in tomography equipment have produced a model small enough to fit into a bus, thereby permitting mobile screening units.

Fig. 2.9 Computer tomography. In this example, the patient's brain is being scanned by a ring of detectors. Their outputs are processed in a computer to give a picture of the cross-sectional structure of the brain. (International General Electric Company of New York Ltd)

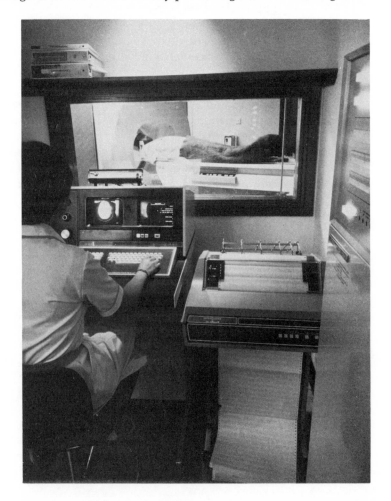

A current development could see the replacement of X-ray photographic film with on-screen digital images, following work undertaken at the Hammersmith hospital. The X-ray image is projected onto a re-usable phosphorous plate which is then scanned by a laser and digitised. Each plate can be re-used up to 10,000 times and the process exposes patients to 15 per cent less radiation. The images can be accessed from any one of the hospital's 150 terminals, viewed simultaneously at several locations or even transmitted to a remote location. The Hammersmith hopes to have become the first film-less hospital by the end of 1994.

Computers are being used, on a limited scale, in applications such as the maintenance of abstracts of medical literature and medical statistics, the monitoring of critically ill patients who require continuous measurement of vital body functions, the automation of certain hospital laboratory tests, and diagnostic tests.

Computers are also being tested in the role of assistants in arriving at a diagnosis of the cause of patients' complaints. In some experiments, the patient answers questions posed by a computer terminal, in a conversational form; in others, the questions are posed by a doctor-figure on a video screen. In either case, the patient keys in the responses, which may be as simple as 'yes' or 'no'. The computer records these responses and comes up with a set of possible diagnoses, in order of their likelihood, for the doctor's consideration. In some systems, the computer holds a vast amount of expert diagnostic experience, accumulated over a life-time by clinicians. Such an *expert system* (see p. 165) can be consulted by medical students, or doctors seeking a 'second opinion'. A variant on this theme is the computer system which allows medical students to experiment with treatment plans, examine the likelihood of various diagnoses, etc., using simulated medical cases.

Communication technology is also being employed in medical practice, on an experimental basis. It is possible, for example, to link medical electronic equipment used by patients in their homes, to a data recorder in a hospital via the telephone. In this way, routine tests on the patient, or on the equipment, can be performed at a distance. In a 'live' telecommunication link-up, using visual and audio channels, a doctor can examine a patient, admittedly only to a limited extent. But with the assistance of a trained nurse by the side of the patient, the range of tests can be extended. Such a system can be of significance where the doctors need to cover a large geographical area.

The 'intelligent' robots of manufacturing industry are gradually coming to the help of people unable to use their limbs, a field known as rehabilitation. The robot supports the user by undertaking the simple tasks we often take for granted, for example exchanging diskettes, turning the pages of a book, or inserting letters into envelopes. In some cases the robot arms can be activated by voice (see p. 224). Current developments separate the operational space of the robot from that of the user, to ensure the safety of the disabled user, but future systems will permit free-roaming robots employing ultrasonic and infrared detection systems.

Information technology has also an important role to play in aiding people with sensory handicaps. There are already a large number of systems in use. Blind people, for example, would benefit enormously from having a device which converts printed text to speech. One such device, developed in the United States, scans the print with a beam of light at a rate of 150–200 words/min. A small computer associated with the device then applies about 1000 rules of grammar and pronunciation (with over 3000 exceptions to those rules). A *voice output* component then converts the resulting signals to comprehensible speech (see p. 223). This development suffers from a number of shortcomings, including its price (about $50,000), size, inability to cope with certain styles of print, newspapers, graphics, etc. However, none of these problems is technically insurmountable. A smaller, lower-cost system enables blind people to use computer terminals by converting words on the screen into speech.

For those with impaired hearing, the arrival of *videotex* and *teletext* systems is of much significance (see p. 143). These systems can already provide a great deal of information in purely visual form, including subtitles for television programs. In the future, when electronic mail is developed to its full potential, deaf people will be able to use it to transmit messages person-to-person simply and rapidly. They would also benefit from low-cost *facsimile* (see p. 132), electronic publishing, *video discs* (see p. 85), and similar display-linked developments.

There are many forecasts which put medical applications of information technology on the top of the list as the most rapidly expanding future market. In view of the current level of usage, this may well be true. But in terms of cost-effectiveness and general acceptability, there is still a lot to be done.

Education and training

In comparison with the number of people involved in education and training, and with the size of the education budgets of most countries, the range of applications of information technology in these fields has so far been rather limited. However, the situation is gradually changing, partly as a result of the increasing accessibility of the products of information technology, and partly due to the need to educate and train people in the use of these new tools.

The most widely used educational technology medium is still *broadcasting*. A large proportion of schools is equipped with television and radio receivers, making use of special education programs transmitted by the public broadcasting stations. Many higher education establishments are equipped with their own closed-circuit TV systems for the relay and recording of lectures, which can then be replayed as required. The Open Universities of Britain and of several other countries use broadcasting as a routine component of their distance-teaching systems. In Britain and the United States, it is also used for the professional updating of doctors.

A recent development is the use of *satellite broadcasting* (see p. 123) for educational purposes. The main advantage of the satellite over terrestrial broadcasting is that it can reach a population over a much wider geographical area. For this reason its use was pioneered in the United States, Canada and China, but over the last few years it has also arrived in Europe. The first regular service was Euro-PACE, or the European Programme of Advanced Continuing Education, started in 1988. As its name suggests, it was aimed at advanced learners who wanted to continue their education as part of their professional development. Other current

European educational satellite broadcasting projects include Eurostep, on the European Space Agency satellite Olympus, and 'Channel e', on the Astra satellite.

The United States also pioneered the application of two-way telecommunication media in education: two-way cable TV and the telephone. *Two-way cable* provides a return channel to a tutor in a remote location who can monitor the students' progress with the video material and offer assistance, vision or voice, as necessary. This is, however, an expensive medium for routine educational purposes and no wide-spread use is expected until a technological advance (such as the wide-spread installation of optical-fibre cables and the two-way use of broadcast satellites) changes the economic equation.

Small-scale projects in this area include the interactive video network of London medical schools, which has successfully demonstrated the possibility of 'live' classes with high visual content, shared by students in several geographically separated sites.

A less costly form of two- or multi-way long-distance link between teacher and student is provided by the *telephone network*. Teaching by telephone is being used on a routine basis in the American state of Wisconsin. The University of Wisconsin provides an Extension Service (i.e. off-campus degree courses) in 20 locations around the state via a dedicated telephone network. The courses are aimed at the adult population, and include professional up-dating and other continuing education courses. The cost of operating the service works out at about $20 per student contact hour. Half of this cost is borne by the student.

The telephone network, and its further development, the *integrated services digital network* (see p. 118), can also provide lower-cost alternatives for two- or multi-way visual link-ups. Although currently of somewhat lower visual quality, *video conferences* using *compressed video* (see p. 90) can be adequate substitutes for satellite or broadband cable based services.

The use of the telephone network for the transmission of computer-compatible signals also supports educational information services and electronic mail. One such service is the British 'Campus 2000'. This links computers in primary and secondary schools and in the further education sector to one another and to sources of computerised information and libraries of educational software.

The availability of computers in schools is now taken for granted in most Western industrialised countries. In Britain, for example, there is at least one computer in every primary school and at least 5 in every secondary school. Significant efforts are being made to integrate the computer into the school curriculum, not only in learning about the computer itself, but also as a resource for other subjects.

In industrial, business and military training the computer is also used as part of more sophisticated (and more expensive) *computer-based training* (CBT) systems. Such systems usually consist of a computer-assisted training (CAT) and a computer-managed learning (CML) component.

In CAT the training material (e.g. drill-and-practice, tutorial, simulation) is presented on a screen-based terminal. An attempt is often made to tailor the presentation to the needs of individual students, and to allow considerable interaction between the learner and the computer. For example, in pilot training the computer can reproduce visually a complete aircraft cockpit and present various flight conditions (e.g. from a video disc) to which the pilot must make the appropriate responses. The responses, and the answers to the tests, are monitored by the CML part of the system. The progress of the learner is recorded and reported by the computer, which also alerts the human tutor to intervene in the training process as necessary.

CBT developments are likely to be boosted by the availability of multimedia PCs, supporting stereo sound, full-motion video and CD-ROM storage devices, but the greatest limitation remains good teaching software. There are, however, some applications where need over-rides costs, such as the teaching of medical students at the University of California. The problem stems from a storage of cadavers and so teaching staff have developed a multimedia package that enables students to practice honing their surgical skills on a virtual patient. Other packages have been created to teach practising surgeons the skills of micro-surgery.

'Intelligent tutoring systems' which act as helpful assistants in the learning process are being devised as part of the current drive towards knowledge-based expert systems. Like text processors, some of the educational microcomputers can be interconnected through *local area networks* (see p. 111). In this way, they may share more expensive and larger capacity data-storage devices and printers, and also enable the teacher to monitor and help with the work of individual students through a central console. This parallel of the educational and business applications of information technology illustrates a more general trend in the penetration of new technology: education is not the first area to adopt such developments. It is only when a technology becomes robust, cheap and extensively available that the educational world is prepared to consider its use on a routine basis.

However, even then the role of computers in education is likely to remain controversial. Their introduction into schools has certainly not had a revolutionary effect on pupils' achievement.

As in several other fields of application, after the initial burst of enthusiasm, there is now a re-assessment of the educational impact of information technology. Its true role is likely to emerge through an evolutionary process in the next few years and decades.

The home

Applications of information technology in the home have so far centred on three main areas: telecommunication, entertainment and information, and personal computing.

Two-way telecommunication is based almost entirely on the telephone network, although in some countries *cable television* and citizens-band radio have been used for this purpose. Although initially intended only for voice communication, the telephone network is now increasingly used also to convey other forms of information. By linking computer terminals or videotex equipment to the telephone socket, distant computer data-bases can be accessed from the home. In this way, people whose work involves using a computer or who wish to look up general or special interest information contained in data-stores can do so without leaving their home.

The provision of entertainment and information have, up to recently, tended to be the exclusive province of the broadcasting and printed publishing media. Now, the *video cassette* and the *compact disc* (see p. 86) provide alternative sources of entertainment material, and *teletext* and *videotex* services (see p. 143) bring additional instantaneous, up-to-the-minute information into the home.

The transition from these products and services of today to some possible future applications of information technology in the home is marked by the promise of low-cost microelectronic systems. Already more than one in 25 homes in the UK have a home computer. Its uses as an entertainment device are already with us, in the form of computer games of increasing sophistication and even of some educational content. It will also serve as a means of *aids to learning* of a more serious type, giving a semblance of a one-to-one relationship between tutor and learner. When linked to other computers via a two-way telecommunication medium, the home computer will gain access to a range of services already discussed in this chapter. These include text processing at-a-distance, *electronic mail* (see p. 132), electronic funds transfer, medical assistance, and distance-learning facilities. They will also be able to make use of computer programs (software packages) from centralised 'program warehouses' or from specialist suppliers. *Voice input and output* (see p. 221), links to home security devices (detectors, locks, etc.) and to other domestic equipment (lights, heating and ventilation control, etc.) for personal computers are also becoming a reality, at least technically, if not economically.

One view of how a 'home information and control centre' of the future may operate comes from the United States (Carne, 'The wired household', *IEEE Spectrum*, October 1980, p. 65). It is summarised in Fig. 2.10.

The computer occupies the central position in this picture. It communicates with other equipment by means of a *local network* of electric or optical-fibre cable, and with the outside world by broadcast signals, and digital signals via a *data network* (see p. 105) and/or a cable TV network (see p. 74). (Whether the telephone, data and cable TV networks are to remain separate entities, or will be combined into one, is a matter of debate at the time of writing.)

Looking first at the new entertainment and information services, we are likely to see the emergence of high technical quality TV transmission; receivers with increased visual and audio fidelity and stereo sound; pay-as-you-view television delivered over the telephone system (Video on demand) and later possibly three-dimensional pictures. Direct-broadcast satellite and multi-channel cable transmissions will offer a wider choice of programmes, including those originating from other countries. The higher technical quality video and audio sets will also exploit to the full the better reproduction offered by digital audio (e.g. 'compact discs') and video (e.g. video discs, satellite transmissions).

Home administration covers services like electronic banking and shopping, electronic mail, the use of computerised office facilities, etc. For some people, working from home via IT-based aids is already possible. We may see a more widespread use of this option as a means of saving on transport costs and as a way of opting out of lengthy journeys to and from work. Jobs that are particularly suited to such '*teleworking*' include management or professional tasks which are largely administrative,

Fig. 2.10 A computer-centred view of the home information ring-main. The computer acts as the central control panel and communication centre for other electronic equipment in the home.

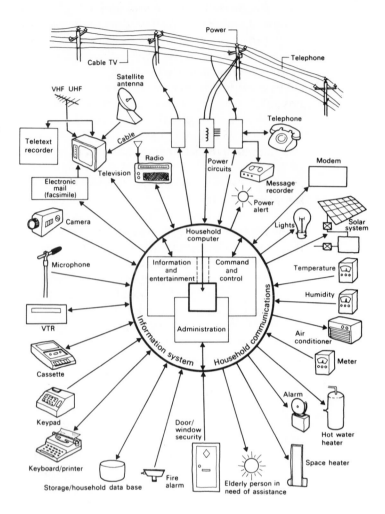

clerical, analytical or creative. People involved in 'teleworking' may be

–   full-time employees of an organization who do not need a conventional office;

–   part-time employees, usually taking on a reduced commitment from their previous employer in exchange for freedom to work partly for themselves; or

–   self-employed people operating on a free-lance basis.

The minimum equipment is a personal computer and telephone, which can also connect the computer to other, remote computers.

In 1993 BT completed a trial of teleworking for more closely supervised staff, a group of directory enquiry operators based in Inverness. Operators working from home were provided with PCs connected to the local exchange by an ISDN line of 128 kilobits per second. Videophones permitted face-to-face contact with the supervisor or any other colleague on the network, thereby reducing many of the problems of isolation felt by teleworkers. In addition to testing the various IT systems, BT also learnt much about the importance of the selection and management of teleworking staff.

An alternative to having such facilities, or more sophisticated and expensive ones, is the 'telecottage' pioneered in Scandinavia and Japan. It usually takes the form of a room, or set of rooms, in a village house which is equipped with information technology products and systems useful for teleworking. People can come to work in the telecottage as if they are going to work in an office, paying for its facilities for remote working. By the middle of 1994 there were over 100 telecottages and telecentres established in the UK and Eire, with estimates of a total of 250 by the end of the decade, serving 10,000 teleworkers.

In Japan, the concept of home working is taken even a step further by the planning of new 'information cities'. Along the lines of 'intelligent buildings' mentioned in the context of office applications, such cities would have all the facilities of Fig. 2.10 built in from the outset.

'Command and control' may refer to facilities like computerised energy control (heating, ventilation, hot water, lights, cooking, etc.) and electronic security devices. For example, in the United States these can already be linked to the police via the cable TV network.

The usefulness of interlinking domestic appliances in this way is yet to be proved. There are also several technical, economic and social hurdles in the way of the home information centre: for example, many households are still without telephone, let alone equipped with the wide-band cable needed for fast, high-volume electronic communication. The economic justification for many of the new products and services will only exist if they are able to offer savings compared with existing ways, or if they satisfy a hitherto unfulfilled need. A government-sponsored survey in Britain has shown that in 1989 about a third of the people interviewed were keen to automate their homes. The majority expressed interest in more restricted, common-sense developments, such as

- warning displays on appliances saying when they have broken down and why (74%)
- home security systems (70%)
- learning at a distance (69%)
- home banking (63%).

At the same time, people were concerned about the reliability of equipment, the need for such systems to remain under human control, and the possibility of centralised accumulation of information about their personal lives.

Summary

A common feature of the current range of tools offered by information technology is that they represent an *alternative* to established media and to existing facilities for handling information. By converting the *form* in which information is expressed to the digital form used by computers, they make it possible to combine a range of tasks hitherto done as separate operations. For example, text translated to this form does not have to be typed out or duplicated when it passes from one person, or section, in an organization to another. Rather, it is the electronic signals representing that text which are transmitted, filed, modified or displayed, using the new tools and products developed for those purposes (see Fig. 2.11).

Whether the alternative offered by information technology is a solution to recognised problems or whether it is an answer in search of questions is the subject of much current discussion. In some areas, such as banking, communications and certain military applications, the amount of information that needs to be handled, or the time available for its processing, make it necessary to employ the electronic alternative. In other areas, such as the home, medicine, education, information technology is yet to make a serious impact. In a third group of applications, in the office, in manufacturing industries, in commerce, the new technology is on trial. Its capacity for performing some of the more mechanical, menial tasks currently done by people is at once its strength and threat.

The use of electronic signals does not provide, in itself, a more attractive alternative to long-established tools of human information handling. If anything, it interposes an additional link in the communication chain, with its attendant 'interface' problems. The contribution of electronic (and optical) representations of information lies in the speed, reliability and reduced physical storage requirements associated with these representations. Furthermore, the existence of automatic equipment (e.g. computers) for the processing of electronic signals holds out the prospect of the automation of tasks which involve representations of information.

There is still a great deal to be learned about information, its use by people and the way people interact with machines before information technology can realise its *full* potential as an aid to human communication and decision-making.

Fig. 2.11 Stages of information management and use in organisations. Arrows indicate the transmission of various representations of information

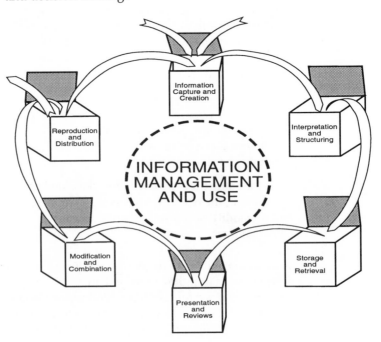

3 Management of information technology

The European Information Technology Observatory reported that total UK expenditure in 1993 on IT related products and services totalled £14,500 million, of which approximately 40 per cent was spent each on hardware and services and 20 per cent on software. These figures exclude the costs of telecommunications services, consumables and salaries. This makes IT into a multi-billion pound business in the UK alone and worth some £245 billion world-wide.

From a management point of view, this level of expenditure needs to be justified, in terms of the overall business objectives of the organisation. Justification for spending on IT is also important at other levels of society, from the individual to national governments and multi-national associations. (The EEC, for example, has multi-billion pound programmes for IT research and development alone.)

In this chapter we shall look, first, at the reasons for introducing IT into organisations, then at some of the issues in producing and implementing an IT strategy, and, finally, at the techniques and results of assessing the 'value-for-money' of IT expenditure.

Making a case for IT

There are four main reasons usually advanced for investment in information technology (Earl, M.H., *Information Management*, Clarendon Press, 1988, p. 33):

1   to gain competitive advantage;
2   to improve productivity and performance;
3   to facilitate new ways of managing and organising;
4   to develop new businesses.

In each of these cases it is also useful to distinguish between the benefits that are associated with the possession of information, and with the effects of investing in technology (for the sake, say, of automating some existing information handling tasks). This distinction is often difficult to make since to acquire and utilise information one also needs to invest in equipment, and, once the equipment is installed, it opens the way to unforeseen resources of information.

So, let us have a look at some examples where the distinction is relatively clear. An organization aspiring to be the first in the market in a product area could subscribe to computerised data-bases reporting on the latest patent applications, virtually as they are filed, on post-graduate theses successfully submitted at leading universities, or market opportunity assessments available virtually as the surveys are completed. This company would be investing in IT essentially with the purpose of obtaining and exploiting new information.

Another company, for example in the travel business, could offer to place free computer terminals, and even two-way communication facilities, into travel agencies in order to ensure that reservations are made with that company and not with its competitors. By offering a convenient and rapid way of conducting business this company may have gained a competitive advantage, improved its productivity (since bookings do not have to be re-keyed once they have been entered by the travel agent), may have introduced more efficient management (through instantaneous access to financial data), and developed new business opportunities (say, by offering not only package holidays, but also tailor-made arrangements which the travel agent and the client can assemble and confirm rapidly from a wide range of computer-listed alternatives). This company, then, justified its expenditure on IT primarily in terms of investment in equipment which then was used to make better use of already available information. Whichever reason has dominated in making a decision to invest in information technology it is important to realise that, if the resulting achievement is to be sustained, a longer-term *IT strategy* is necessary.

IT strategy and its implementation

An IT strategy is concerned with the planning, introduction and use of IT resources, for the benefit of the entire organisation. Although the creation of an IT strategy is primarily a matter for specialists, and in particular technical experts, the strategy itself must be closely linked to the strategies for other aspects of the organisation:

– business strategy;
– personnel strategy;
– general infra-structure development (internal services);
– relations with suppliers and customers, etc.

Information technology has an impact on all of these, and is, in turn, influenced by them.

One approach to the development of an IT strategy is to identify the requirements for information in the various areas of the organisation, and then to provide the technology which delivers the information. This approach often results in changes of the technical infra-structure of the organisation, which then enables it to undertake new projects and access new information. An alternative approach is built around the emerging capabilities of technology: in areas such as computer-integrated manufacturing or electronic publishing, where the availability of complete systems offers new business opportunities. This approach is usually motivated by a specific project – to introduce a new process or product. An example of the former approach is the computerisation of the pay-as-you-earn system (COP) by the Inland Revenue in Britain. The objectives for the strategy were stated as follows (S. Matheson in Earl, op.cit.):

– save staff costs;
– improve service to the public;
– improve facilities and job satisfaction;
– provide flexibility for change.

The timetable for the introduction of a combination of computer, telecommunication and office system is shown in Table 3.1. It was modified in 1984 to allow for its extension to the taxation of the self-employed – a system known as CODA. The overall cost of introducing the system to cover 11 processing centres, 33,000 staff, 32 million taxpayer and employer records using 25,000 computer terminals and 900 telecommunication circuits was £319 million (at 1986 prices).

In 1994 the Inland Revenue transferred its information technology staff and systems to the large American services specialist EDS.

Table 3.1 (From S. Matheson in *Information Management*, ed. by M. Earl, Clarendon Press, 1988)

Preliminary study	1977
Feasibility study	1978–9
Initial approval	1980
Procurement and initial design	1980–1
Detailed design and development	1982–3
Pilot implementation and review	1983–4
Approval for nationwide extension	July 1984
Setting up of COP nationwide	1985–7
Specification and introduction of CODA, including user testing and staff training	1984–9

Some well-publicised examples of businesses which were started from technological considerations come from the newspaper industry. A totally new paper in Britain went through a difficult period with production problems, but has now managed to integrate information technology into its operations, along with several other national dailies and weeklies, which followed the first approach.

The introduction of 'new technology' into the newspaper industry has also called attention to the impact of IT on the employees. The need for training for working with new systems has already become apparent in most applications. Indeed, the rate of innovation tends to outpace the rate at which many organisations provide training for their employees.

Other human issues which arise in the implementation of IT strategies concern health hazards (see chapter 25), job satisfaction industrial relations, organisational re-structuring and consequent changes in decision-making, power and leadership.

Among the technical issues consideration must be given to the reliability of the overall system, in particular in safety-critical applications, its susceptibility to breaks or fluctuations in the electrical power supply, the possibilities of accidental or criminal misuse, the compatibility of equipment and services supplied from different sources, compliance with local, national and international laws and regulations, etc. We shall return to most of these issues in greater detail in Part 2.

Is IT 'value for money'?

A number of surveys have suggested that some 80% of UK financial institutions felt disappointed by the results of their investment in IT, but none have found any simple relationship between IT investment and performance. Wrongly applied IT becomes a competitive handicap rather than a competitive advantage. At the same time, there are doubts whether the return from IT is being properly measured.

The traditional measure in business for investment in capital equipment is return on investment. For IT this should be a complex measure which includes quantifiable improvements in performance, as well as an assessment of new business opportunities, risks and uncertainties arising out of the investment. Some of the most useful improvements in performance come from well-managed introductions of off-the-shelf applications, such as packaged software, or access to commercial data-base and value-added services. These usually carry a low level of technical risk. More risk and uncertainty is associated with IT which is introduced specifically to gain new business and competitive advantage. Such investment is frequently in leading-edge technology and custom-made software, involving innovation and invention.

In addition to return-on-investment, information economists suggest other measures which take into account the pervasive nature of IT:

- *traditional cost-benefit analysis* (e.g. cost-displacement and cost avoidance);
- *value-linking* – benefits achieved in areas other than where the costs are incurred;
- *value-restructuring* – the use of IT to empower employees to perform higher-value functions in the organisation.

There is no general agreement on what the appropriate measures are which determine whether IT offers 'value for money'. What experience has shown is that spending money on IT in itself does not guarantee business success. Nor is IT the solution if the expected benefits can be obtained by some simpler, cheaper actions. The process, however, of assessing the goals, functions and infrastructure of an organisation, prior to investment in IT, may in itself prove beneficial. Proper application of IT will help to release some of the constraints on the organisation, such as time constraints (more rapid feedback on actions, working across time-zones, etc.) and distance-related constraints (wide coverage, distributed operations, etc.).

Finally, it needs to be borne in mind that the IT scene is changing very rapidly, particularly in relation to the conventional planning and investment horizons of many organisations. The most obvious effect is in terms of improved price/performance of IT hardware. There are, in addition, significant changes in the standardisation and inter-operability of IT systems, reducing some of the risks associated with investment. Changes in the laws and regulations in IT-related fields (e.g. copyright and data protection laws, the de-regulation of telecommunication monopolies) will also affect whether IT is perceived to offer value for money. These considerations will also receive attention in Part 2.

Summary

From a management point of view, we again see information technology as involving the three key components of Fig. 1.4:

- people (as individuals and in organisations),
- products (and the infrastructure based upon them), and
- applications (the combination of people and IT systems for specific tasks or functions),

linked together by the flow of information between them.

Part 2

4 Introduction to Part 2

Part 1 has already referred to a range of products and systems which form the technology component of information technology. In this part of the book we shall look in some detail at the technical aspects of the products and services mentioned in the context of their contribution to the handling of information. The areas discussed cover, between them, the historical roots and some recent branches of the 'tree of information technology'.

The 'root' technologies of IT are the telecommunications and audio-video systems of the pre-digital era. The digital computer formed their first healthy off-shoot (it has evolved from the basic techniques of switching and recording from its predecessors). The requirement of communication between computers has contributed to the development of the branch designated as Digital Networks. Part 2 starts with a review of these technologies, as the concepts and terminology employed there provide a good foundation for the later chapters.

With the rapid development of micro-electronic and optical technologies, and the growing emphasis on information services, many new off-shoots ('application technologies') have emerged and are continuing to grow at the same time as the longer-established branches. Figure 4.1 attempts to show these growth points.

Fig. 4.1 New branches of the 'information technology tree'

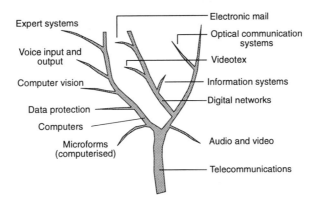

5 Telecommunications

Introduction and fundamentals

The main purpose of telecommunications is to transmit representations of information (*signals*) between remote locations. Most telecommunication systems in operation today employ electrical or electromagnetic media (including light waves) as carriers of signals. These media are harnessed to provide world-wide telecommunication networks. The characteristics of the signals to be transmitted (which will be our first concern below) largely determine the type of network (e.g. data networks, television networks, etc.), and whether a transmission link is dedicated to a particular use, or, as is more often the case, it is shared among a number of uses, e.g. in switched networks used for speech or videotex.

Fig. 5.1 A tele-communication network used for speech transmission requires equipment to convert between speech and its electrical signal representation. The electrical signals are used in the transmission and routing processes

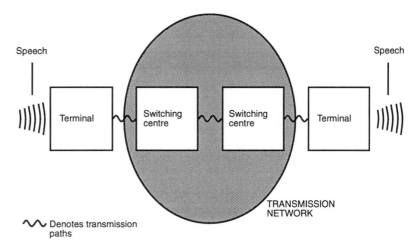

The main components of a telecommunication system are shown diagrammatically in Fig. 5.1. They include terminals which convert representations of information to, and from, the form used within the system and other forms used outside it. The telephone is an example of a terminal, converting the acoustic waves of speech into a fluctuating electrical signal, and the signal back to audible form. The network contains *transmission paths* and *switching centres*, so that the terminals can exchange messages with each other, and optionally, with terminals of other telecommunication systems, through inter-network links.

This generalised view of the network assumes that the terminals connected to the network are capable of acting both as senders and as receivers of signals (a telephone, for example, is equipped with both a microphone and a loudspeaker enabling it to act in *one-to-one*, *one-to-many* or *many-to-many* link-ups). Some systems, such as public broadcast networks, provide only a central sender and many receivers in a *one-to-all* configuration. In such a configuration, there is no need for switching centres (see also Fig. 5.10).

Signals and terminals

Representations of information (speech, text, pictures, measurements, etc.) must be converted to signals for the purpose of telecommunication. Signals themselves are also representations appropriate to the medium which has been chosen as the carrier. A signal is usually represented by the *variation* of some property of the carrier with respect to time. For example, the variations in electrical current representing speech in a telephone system may look as shown in Fig. 5.2. These variations mimic the changes in air pressure at the microphone. Both the air pressure and the electrical signal can vary over a continuous range of possible values; they are called *analogue* representations.

Fig. 5.2 An analogue signal can take on values from a continuous range of possible values over a length of time

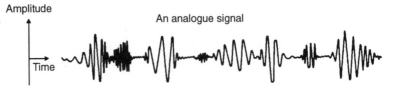

An example of the other main type of signal is that used within computers, as a means of internal communication. It is of the form of electrical *pulses* (Fig. 5.3) which can take only a finite number of values (in this case two) from a discontinuous range. These are *digital* signals.

Fig. 5.3 A digital signal can take on only a limited set of possible values (one of only two values for a binary signal) and transitions between these values occur rapidly

The distinction between analogue and digital signals has been expressed in terms of the size of the variation of the carrier (also called the *amplitude* of the signal). But there is also the other dimension of variation – time. The rapidity (rate) of variation of either type of signal determines the *bandwidth* occupied by it (see p. 66). Bandwidth is expressed on a scale of frequencies, and is measured in units of hertz (Hz), thousands of hertz (kHz), millions of hertz (MHz), etc. Human speech has a bandwidth of about 4 kHz, orchestral music about 15 kHz, a colour TV (video) signal, on the 625-line system, about 5.5 MHz, and on 525-line systems, about 4.2 MHz.

The bandwidth of a digital signal depends on the duration of the shortest pulse used in the particular application. This determines the maximum number of pulses that can be sent per unit time. If the unit of time is the second then the pulse rate is expressed in *bauds*. In most computer applications, where the representation is based on a pulse being present or absent, the pulse rate in bauds is the same as the number of data *bits* per second. (A bit is an elementary data unit, a 1 or a 0.) Computers can communicate with each other at data rates as high as hundreds of Mbit/s (1 Mbit/s = 1 million bit/s) by means of optical fibres, but the rate falls significantly over copper wires. Additional equipment may also be necessary to convert the digital pulses to analogue signals, such as the *modems* (modulator-demodulator) used for communication over voice-grade telephone lines.

Terminals act as the interface between the source/destination of a message and the network. They must be able to reproduce, or convert, the form of representation of a message without appreciable distortion.

Table 5.1 gives examples of terminals which match particular types of message source/destination to particular transmission media and signal representations.

Type of communication	Message source	Transmitter terminal	Transmission channel	Receiver terminal	Destination
Own-exchange telephone call	Speech	Telephone	Local lines and exchange	Telephone	Human listener
Transatlantic telephone call	Speech	Telephone	Local and trunk lines; local, trunk and international exchanges; communication satellite or submarine cable	Telephone	Human listener
Public broadcast radio	Speech and music	Studio, RF transmitter, and links between them	Radio waves	Radio receiver	Human listener
Telegraph	Human operator	Teletypewriter	Lines (wire pairs) and exchanges	Teletypewriter	Human addressee
Data link to a computer	Human operator	Terminal and modem	Data link	Modem and computer input/output devices	Computer
Local and wide area networks	Human operator or PC	PC	Wire pairs, coaxial cable, or optical fibres	PC	Computer

Transmission media

The media used to carry representations of messages differ widely in physical form, speed, capacity and the fidelity with which they are capable of transmitting messages. Engineers are in constant search of physical phenomena, and methods of their utilisation, which can lead to faster, cheaper, more faithful transmission of signals.

The fastest transmission media operate almost at the speed of light, 300 million m/s. The two most widely used forms can be classified as *bounded media* and *free space*. Both make use of electromagnetic wave propagation as the carrier of signals. Bounded media include twisted pairs of wires, coaxial cables, waveguides, optical fibres (light-guides), illustrated in Fig. 5.4. Free space (or unbounded media) is utilised for transmission between aerials (antennas), or radiation sources and sensors.

Figure 5.5 shows how electromagnetic waves of various frequencies (the electromagnetic spectrum) are exploited as carriers of telecommunication signals. The fidelity of transmission in these media is dependent on the signal being able to retain its pertinent characteristics (shape, amplitude,

Fig. 5.4 Some
examples of bounded
transmission media:
(a) Twisted pairs of
wires formed into a
cable

(b) Coaxial cables:
submarine type (top)
and underground type
(bottom)

(c) Waveguides: metal
tubes, about 7.5 cm in
diameter.
(From *Communication
channels*, Henry
Busignies. Copyright
1972 by Scientific
American, Inc. All rights
reserved)

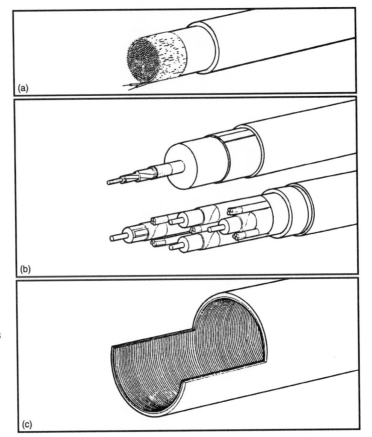

etc.). The main factors influencing this are the effective *bandwidth of the
medium* and *noise*.

The concept of the bandwidth of a medium is similar to that of a signal:
it is the range of frequencies which it can transmit efficiently (the
'efficiency' being strictly defined in engineering terms). That is, for a signal
of a given bandwidth to be transmitted with a defined fidelity by a
medium, the bandwidth of the signal must be within the bandwidth of the
medium. As an example, Fig. 5.6 shows the range of frequencies present in
human speech. By experience, it has been found that speech remains
comprehensible even if its bandwidth is electronically limited to 3.5 kHz.
So, in telephone transmission, the bandwidth of each speech circuit is
engineered to be 4 kHz. In this way, it can contain the (truncated)
bandwidth of speech together with a small 'guard-band' to cater for
imperfections in truncation and transmission.

The notion of the bandwidth of a medium is complicated by the fact that
its value is dependent upon distance from the source. The bandwidth gets
smaller with increasing distance, unless devices known as repeaters are
used to compensate for this effect.

For example, with repeaters, twisted pairs of wires can have a
bandwidth of 500 kHz over some 75 km. Without repeaters, the effective
bandwidth drops from about 100 kHz at 1 km to virtually zero at 75 km.

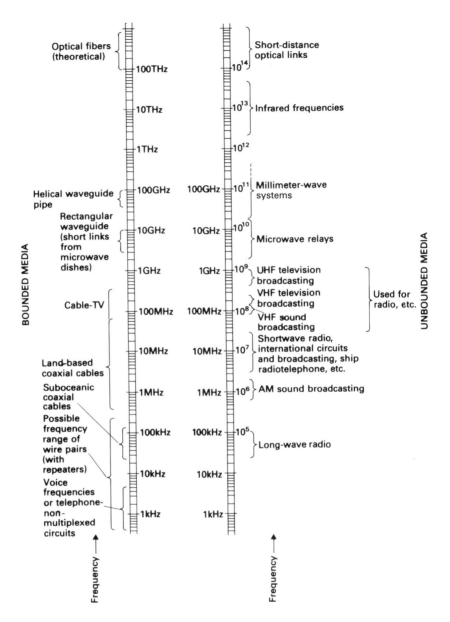

Fig. 5.5 How the electromagnetic spectrum is exploited as carriers of telecommunication signals

Coaxial cables, with a repeater spacing of 1.5 km, can have an effective bandwidth of over 60 MHz, while waveguides with an effective bandwidth of more than 2000 MHz have been fabricated.

Optical fibres operating in excess of 600 Mbit/s form part of the backbone of the trunk network in the US, but these are relatively old technology. August 1993 saw the ordering of the latest Atlantic submarine optical cable, TAT-12, due for installation by the end of 1995. The cable will be 6000 km long, operate at 5 Gbit/s (giga bit/s) and provide a capacity equivalent to 600,000 simultaneous telephone calls.

Communication satellites, which use free space as the transmission medium, can provide up to 2300 MHz bandwidth in the current range of Intelsat V satellites, compared with the bandwidth of 50 MHz of Intelsat I launched in 1965. Unfortunately, the length of a satellite link (about 35,786 km each way) is such that the returning signal is very weak, hardly distinguishable from noise. To exploit the full bandwidth, expensive ground-station equipment is required.

Noise, the other important factor affecting transmission, takes on a special meaning in the field of telecommunications. It includes all the unwanted signals which corrupt the message signal. Noise may be due to electronic components, say in the transmitter or repeater, or to natural disturbances.

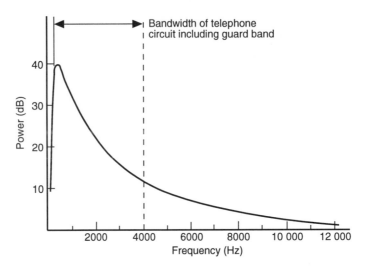

Fig. 5.6 Human speech is represented here by the intensity (power) of vibrations at different frequencies. Superimposed is the bandwidth of speech circuits in telephone transmission

The relative strengths of the message signal and of noise in a transmission link determine the maximum rate at which it can transmit signals without error. This maximum rate, which is also dependent on the bandwidth of the link, is called the *capacity* of the link. The mathematical expression which defines capacity in terms of these quantities is known as Shannon's law (Shannon, 'Mathematical theory of communication', *Bell System Technical Journal*, July/October 1948, p. 401). The theoretical capacity of a transmission link is seldom even approached in practice. An important reason for this is the cost and complexity of the necessary terminal equipment, which has to separate the wanted signal from the unwanted noise. When added to the cost of the link itself (e.g. the coaxial cable or satellite construction and launch costs), the investment needed to establish a long-distance telecommunication network is quite substantial. (It represents about two-thirds of the total cost of the system.)

One way of exploiting the bandwidth of transmission links more effectively is by accommodating more than one signal in the available bandwidth. This is done by a technique known as *multiplexing* (see Fig. 5.7, also p. 112).

Multiplexing is the sharing of a wide-band link among signals of narrower bandwidth requirements. For example, as noted earlier, a single signal in the telephone network requires a bandwidth of 3.5 kHz.

The various transmission media used in telephone networks have bandwidths much in excess of this, so they are split into *channels* of 4 kHz bandwidth (again with a 'safety margin') for better utilisation. A

Fig. 5.7 A tele-
communication channel
can be represented by
its bandwidth available
over a length of time.
The telecommunication
channel of Fig. 5.7(a)
can be fully utilised in
one of two ways:

Multiplexing

Multiplexing is the use of a single telecommunication link to transmit
a number of different signals, either simultaneously or in rapid
succession.

As shown in Fig. 5.7(a), a telecommunication link may be visualized
as a medium with some bandwidth, available over a length of time. If
each of the signals to be transmitted requires a smaller capacity than
that available in the link, the available capacity may be split up either
into (1) frequency bands or (2) time bands, as shown in Fig. 5.7(b), (c).

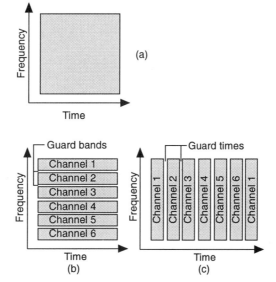

(1) By subdividing it
into narrower frequency
bands, or channels, as
shown in (b)

(2) By allocating its full
bandwidth to one of a
set of channels one
after another, as shown
in (c)

In frequency-division multiplexing, electronic frequency translators
(modulators and demodulators) are used to ensure that individual
signals occupy their allocated channels. The widths of the channels
need not be the same - optimum utilization of the link results if
each channel occupies only the bandwidth it requires.

waveguide with a 2000 MHz bandwidth, say, could be split up in this way
into about half a million speech channels, each carrying a different speech
signal. To slot into these channels, the speech signals are modified
electronically (by *modulation*) at, or after leaving, the transmitter and
unscrambled (by *demodulation*) at, or before reaching, the receiver (see Figs
5.8 and 5.9). The process of tuning a radio or TV to a particular
station is just the selection of a particular channel out of the many which
share the available bandwidth. (The VHF band, for example, is 270 MHz
wide, and is divided into channels each 200 kHz wide.) Another technique
available for radio transmission is *polarisation* of the propagated signal. TV
transmitters and satellites can reuse frequencies if one is horizontally
polarised and the other vertically polarised. Alternatively transmitters can
use clockwise and anti-clockwise polarisation.

Modulation

Modulation is the variation of some characteristic of a signal (called the carrier signal) in accordance with the instantaneous value of another signal (the modulating signal).

If the carrier signal is a sine wave, as shown in Fig. 5.8,

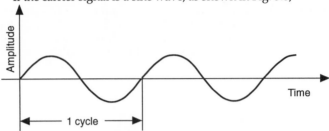

Fig. 5.8 A sine wave is characterised in terms of its amplitude (instantaneous value), frequency (number of repetitions of the wave per second) and phase (starting point relative to some timing mark)

the characteristics which may be varied include its amplitude, frequency and phase, corresponding to amplitude modulation (AM), frequency modulation (FM) and phase modulation (PM) respectively.

These are illustrated in Fig. 5.9 for the case of a modulating signal which is a sequence of pulses.

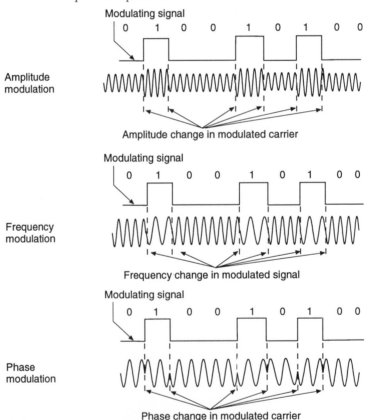

Fig. 5.9 Three methods of modulating a carrier sine wave by a digital modulating signal:

Amplitude modulation: A binary 1 corresponds to a higher amplitude than binary 0.

Frequency modulation: A binary 1 corresponds to a lower frequency of oscillation than binary 0.

Phase modulation: A binary 1 corresponds to a sine wave whose phase is one half cycle different from that of a sine wave representing binary 0

The carrier signal itself may be a train of pulses. In that case, pulse-code modulation (PCM), the characteristics available for variation include the amplitude, width, phase, position, and number of pulses.

The purpose of modulation is to translate or code the modulating signal so that it becomes better matched to the available transmission link. At the receiving end of the link, the signal is recovered, i.e. demodulated, electronically.

The improved utilisation of a transmission link by means of multiplexing is not the only way of sharing out its capacity. An additional possibility is to allocate each channel to a new user when the current user no longer requires it. This is achieved by connecting different terminals to the channels, in other words by *switching*.

Switched networks

The need for switching arises in a network when more than about a handful of terminals are connected to it. The reason for this is illustrated in Fig. 5.10 for the case of ten terminals. Figure 5.10(a) shows that, to enable each terminal to communicate with all others, it is necessary to provide 45 links. The number of links increases disproportionately with the number of terminals; for example, for 100 terminals, 4950 links are needed, while for the total number of telephones in use in Britain today the number of links would run to 15 digits.

Fig. 5.10 Three possible arrangements for a small network:

(a) Direct connection between the terminals, requiring many lines.

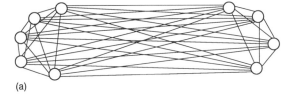

(b) The use of a switching centre reduces the required number of terminals.

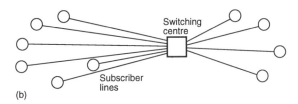

(c) Local switching centres may be interconnected by trunk lines

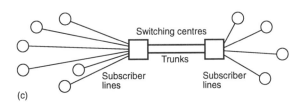

Figure 5.10(b) illustrates that if each of the original ten lines is connected to a switching centre, instead of directly to each other, the number of lines reduces to ten. Note that this approach will not reduce the number of possible interconnections, it merely cuts the number of transmission channels.

Figure 5.10(c) shows a further improvement: the individual lines between the terminals and the switching centre can be reduced in length by introducing more switching centres, local to a group of terminals, and linking these by trunk lines. The trunks are just wide-band links which can carry a large number of channels along the same link. In large networks, such as a national telephone network, the trunks themselves may be switched, for example, to offer alternative routings and so to improve the reliability of the network. This usually results in a hierarchical arrangement of lines and switching centres (exchanges), as shown in Fig. 5.11. The analogy here is to the road or railway network of a country: the switching centres can be likened to major road or railway junctions, and the trunk lines to the inter-city road or railway routes.

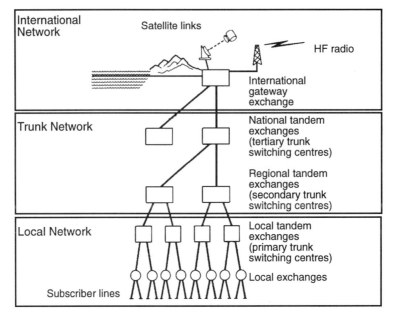

Fig. 5.11 The national telephone network is organised in tiers. The international network is structured similarly

A switching centre may be visualised as a large number of electrical contacts, each of which may be open or closed, forming a switching network (see Fig. 5.12). The action of each switch is under the direction of a control unit.

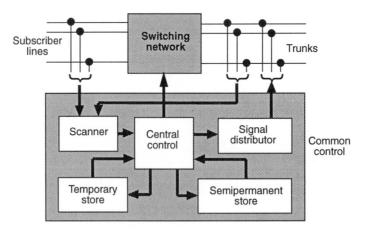

Fig. 5.12 An electronic telephone exchange

The scanner monitors the incoming subscribers' and trunk lines and the data relating to calls in progress are stored in the temporary store. General procedures for establishing calls are stored as computer programs in the semi-permanent store and pairs of lines are connected and disconnected in the switching network. The signal distributor supplies the dialling, engaged, ringing and other tones.

The switches are so organised that any line connected to the centre, including trunk lines, can be connected to any other line, in a temporary manner. This latter restriction is because, for practical and economic reasons, the number of switches is less than that required to interlink all the lines, in pairs, at the same time. So, the same switches are shared out among successive calls. The size of the switching network determines the number of simultaneous calls an exchange can handle.

Switching centres have gone through a century of development (see Fig 5.13) from the early mechanical exchanges, through the computerised electronically switched exchanges of ISDN, towards the optically switched exchanges that will be needed for broadband ISDN.

Fig. 5.13 Phases of development of switching technology

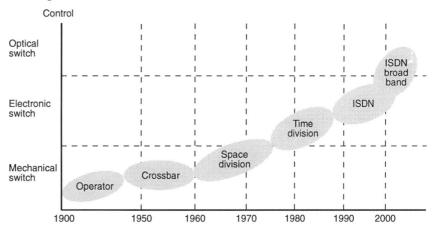

Computers are employed in present-day exchanges in the role of the control unit. This is known as *stored-program control* (SPC). In an even smaller number of ultra-modern exchanges (but an increasing number of future ones) the switching network is also computerised. The technical name of this is *digital switching*. It is particularly applicable where all signals travelling in the network, including the speech signals, are digital in form. The long-term plans of many telecommunication organisations include the conversion of the present analogue-signal transmission network to an all-digital-signal data network. The conversion, however, has to be a gradual one, owing to the scale of the task, and its cost. This means that the switching centres being introduced now will have to cater for both analogue and digital signals, as the amortisation time of a large switching centre is 20 to 30 years. An example of this dual-purpose switching centre is the British System X range of exchanges.

System X
System X is a collection of equipment and computer program modules which can be combined together in various configurations to produce switching centres of varying sizes, for different applications. The applications may be a simple multiplexer to a large trunk exchange or an international network switching centre. The larger exchanges can handle up to 500,000 busy-hour call attempts.

The exchanges use distributed microprocessors, stored-program control, and digital switching (within the system, speech is handled as digital signals, with any necessary conversion and reconversion performed by special modules). The exchange modules are capable of being interfaced to analogue-signal lines, and to digital-signal lines operating up to 2.048 Mbit/s (equivalent to 30 speech channels at 64 kbit/s each), including optical-fibre links.

Cable television networks

Another established area of telecommunications is broadcasting. The use of unbounded media (e.g. radio waves) for the communication of signals is considered in the section on Mobile Communications (see p. 76 and p. 124) and in the chapter on Audio and Video. Here we shall concern ourselves with the distribution of television signals by cable. The cable TV network has grown in parallel with the telephone network in many Western countries. With the advent of computers and the wider use of digital signals, the two networks are set for convergence, as discussed in the chapter on Digital Networks.

Cable television networks were initially installed in the 1950s to provide a television service for those areas where the signal strength of broadcast TV was inadequate for good quality reception. These networks operated under the names of relay systems or communal aerial TV (CATV) systems. They retransmitted TV signals picked up by favourably positioned mast aerials.

Cables have come back into favour for the provision of new subscription television services (Cable TV) delivering both national and satellite broadcast programmes. The subscription services are normally scrambled to prevent unauthorised viewing.

A single coaxial cable has a capacity of up to 55 channels, each 6 MHz wide. In some recent systems the number of possible channels has been doubled by the installation of two coaxial cables.

One reason for going beyond the initially small number of channels is the proliferation of commercial companies and services which aim to exploit this channel into the home and office. Examples are pay-TV, business and financial services, and telephone services, all supplied via cable TV networks.

The availability of a range of services and many channels, and the commercial element, introduce the technical problems of channel selection (by the user) and charging and billing (by the service provider). CATV channel selection is achieved by a selector switch, and charging by a system control box which registers the usage of various channels by each user connected to it.

In ordinary TV receivers and in conventional CATV systems the selector switch is built into the set. This solution usually limits the number of channels that can be received. It also makes it difficult for the system operator to deny access to those pay TV channels to which a particular user did not subscribe. This is because in these systems every channel is available to every subscriber. Modern Cable TV services are financed by annual subscriptions and users provided with a combined channel selector and unscrambler. Access to the services are controlled by a *smart card* inserted into the selector unit.

Figure 5.14 shows the lay-out of the currently most frequently used '*tree-and-branch*' method of arranging cable TV networks – using a street-long cable with 'taps' for each user. In coaxial cable systems the selector switch is in a set-top box, and it is controllable not only by the user but also by the system controller, via a remote link. This facility enables the service provider to make available only certain channels to certain subscribers, or indeed to discontinue the service in the event of non-payment. The set-top box may also contain remotely controllable descrambling circuits for services which are transmitted in a scrambled form.

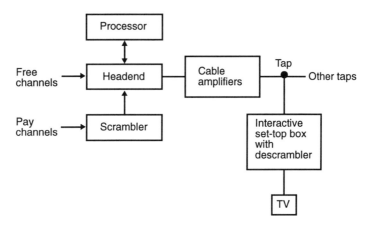

Fig. 5.14 'Tree-and-branch' structure for a cable TV network. A street-long cable from a local head-end is tapped at each house/apartment which it passes

In a few systems the remote link is two-way, that is signals may also be sent from the receiver to the system controller. Typically, signals in the outward, or broadcast, direction are in the frequency range 50 MHz – 400 MHz and in the return direction 5 MHz – 30 MHz. This makes it possible to also use the return channel for other purposes, like home security, remote meter reading, keyboarded data, etc.

The main alternative to the 'tree-and-branch' lay-out, with its set-top selector box, is the '*switched-star*' system, shown in Fig. 5.15. This system is rather similar to the switched telephone network described earlier. Subscribers are connected, via their individual broad-band cables, to a bank of central selector switches which they, as well as the system controller, may remotely control.

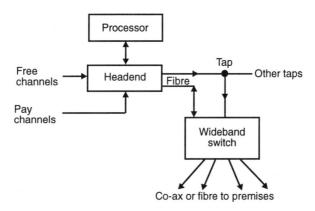

Fig. 5.15 'Switched-star' structure for a cable TV network. One-way (broadcast) services are delivered on the main line, via taps; two-way (interactive) services require individual connections

In the 'switched-star' system proposed by some comapnies any two out of 30 video channels may be switched to a user at any one time. A return video (broad-band) channel can also be provided from each customer, either to the centre or to other customers being served by the same local network.

An increased bandwidth in cable networks can be obtained through the use of optical fibres rather than metallic cables (see Chapter 10 on Optical Communication).

A new service currently on trial in the UK is *view-on-demand TV*, where users can request films to be delivered into their homes via the telephone network. Using digital video compression techniques (see p.89) it is possible to reduce the data rate of video from several tens of Mbits/sec to less than 1.5 Mbits/sec. British Telecom is has invested in new computer technology that is capable of enabling several viewers to receive the same film at slightly different times. It is not yet clear whether the service will be offered commercially.

Mobile communications

The cable-based techniques of telecommunication have been increasingly challenged since the mid-1980s by systems and services using radio links for transmission. The main advantage of this technology is that it enables its users to connect to the telephone network from portable phones or from cars, trains or planes, that is while on the move.

The two main types of mobile communications are those allowing one-way or two-way communication. One-way (exchange to user) links are provided by *pagers*. These alert their users that someone is trying to contact them. The call then can be returned from a convenient two-way telephone. This service is now being extended over national frontiers. Two-way mobile communication includes *cellular radio* and *private mobile radio*, as well as variants, such as Band III, CT2, CT3, DECT and PCN.

Before the development of the concept of cellular radio (at the Bell Laboratories, USA, in the 1970s), mobile telephone users were linked to the rest of the (wired) telephone network via a small number of high-powered radio transmitters. Each of these covered an area, say, 20–30 km in radius, and may have carried about 50 channels. The transmission frequencies of these channels could not be re-used by another transmitter within perhaps 150 km for fear of interference. This severely restricted the number of possible simultaneous users of radio telephones, and made the system economically unattractive for crowded city areas.

With cellular radio, the power of the transmitters is reduced, so that the area of coverage of each is now only a few km across (see Fig. 5.16). So channels can be re-used in non-adjacent cells. As a result, a network of cells can easily handle 50,000 calls an hour, as compared with the 1400 or so in a conventional radio telephone system. In principle, there is no reason why the power of the transmitters should not be further reduced, and so the number of possible channels increased. This is the basis of the European Personal Communications Network (PCN).

To make a call, the user of cellular radio keys in the required number. This is then sent over a special digital control channel to all the adjacent cell-bases. The cell-base receiving the strongest signal takes control and relays the call request to a computer-controlled switching centre. The cell-base then allocates a transmission frequency to the call and asks the mobile to tune to it (automatically) via the control channel. It also dials the required number into the public telephone network and sets up the call.

As the mobile user moves away from the cell-base the signal strength decreases, but before it gets too weak a new frequency channel is negotiated from an adjacent cell-base. At the same time the call is transferred between cell-bases using the terrestrial network. The transfer is very rapid, but just discernible by the user.

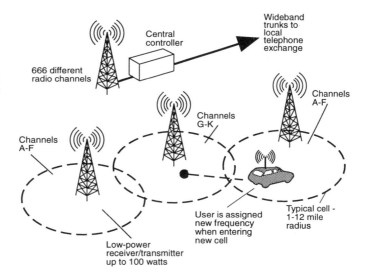

Fig. 5.16 A cellular radio network. Upper diagram shows the link between a local transmitter/receiver and the fixed network; lower diagram the re-use of the 666 30-kHz channels, in a pre-established pattern

Even when no call is in progress the mobile handset keeps the cellular network informed of its location by 'logging-in' to each cell, this way the system knows where to pass on incoming calls.

The popularity of cellular radio (a UK market of 1.6 million in 1993) has led to a shortage of channel capacity. To deal with this problem the UK Government first released a range of frequencies (Band III) previously used for 405-line TV transmissions, and then re-allocated some frequencies previously used for military purposes. In the meantime, private mobile radio (PMR) services cater for those mobile users (e.g. taxis, police and other emergency services) who do not necessarily require linkage to the public telephone network.

The 'telepoint' or CT2 facility has extended the principle of the cordless phone to a public mobile service. The usual cordless phone needs a base station joined by cable to the telephone network, with a mobile handset communicating with it by radio. The CT2 service makes the base station public and allows more than one mobile user for each station but restricting all calls to outgoing ones (i.e. *from* the mobiles), and distances not greater than 100 metres between the mobile and base. The major UK version of this service, Rabbit, has already been withdrawn due to lack of interest, arguably because there was no out-going call facility.

Future developments in the field of mobile communications include the introduction of a standardised form of digital cellular radio on a European scale: the Pan-European Cellular Network, using the 1.7–2.1 GHz range for transmissions.

The *Groupe Speciale Mobile* or GSM, operating in the 900 Mhz band, is another European standardised digital service. Users will be supplied with a personalised smart card which locks into the GSM handset to provide user access codes and accounting information. A user travelling within Europe will rent a handset within the destination country and plug in their smart card, alerting the GSM system of their location and so permitting automatic redirection of calls.

Other digital mobile systems being developed include CT3 (cordless telephones), DECT (digital European cordless telecommunication), PCN (personal communication network) and ERMES (European radio messaging system).

Cellular technology is also being applied to satellite systems. Motorola's multi-satellite Iridium system proposes the use of 66 low earth orbit (LEO) satellites in 11 circular polar orbits. Inmarsat is also considering the development of a satellite-based mobile system, but utilising either 10-12 satellites in intermediate circular orbits (ICO), or 4 to 6 geostationary stationary (GEO) satellites. The first satellite of the Inmarsat P service is due for launch in 1998.

Applications

Telecommunication services are at the heart of many applications of information technology. In the office setting, the internal telephone network is based on wire-pairs or cables, linked to a private (in-house) exchange, with a wide range of facilities, not always found in public networks. These may include automatic call transfers, signalling urgent calls arriving when another call is in progress (this may then be taken while the original call is on 'hold'), call monitoring, automatic dialling, abbreviated dialling of long or frequently used numbers, paging, pre-recorded messages, automatic answering, dictation recording, etc.

One service of particular interest to many organisations with offices or branches on distant sites or those wishing to replace travel by telecommunications is *telephone conferencing*. This facility is available on many private exchanges and, via the operator, on the public network as well. It involves the interlinking of more than two parties in a single call, so that everyone can hear everyone else. At any site there may be a single participant, using an ordinary telephone, or a group of people with a loud-speaking telephone. Push-button-activated light signals can be used to indicate to the chairman that a participant wishes to speak. Other signals may control local visual or graphic display media which show previously distributed illustrations.

One method of distributing documents or graphical information in advance of telephone conferences is facsimile transmission (discussed in greater detail on p. 134). Another is *slow-scan television* transmitted over the telephone network, available commercially in the UK as *videophone*. Alternatively, a telephone conference may be combined with a video (television) conference link so that the participants can see each other and view presentations involving movement. Unfortunately, the cost of multi-site conferences of this type is still quite high, and the technical and human problems have not been fully resolved. With the wider-scale introduction of digital wide-band networks and computerised exchanges into the public telecommunication network, the cost and technical problems at least may find a solution.

Remote control and measurement in industrial environments forms an increasingly important application area for telecommunications. They make it possible to monitor and control equipment in hostile or dangerous situations, at unmanned remote locations, etc.

In financial and commercial applications, telecommunication is already widely employed for ordering, business negotiations, news and wire services, message transmission, etc. The services discussed in the chapter on *electronic mail* (p. 133) are also relevant here, and in the previous two application areas. Electronic funds transfer and direct-mail ordering systems are likely to become greater users of telecommunication services. In the field of communications, the public telephone and broadcast systems will expand, but are also likely to be joined by privately operated ('value-added') services, exploiting the wide-band transmission facilities of cable networks and telecommunication satellites. The spread of microcomputer-based telephones and exchanges will provide an increasing range of facilities to telephone users.

The educational and health services are so far not major users of telecommunications. However, with other technological developments, applications such as education and training at a distance, better assistance to the disabled and elderly, access to remote information sources, become possible. For the home user, improved telecommunications may mean a reduction in information-related travel.

6 Audio and video systems

Introduction

Audio and video systems are among the earliest products of information technology, dating back to the late 19th century and mid 20th century, respectively. They involve the conversion of sounds/images into electrical signals, the transmission or recording of these signals in some agreed format, and their subsequent re-conversion into audible/visible form.

In addition to being well established but still developing technologies in their own right, audio and video have found their way into many systems where spoken or visible information play an important role, e.g. in broadcasting, videotex and teletext, visual displays, etc. In this chapter we shall concentrate on the recording of audio and visual signals and their transmission in analogue form, whilst digital transmission is discussed in Chapter 8, Digital Networks.

The first recordings of sound in the early years of this century were based on the principle of 'engraving' the variations of the shape of the analogue signal, representing the sound, on the grooves of a disc, or record. On replay, a stylus reproduced these variations as mechanical vibrations, which were then converted into audible sounds by a loudspeaker. Electronic methods of signal handling improved the recording and replay quality but did not completely eliminate noise and distortion.

The next stage of development in audio recording came with the introduction of the magnetic tape as the recording medium. An important feature of magnetic tape is that recordings can be erased, edited and the tape re-used. The quality of recording and reproduction of analogue signals on magnetic tape has been enhanced by various noise reduction methods. The Dolby system, makes 'hiss and hum' noise virtually inaudible, by selectively increasing the recorded level of those frequencies where the signal is relatively weak.

Video tape and disc systems have been developed, from the late 1950s, for the recording and subsequent display of television images and sound. Historically, video tape was the first to be exploited for this purpose, by the Ampex Corporation, which still holds the original patents. Sony of Japan showed the possibility of recording video by the 'helical scan' method, with Philips leading the way to the video-cassette tape (commercially available first in 1972).

In theory, the recording and replaying of TV pictures are simple processes. There must be a sufficiently detailed representation made of the pictures on the recording medium (about half a million picture points per frame), and this must be replayed at a speed sufficient to give the impression of natural movement between each frame (there are 25 frames/s in the European standard, and 30 frames/s in the US standard). The television picture is produced by a process of scanning each image frame by a beam of electrons. The variations in the details of the picture are transformed into a coded signal for transmission and/or recording. The bandwidth of this signal is about 5.5 MHz, some 350 times greater than the 15 kHz bandwidth of audio transmission/recording.

In practice, the ability of a recording-replay machine to cope with this bandwidth depends on the relative speed of motion of the recording medium and the signal converter, or 'head', in the machine. In a video-tape recorder, the medium (tape) moves rather slowly (at a few centimetres per second) past an array of rapidly rotating heads (1500–1800 rev/min). In a video-disc player, the head moves slowly across a rapidly rotating disc. Beyond these simple principles, there lies a confusing range of implementations. Apart from the variety of methods used by different manufacturers to produce high-quality images and sound in a reliable, low-cost system, there are also national differences in the way television pictures are produced in the first place.

The United States was first to introduce colour television, in 1954. The National Television System Committee (NTSC) standard, still in use there and in Japan, uses 30 frames/s and 525 lines of scan per frame. It requires a bandwidth of 6 MHz*. Due to the way it encodes colour data, it is prone to errors in the true reproduction of colour. To improve on this, two new TV standards were introduced in Europe in 1967:

(a) the PAL (phase alternation line) system, used in most of Europe, in Australia, and many countries of Africa and the Far East;
(b) the SECAM (sequential couleur a memoire) system, used in France, the republics of the former USSR, and many Middle East countries.

These employ a bandwidth of 7–8 MHz*. PAL is in many ways similar to NTSC, but uses 25 frames/s, 625 lines/frame and codes colour data differently. SECAM is totally incompatible with either of the other systems. In spite of this, the original division persists, due to the large investments already made in studio equipment and receivers. So, any recording and playback system for TV signals must follow one or another, or several, of these standards, and thus be either incompatible or costly. These problems, from the users' point of view, are compounded by the differences between the various manufacturers' products, and by new developments.

High-definition television
One such new development is high-definition television (HDTV). The main differences between HDTV and its predecessors are an approximately doubled number of scan lines and a different aspect ratio of the screen – the ratio of the width of the screen to its height is 16:9 in HDTV as opposed to 4:3 in older systems.

Even before its commercial introduction, a variety of HDTV 'standards' have emerged. The Japanese 'Hi-Vision' system (under development by NHK, the Japanese broadcasting organisation, since 1968) used 1125 horizontal scan lines, and is incompatible with existing TV receivers. The European 'Eureka' system employs 1250 lines, and is incompatible with

---

* These figures include the bandwidth needed for sound.

Hi-Vision; but in combination with an American development called ACTV (advanced compatible television) can make use of existing studio and receiving equipment (but, of course, at the lower resolution).

A compromise solution, called Clear Vision, was introduced in Japan in 1989. It uses a Hi-Vision camera to produce a high-resolution picture, but only every second line of this is transmitted, in the conventional NTSC 525-line format. At the receiver, which is also of high resolution, each line is displayed twice. This results in a much improved picture quality. However this option has already been ruled out by US and European standards groups because it is based on analogue technology.

The transmission standard adopted for HDTV is of considerable importance in terms of the bandwidth required. The doubling of line numbers would more than double the bandwidth occupied by the HDTV signal to 25–30 MHz. This increased requirement cannot be satisfied within existing channel allocations for TV broadcasts or cable transmissions. For this reason, HDTV signals must be electronically processed (compressed) before transmission and de-compressed on reception. The standards for this processing are even more elusive than for the common image format (CIF), and are further complicated by the requirements of *satellite broadcasting* (see p. 122).

As of June 1993 the Telecommunications Ministers of the members of the European Union agreed to commit £180 million over four years to HDTV. These funds will only be available to assist broadcasters and programme makers to upgrade their equipment and to convert existing programmes to the new wide-screen format. Funding is also conditional upon matching funds from industry or financial institutions. As of June 1994 there is still no agreement on an HDTV standard for Europe and it appears as though Europe will fall-in with whatever system is eventually adopted by the US.

Video-cassette tape systems

There are two main types of cassette system: those intended for the large-volume consumer entertainment market, and that for the higher-cost, professional applications. VHS dominates the former, and Sony's U-Matic and Betacam and JVC's S-VHS are representative of the latter.

One historical difference between the two types is that consumer systems used half inch wide tape, whilst professional systems employed three-quarter inch and one inch tape. On both, the video signals are recorded in adjacent tracks at an angle across the tape, as shown diagrammatically in Fig. 6.1. This makes good use of the available recording surface. Sound is recorded as a separate track, along the length of the tape, in the usual way. Another length-wise track controls the position of the heads during replay, to ensure that they are precisely aligned with the tracks. This control track ensures that during replay the head follows the same path as during recording .

The various manufacturers' systems differ mainly in the way the tape is wound on the cassette spools, and in the path the tape follows in relation to the rotating drum which carries the record/replay heads.

Figure 6.2 (a), (b) shows the VHS (Video Home Systems) domestic format, and Fig. 6.3 the Betamax professional format. In each case, although the threading of the tape is automatic, the operation is

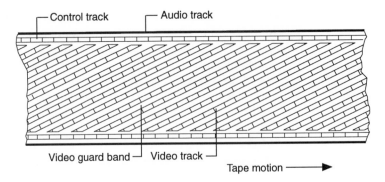

Fig. 6.1 Video tape track layout. The video data are laid down as continuous 'tracks' of magnetisation. Since the head moves across the tape, and the tape moves as shown, the tracks are at an angle

dependent on a high-precision, complex electromechanical system. Other drawbacks include the wear-out of heads, after about 1000 hours use. In the VHS and Beta systems, the tape is pressed against the head drum as soon as the power is on, so that if the tape is not started within a few minutes the tape may also get badly worn. These problems are the subject of intense research, and the technology of video-tape systems is undergoing rapid development.

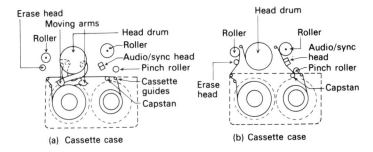

Fig. 6.2 Video-cassette formats: VHS –

(a) unthreaded tape

(b) threaded tape

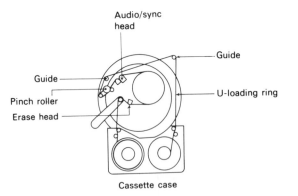

Fig. 6.3 Video-cassette formats: Betamax – threaded tape

More recent developments include Super-VHS (S-VHS) and Hi8 formats. S-VHS, launched in 1987 by JVC, was aimed at the semi-professional market and extends the recording bandwidth from 2.5 MHz to 4 MHz. The recording format and cassettes are upwardly compatible with VHS. Hi8 was developed by Sony for use with camcorders and utilises a small 8 x 6 cm cassette but still offers comparable technical performance to S-VHS.

Turning now to video-tape systems for professional use, the U-Matic system was introduced by Sony in 1972. From the start, the U-Matic machine have catered for both the PAL and NTSC systems simultaneously; some of the later models also included an ability to replay U-Matic format tapes on SECAM-standard receivers. The U-Matic system produces a high-quality picture, can incorporate electronic editing facilities for program production, and is available in battery-operated, portable units.

The Professional S-VHS series of cameras, recorders and electronic editors from JVC appeared in 1988 and offered comparable performance to U-Matic.. Their small size and light weight made them ideal for the news-gathering and corporate advertising markets, but at reduced cost.

Sony has also launched a replacement for U-Matic, the Betacam range of cameras, recorders and editing equipment. Betacam also employs half-inch tape, but the extensive use of VLSI components has increased reliability but reduced the weight of individual units. Betacam is employed extensively by national broadcasting organisations, such as the BBC and has effectively replaced 16mm film for all location and studio recording.

There are several developments that may eventually lead to the demise of professional video tape recording systems, all based on direct recording to magnetic disks. At present the majority of video tape editing requires copying from several tape players onto a single tape, but each copying stage introduces some degradation in the final tape quality. The process is also time consuming because each of the source tapes has to be positioned to the correct starting point before the edit can take place.

The latest developments involve digitisation of the source video material onto fast hard disks within the camera itself. Avid Technology of the US and Ikegami of Japan are currently developing a news gathering quality camera system capable of storing about 10-20 minutes of video on a removable disk. The camera relies on new data compression techniques which reduce the storage requirement by tenfold. Back in the editing suite all copying is performed digitally, without any loss of quality. Last minute changes become a simple reordering of the sequence of reads from disk. Furthermore, the video can be broadcast directly from the hard disk.

Video-disc systems
As noted earlier, in video-disc systems it is the medium (the disc) that rotates fast, rather than the head. The necessary bandwidth can be achieved by rotating the disc at 1500 rev/min (for 25 frames/s operation) or 1800 rev/min (for 30 frames/s operation). At these speeds a full picture frame is recorded per revolution. Consequently, a freeze-frame or still-picture effect can be achieved by simply halting the movement of the head across the disc. The slower speed has the advantage of longer playing time per disc.

As with video-cassette tape systems, there were several incompatible video-disc standards on the market. The differences lay in the physical principles employed at the recording and replay stages, the size and material of the disc, and the optional facilities provided. Today the only commercial system remaining is Laservision.

Laservision
The Laservision system, developed by Philips, utilises a plastic, 305 mm

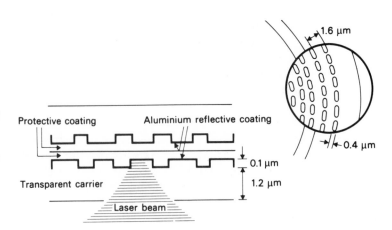

Fig. 6.4 The Laservision video-disc system. The diagram on the left shows the disc in cross-section. The magnified area on the right is a top view, showing the pits whose presence or absence carries the message. The disc is replayed by detecting the reflection of laser light from the pitted grooves

(12 in) disc coated by a reflecting silvery metallised layer. The video data are carried by a pitted spiral track, as shown in Fig. 6.4.

The head contains a tiny laser, the light from which is reflected back from the disc to the head. A sensor there picks up the variations in the reflected light caused by the pits, and generates an electrical signal which represents the recorded data. The playing time of each side of the disc is 1 hour, but with an add-on option, a random-access facility to any frame on the disc is available. In this case, however, the continuous playing time is reduced to a half hour on each side.

Optical systems, such as this, are not sensitive to surface contamination because, just as a dust particle on a camera lens, it is out-of-focus. Also, there is no mechanical contact between head and disc so there is no wear-out. On the debit side, the need for a laser and for a very high accuracy in the positioning of the head imposes considerable demands on the engineering cost and reliability of the system.

The use of video discs for data storage offers the prospect of a low-cost storage medium. Theoretically, the density of data recorded on a video disc can be 100 times higher than on a magnetic disc (an upper limit of 10^{10} bit/cm^2, compared with 10^8 bit/cm^2). However, at the present state of development, video discs cannot be re-used once a particular data pattern has been recorded on them, whereas the magnetic disc is re-usable.

The re-usability of the magnetic medium is exploited in *still video cameras* of the size of an ordinary 35 mm camera, and able to record up to 50 images on a computer-type 2 inch floppy disc. The images then can be played back on a TV set or high-resolution monitor.

Compact discs

Video disc technology has also been applied to the recording and replay of audio signals coded as digital data. (For the principles of coding see Chapter 8, Digital Networks.) Philips of The Netherlands and Sony of Japan announced in 1980 the basic idea of a compact disc system, illustrated in Fig. 6.5.

The 120 mm diameter disc contains more than 20,000 tracks within which sound is represented in the same physical form (by microscopic pits and plateaux) as in an optical video disc. With the tracks 1.6 μm apart, the disc can hold more than a 300 mm LP disc holds on both sides. High recording density is also aided by rotating the disc at a constant linear velocity (CLV) with respect to the laser beam, rather than at a constant angular velocity (CAV), as is done with conventional audio discs and some video disc systems. This means that when the beam is tracking close to the centre of the disc the angular velocity is 458 rev/s, while at the outer tracks it is 197 rev/s. Digital signals can then be read off the disc at a rate of nearly 2 Mbit/s.

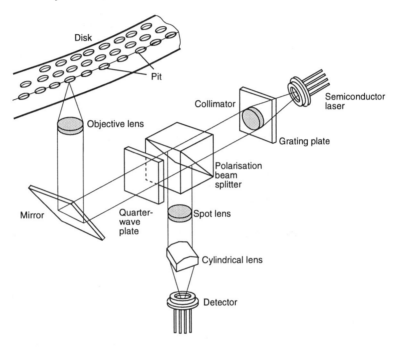

Fig. 6.5 The 'optical pickup' of the compact disc. Light from the semiconductor laser passes through the beam splitter and is focused onto the surface of the disc. The beam reflected from the surface is 'modulated' in intensity by the pits and plateaux. It is deflected by the beam splitter onto the photodiode detector where it is converted into electrical signals

This rate is well in excess of the theoretically necessary rate of 320 Kbit/s necessary to reproduce hi-fi music. The excess is used to carry control information for the replay mechanism and redundant (error detecting and correcting) code to combat the effects of noise. The high data capacity also presents an opportunity to employ the compact disc not only for the recording of digitised audio signals but also for digital data of any origin. It can, therefore, be used to carry, say, a combination of computer software, pictures and sound. (This opportunity exists, of course, with any digital recording system.)

The technology of compact discs is not restricted in application to music. Because it stores data in digital form it can be used for any application where a digital representation of information is employed – be it text, still pictures, numbers, or a mix of these.

In the mid-1980s compact discs employed for other than the recording of music became known as *CD-ROM* (compact disc read-only memory). The format in which data is recorded on CD-ROM became standardised (the so-called High Sierra format). This enables a disc to store more than 600 Mbytes of data – roughly a hundred million words of text, or about 270,000 printed pages corresponding to 200 lb of paper. A CD-ROM drive is an essential component of the MPC-1 and MPC-2 multi-media computer standards (see p. 92)

Connecting a CD-ROM player to a computer makes it possible to find and display any particular item in this vast collection of information within seconds. However, adding new information to the disc is not possible, because as its name suggests, a CD-ROM is 'read-only'. A newer generation of writable and re-writable optical discs is now available although at somewhat higher cost.

Writable discs, known as WORM (write once read many), utilise the changeable properties of crystalline materials when subject to intense heat. The active layer is sandwiched between two layers of polycarbonate or glass and can have its optical properties permanently altered by applying a high-powered laser beam. The local heating effect changes the material from its normal amorphous state (atomically unstructured) into its crystalline state (atomically ordered) which is more reflective. Reading the disc is performed by the same laser, but at much lower power, and follows the same pattern as that for CD-ROM.

There are currently two forms of re-writable disc technology, commonly referred to as *phase-change* and *magneto-optic* respectively. The phase-change disc also uses an active layer between two transparent layers, but the normal state of the layer is crystalline (reflective). To write to the disc a very high powered laser locally heats this layer, causing it to change from crystalline to amorphous (low reflectivity). Reading again relies on detecting the intensity of the reflected beam of a low-powered laser. Re-writing to the disc is performed by re-heating the active layer, which then returns to its crystalline state (reflective). Since only the temperature of the laser beam varies, the disc can be re-written in a single pass. Capacities of phase change discs are typically of the order of 1000 Mbytes on a 130 mm (5.25 inch) disc.

The magneto-optical disc utilises a magnetic active layer whose properties are stable at room temperatures. Above a certain temperature (the Curie point) however, the magnetic polarity is readily 'flipped' by an external magnetic field. Fig 6.6a shows the arrangement of the high powered heating laser and electro-magnet for writing on the disc.

Fig. 6.6 Magneto-optical disc
a) writing to disc
b) reading from disc

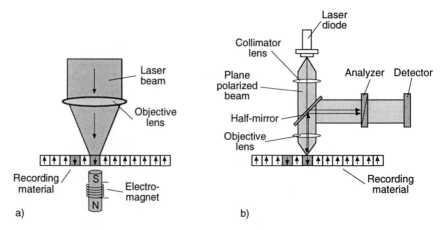

Reading from the disc requires that the 'flipped' locations be identified.

A plane-polarised beam reflected from the magnetic surface will have its plane of polarisation rotated either clockwise or counter-clockwise depending on the polarity of the surface (the Kerr effect), as shown in Fig. 6.6b. By combining the original and reflected beams, the detector can distinguish between the 0 and 1 states of the digital data.

Re-writing onto the disc is a two-stage process. First the disc must be erased by heating with the laser and applying the opposite magnetic polarity, thereby returning each bit to its original magnetic state. New data can be written on a second pass of the disc, again by heating and applying the external magnetic field. It is estimated that these discs can be rewritten over 1 million times.

Rewriting to this type of magneto-optical disc is a much slower process than that of either a conventional hard disk or the phase-change optical disc. However, Sony have found an alternative magnetic active layer (utilising the rare-earth element 'terbium') which permits re-recording in a single pass. Instead of varying the power of the laser beam, so as to heat the layer above its Curie point, the Sony system heats the active layer to a constant 200 degrees Celsius and varies the external magnetic field to produce the appropriate polarity on the disc. The detection system is essentially the same, that is it relies on determining the plane of polarisation of the laser beam upon reflection from the active layer.

Digital video

Among the various kinds of information which were listed above as suitable for storage and replay by CD-ROM one important representation was not included: *digital video*. The reason for this is that even the vast storage capacity of the CD-ROM is insufficient to cope with the amounts of data required for full-motion video: up to half a million bytes per TV frame (depending on the picture quality) and up to 25 frames a second (depending on the TV system used).

Two recent developments have taken up the challenge of digital video linked to personal computers and employing compact discs. In both *CD-interactive*, or CD-I, and *digital video interactive*, or DVI, the digital signals are compressed for recording and expanded for replay by complex electronics, giving some 72 minutes of playing time. Intel, the developer of DVI, has since withdrawn from further development of hardware-only solutions due to cost, but has launched the Indeo software compression standard which permits replay of full-motion video at up to 30 frames per second.

CD-I has lower resolution and occupies only a fraction of the TV screen on replay. The interactive aspect of both systems is due to the ease of control over the selection of video sequences from the disc by the computer.

Perhaps the most important developments for digital video (including HDTV transmission) are the MPEG (motion picture expert group) set of standards. These utilise the fact that much of the information in sequential TV frames does not change, hence all that needs recording is an initial picture plus the changes. The changes can also be encoded using the discrete cosine transform to give what is referred to as 'full motion video', that is 25 (Europe) or 30 (US) frames per second. A further advantage of the MPEG standards is that decompression can be carried out by either hardware or software.

MPEG-1 sets out a compression standard for data rates of about 1.5 million bits per second, compatible with current CD-ROM replay data rates. Of this data 1.2 Mbit/s are used for the video element and 300 Kbit/s for the stereo audio element.

The MPEG-2 standard covers compressed data rates from 2 Mbit/s to 20 Mbit/s. The low end is regarded as suitable for electronic news gathering, whilst the high end will meet the requirements of general broadcasting, video recording and ultimately HDTV.

The last in the group is MPEG-4, which is designed for very low data rates (tens of kilo bits per second) such as used for videophones. The planned launch of MPEG-4 is 1997 and it is likely to be based on 'fractal' compression techniques.

A number of US companies have already developed video codecs based on MPEG-1 and these will be built into professional and consumer CD players for displaying full-motion video. A typical 650 Mbyte CD-ROM will be able to deliver about 70 minutes of video.

Audio recording systems

Audio recording systems have also undergone a wide range of improvements and enhancements over recent years, but with a general drift towards digital recording systems. The reasons are simple: better quality recording, simpler editing and no degradation during editing and copying. Digital audio is now an essential component of multimedia PCs.

The basic principles of converting analogue music and speech signals into digital form are covered in Chapter 8, here we simply review the three primary recording options, DAT, DCC and Master Disc.

Digital audio tape (DAT) was developed by Sony for both the professional and consumer markets and provides direct 16 bit stereo data sampling at frequencies of 44.1 kHz, and 48 kHz. A long-play mode is also available for storing 12 bit samples at 32 kHz. At the highest sampling rate the tape must store the equivalent of 192 Kbytes per second which together with the error detection and correction bits results in a data rate in excess of 307 Kbytes per second, or 2.46 Mbits per second, as shown in Table 6.1. This is well beyond the capability of conventional linear tape recording heads.

Table 6.1 Operational specifications of a DAT audio recorder

Function	Standard play	Long play
Recording time	120 minutes	240 minutes
Tape speed	8.15 mm/sec	4.075 mm/sec
Drum rotation	2000 rpm	1000 rpm
Data transfer rate	2.46 Mbit/s	2.46 Mbit/s
Frequency response	2 Hz - 22 kHz (±0.5 dB)	2 Hz - 14.5 kHz (±05 dB)

DAT therefore employs the spinning head technology of video recorders, with the data stored on inclined tracks across the width of the tape (see Fig 6.1).

In addition to the analogue sampled data, sections of each track store timing information (for high speed searching) together with markers for the start and end of individual recordings (e.g. songs).

Special oxides are utilised for the DAT tapes, resulting in much smaller particle size than conventional ferric-oxides, in order to reduce distortion and loss of quality due to tape drop-out. Nevertheless drop-outs can still arise and so a double Reed-Soloman error detection and correction scheme is employed. The basic operational specifications for a typical DAT recorder are listed in Table 6.1

DAT has failed to make any headway in the UK consumer market, perhaps because unit prices have stayed above £500. It has however taken a firm hold in the professional recording market and multi-track machines are now available complete with computer-controlled positioning to simplify editing.

A DAT tape offers about twice the storage capacity of CD-ROM: 1300 Mbytes in a standard R-DAT format cassette of 60 m tape length, hence the technology has been developed for use as a disk back-up medium. DAT, however, is not an interactive medium; it takes on average about 20 seconds to locate a particular set of data on the tape.

Digital Compact Cassette (DCC) is one of two new analogue recording systems that employ data compression to reduce the complexity of the actual recorders. Pioneered by Philips of the Netherlands, DCC offers comparable audio quality to CD-Audio, but retains the ability to play existing analogue compact cassettes. This latter feature it is hoped will ensure commercial success.

DCC tapes run at 4.76 centimetres per second, as per compact cassettes, but this is far too slow to record digital stereo, hence Philips developed precision adaptive sub-band coding (PASC). This scheme draws on features of the human ear, in that a loud note swamps a softer note of similar frequency. The stereo bandwidth is split into some 32 bands, each about 750 Hz wide. The PASC system only encodes those bands containing information and allocates more bits to the channel with the loudest sounds. On average the PASC system uses an equivalent of four bits per sample, a quarter of the data volume of DAT.

The binary data is recorded onto nine parallel tracks along the length of the tape. Eight tracks carry the recorded samples and the ninth track stores control and timing information. An additional pair of read heads are provided to replay conventional compact cassette tapes, but there is no facility to record to these tapes.

Tests of the encoding system suggest that many users perceive DCC as producing a higher quality recording than CD-Audio and that the dynamic range is comparable with that of an 18 or 20 bit sampling system.

Mini Disc is Sony's optical disc audio recording system based on 86 mm magneto-optical disc technology (see p. 88). Like DCC it employs data compression to reduce the storage requirement to about a fifth of CD-Audio, whilst retaining comparable quality. Sony's compression system is known as ATRAC (adaptive transform acoustic coding) and filters the sound into 52 variable width frequency bands, each band some 20% wider than the one below it. The result is a band 100 Hz wide at 500 Hz, increasing to 3500 Hz at 13.5 kHz. Further compression is obtained by varying the sampling rate, so that during long constant sounds sampling may stretch to more than 10 ms whilst for short duration sounds the sampling intervals are about 1.5ms.

A professional version of Mini Disc (Master Disc) has also been launched by Sony. The main differences are that Master Disc does not use data compression and it is capable of storing 100 minutes of 16 bit samples, 80 minutes at 20 bits or 65 minutes at 24 bits. The extra storage capacity results from employing a 130 mm disc rather than the 86 mm of Mini Disc.

Multi-media

The term multi-media has come to dominate recent sales of personal computers, particularly those based on the Intel family of microprocessors. Essentially the term applies to any computer capable of simultaneous output of video and audio material under software control. Programme material is typically provided on CD-ROM, but could equally well be stored on a large capacity magnetic disk.

Microsoft and Apple have both developed multi-media tools for programme providers and users. The Microsoft tools are often referred to as the multi-media extensions, but are in fact an integral part of release 3.1 of the Windows user environment. The tools permit users to purchase a variety of multi-media components, including: laser-disc player, computer-controlled VCR, video frame-grabbers, video overlay cards, digital audio cards, music synthesisers, etc.

In order to promote the marketing of multi-media platforms, a number of manufacturing organisations joined together to form the Multimedia PC Marketing Council. This council has published two specifications for multi-media PCs, referred to as MPC-1 and MPC-2 and these are listed in Table 6.2 and 6.3 respectively.

Table 6.2

MPC-1 minimum specification	
Processor	386 SX
Memory	2 Mb
Graphics	640 x 480 pixels, 16 colours
Disk storage	30 Mb
CD-ROM transfer rate	audio and video 150 kbytes/sec
Sound card	8 bit mono at 11.025 and 22.05 kHz
	8 voice synthesiser
Software	Windows 3.0 with multi-media extensions
	Windows 3.1

The MPC-1 specification is based around the 80386 microprocessor and has minimal memory, storage and graphics requirements. The CD-ROM data transfer rate is too slow for full-screen video and so images have to be kept smaller than one quarter of the screen. The sixteen colour capability of the display screen also restricts video applications to little more than specially crafted animations and marketing presentations. The 8-bit digital audio is not much better sounding than some telephone conversations due to the high levels of background hiss, and falls very short of the CD-Audio performance of the CD-ROM drive.

The recent developments in microprocessors and interface standards has enabled a considerable improvement in performance with the publication of the MPC-2 specification built around the 80486 microprocessor and higher bandwidth interfaces. Memory, storage and graphics requirements have all been upgraded to permit good quality displays of photographic and video colour images.

The CD-ROM transfer rates have been increased to permit replay of quarter-screen video at approximately 15 frames per second, not quite the performance of television and film, but perfectly adequate for education and entertainment. The 150 kbytes/sec transfer rate for audio has been retained to maintain compatibility with CD-Audio and hence permit replay of audio discs under the control of the computer. The multi-session requirement provides compatibility with the Kodak Photo-CD standard for 35mm photographs and XA is a forthcoming extended-audio recording format.

Sound input and output has been upgraded to 16-bit stereo at CD-Audio sampling rates, an enormous improvement over the 8-bit mono of MPC-1.

Table 6.3	MPC-2 minimum specification	
	Processor	486SX running at 25 MHz
	Memory	4 Mb
	Graphics	640 x 480 pixels, 65,536 colours
	Disk storage	160 Mb
	CD-ROM	multi-session. XA-ready
	transfer rates	average seek time <400ms
		video 300 kbytes/sec
		audio 150 kbytes/sec
	Sound card	16 bit stereo at 11.025, 22.05 and 44.1 kHz
		8 voice synthesiser
	Software	Windows 3.0 with multi-media extensions
		Windows 3.1

Applications

The main application areas of video-tape and disc systems at present are in the home, for entertainment and education, in commerce and industry as a means of presentation, advertising and training, and in the information industry as a means of electronic publishing and electronic news gathering. News gathering is still dominated by video-tape systems, because recording on video discs is still a complex and costly process, but there are signs of a shift toward disks within the next few years.

The range of applications of both tape and disc systems depends also on the availability and perceived value of programme material. With the diversity of incompatible disc systems on the market, this factor currently favours video-tape systems: broadcast material can be recorded on any VHS tape machine. A domestic disc player, however, is unable to record 'off-air' and can only play compatible discs. Each disc system (LaserVision, CD-I or CD-ROM), therefore, has to develop its own programme 'library' separately.

LaserVision offers a generally much higher picture and sound quality and, on some systems, rapid access to any frame, or sequence of frames, on the disc. Its ability to give a high-quality reproduction of a single frame, combined with the freedom to move from that frame to any one of a set of logically linked frames, makes the disc of particular interest in educational, training and retailing applications.

The cost factor is also in favour of the disc: disc replay machines can cost less than tape machines, primarily because of the greater mechanical complexity of the latter. The disc is also cheaper as a distribution medium for programme material: the production costs of full-length feature films (the only current means of comparison) on disc are about one-tenth of the price of the same films on cassette. This ratio is, of course, sensitive to the volume of production and sales, and to advances in technology and standardisation.

7 Computers

Introduction

In the context of information technology, computers take on the role of *automatic data processors*. The processing operations which they can perform on data are limited only by the demands of complete and unambiguous specification of the processing task – at least in theory. In practice, these demands are often difficult, if not impracticable, to fulfil, as in the case of tasks modelling human intelligence (e.g. expert systems – see p. 165). In other cases, the capacity and performance of computer equipment prove to be the limiting factor, although continuing advances in fields like data networks (see p. 105), voice input and output (see p. 221), and computer vision (see p. 161) keep pushing these limits further and further back. Yet other practical constraints on computers include cost, reliability, physical size – again, these have become less significant in the last few years, with advances in microelectronics. In the final count, therefore, the use of computers by information technology is likely to be determined by the extent to which people find tools based on them helpful and acceptable.

Within the space available, this chapter can give only a broad overview of these theoretical and practical considerations. For a more detailed understanding of specific aspects, the reader is urged to turn to sources such as those listed on page 237.

What is an automatic data processor?

Computers deal with representations of information rather than with information itself (the distinction between information and its representation was discussed in Chapter 1). The representations which a computer can manipulate and communicate are a form of *data*. In the context of information technology, data can include a variety of formalised representations (of speech, handwriting, physical measurements, etc.) but the most widely used type of computer, the electronic digital computer, employs only *digital representations*. As described in Chapter 1, 'digital' does not only relate to digits, or numbers, but includes any finite set of symbols or characters. So, digital data can take the form of letters of an alphabet, or words of a natural language made up of those letters, or speech coded into numbers or symbols, or results of measurement expressed by a finite sequence of digits, etc.

The reason behind this requirement of digital data lies in the engineering aspects of digital computers: they can only manipulate digital signals. Indeed, within the computer, the digital signals must be of a special kind: binary signals with only two possible values – on or off, or pulse or no-pulse. (An item of digital data or digital signal represented by a 1 or a 0 is called a *bit*, short for *binary digit*.) Computers use binary signals because low-cost electronic circuits are available for their fast, reliable, accurate processing and storage.

But the real world does not often oblige the computer with digital data, let alone with binary ones. So, the computer usually includes devices for converting real-life data into the binary representation of the computer, and back again into an appropriate form. In between the two conversions, the data can be simply stored for later use, or it may be subjected to some processing operations. The simplest graphical representation of a computer therefore includes four interlinked boxes, as shown in Fig. 7.1.

Fig. 7.1 The simplest model of a computer consists of a data processor linked to devices for storing and converting data (peripherals). The data conversion necessary between the internal and external representations of information is carried out by the input and output devices

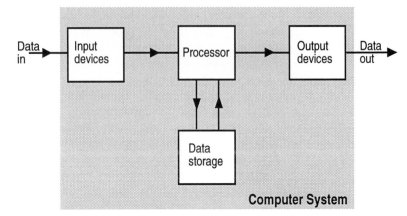

The *input devices* can take the form of a keyboard, or a digitiser for graphics or speech, or some other data converter. The *processor* is an assembly of electronic circuits. The *memory*, or *store*, can employ electronic, magnetic or optical media. *Output devices* again may be chosen from a variety of data conversion units, such as printers, visual displays, voice output devices. Input and output devices may also include links to other computers and to data networks, for the direct transfer of digital data. The devices making up a computer are referred to collectively as the *hardware*.

The hardware may appear, in some cases, to be able to perform certain tasks *automatically*, that is without any routine human intervention. For example, a computer on board a space module, or even in some cars, takes in data, works out settings, displays results completely automatically. However, what is happening is that the computer follows a routine which has been worked out for it in advance and stored in its memory. The routine consists of a sequence of steps, or elementary operations, which completely define the task in hand, be it as complex as the navigation of a space module, or as simple as the calculation of the fuel consumption of a car. The prime requirement, however, is that the prescription of what the computer is to do with the data is to be complete and unambiguous – complete in the sense that it deals with all eventualities that may affect the performance of the task, and unambiguous in the sense that for any eventuality the required action is uniquely defined.

The prescription itself must be expressed in a form and in a representation which the processor is equipped to interpret. Built into the circuitry of the processor is a finite set of elementary operations which it can perform on given data. These will include, as a rule

(a) mathematical, logical, comparison and other processing operations;
(b) *storage operations*, for storing and retrieving specified items of data;

(c) *input* and *output operations* which accept data from input devices and send data to output devices, in a specified format;

(d) *control operations,* which organise the order or sequencing of other operations.

These operations are each invoked by specific codes, which activate appropriate circuits of the processor. The operation codes, together with the relevant data, form the *instructions* to the computer. A sequence of instructions to accomplish a specific task is known as a *program.* The collection of programs prepared for a computer is called its *software.*

The power and versatility of the computer derive from the way its hardware and software combine in the processing of data. The hardware contributes a variety of possible processing operations which have been designed so as to make the computer a *general-purpose data processor.* That is, a program can be constructed to accomplish *any* completely and unambiguously defined task. What the software does is to select a sequence of these operations which convert the computer to a *special-purpose processor* for that task, for the duration of the program's working.

The hardware also contributes speed of operation and memory. Once a program has been worked out, it can be stored as a form of data in the computer's memory. The processor can then be made to perform this program by a single instruction from its operator, *at its own speed.* Present-day computers operate at speeds of up to hundreds of million instructions *per second.* So, highly complex and lengthy programs which may have taken a team of specialists years to develop can be performed in a small fraction of that time, repeatedly and repeatably.

The assumption here, though, is that the program is complete, that is, all the data required to accomplish a task are already stored inside the computer. In many cases, however, some of the data will arise outside the computer while the program is in operation. These cases are called, in computer jargon, *real-time* tasks. They include interactive uses of the computer, such as the monitoring and control of other equipment, text preparation, computer-assisted learning. In these situations, the computer still operates at its own fast speed on the data at its disposal, then waits for the new data to arrive so that the program can be resumed. If the waiting time is a significant proportion of the total time, the computer may be able to handle more than one task, yet give full service to them. This mode of operation is described as *time-sharing.*

So, we see the computer as a combination of electronic and other devices (hardware) and programs (software). The programs prescribe, in complete detail, the operations which the hardware is to perform upon suitably coded data. The programs are stored in the computer, again as suitably coded data. When a program is started off, the processing is carried out automatically, at high speed and with great precision. In this sense, the computer is an automatic data processor. But whether a computer is the right tool in an information technology application depends on practical considerations; to these we turn next.

Computer software

Computer software is of two kinds: system software and application software.

System software

System software is produced to improve the general usability of the computer, rather than to cope with particular applications. Without system software, the detailed control of the computer's operation and the preparation of application programs would be rather tedious. The tasks performed by the system software include the translation of the operator's commands from a near-natural language to the elementary instructions for the processor. They assist people in the editing, testing, modification and storage of new programs, in the rapid re-allocation of hardware resources in the time-sharing mode, in maintaining files of data and making them available as required by user programs, etc.

System software is usually supplied ready-made, rather than having to be produced by each user of a computer. However, a particular item of system software is unlikely to work in computers of other manufacturers. The reason for this is that different makes of computer tend to use somewhat different sets of elementary instructions from which the programs are built up, as well as different codes for specifying these instructions. There have been attempts to standardise at least those items of system software which help users to create new application programs in near-natural computer languages. Computer languages (allowed symbols and rules for their use) such as Cobol, C, Basic, Pascal, Fortran which are widely used around the world, have unfortunately their 'dialects', or minor variations, which prevent the wide-scale interchange of programs expressed in them. These dialects are not geographically related, though, but rather differ from manufacturer to manufacturer, each of whom claims some advantage for the variants specific to them.

Two particular items of system software deserve special mention here: operating systems and data-base management systems.

An operating system is the hub of system software: it accepts and executes the computer operator's commands so as to control in detail the operation of all other software and hardware resources of the computer. It therefore automates many of the tedious tasks that would otherwise have to be done by the operator. These include, for example, the checking of the readiness and availability of input and output devices, the transfer of data to and from these devices (including external storage devices such as magnetic discs), the organisation of orderly operation when the same processor is shared among several users or programs, etc. It also ensures that the various programs and their data are handled and stored as single entities (files).

Finding individual items of data very rapidly among a very large number of others in a data-base (e.g. the state of a person's bank balance, or his address) is a task usually devolved to a separate data-base management (DBM) program. If a data-base is thought of as a single pool of inter-related items of data, DBM systems differ from one another in terms of how they represent these relationships. In a *relational* data-base, for example, data are stored as pairs, linked by some relationship. Thus, an account holder's name may be linked to his address, his account number to his current balance, his name to his address, etc. In this way, any item of stored data can be found from its relationship with other data. The DBM system checks the inquirer's right to access the data, up-dates and checks for the consistency of the stored data, etc.

Some operating systems, such as Pick (used mainly with business computers), include a relational DBM system as a standard component. Other popular operating systems, such as Unix (used largely in technical and academic environments), concentrate on helping the user with the handling of files (collections) of data, and with the production and running of application programs. Many operating systems also include a 'library' of application programs which are likely to be of interest to a range of users, and which thus save them the need to write their own software.

Application software

The production of application programs still tends to be a relatively small-scale, highly labour-intensive activity, which is reflected in the high cost of software. In the early days of computing the ratio of hardware to software costs was about 4:1. Now it is closer to 1:4. This is not only due to the lack of standardisation of computer languages. Economies of scale are difficult to achieve in adapting the general-purpose computer to specific tasks when the detailed requirements vary from user to user, from situation to situation. The only viable alternatives open to would-be users were to produce or commission the production of custom-made application programs, or else to adapt their specific requirements to the programs which may already exist for a particular make of computer.

The emergence of microcomputers brought some relief to this dilemma: certain makes of microprocessor have achieved sufficient sales to stimulate the production of a wide range of off-the-peg application packages. Many of these packages are aimed at the fairly predictable requirements of business applications (e.g. text processing, payroll, inventory), research applications (e.g. mathematical and design problems), or personal uses (e.g. graphics, games, money management) in fields where microcomputers enjoy large sales. Some of the most successful software packages combine several of these functions into a single product. Thus one currently well-known package includes financial planning, word processing, data-base management, graphics generation, communication with other computers, together with a self-teaching tutorial on the use of these facilities. What is more, the various functions are becoming usable simultaneously on the same personal computer through a set of 'windows' on the display screen, each devoted to one of the facilities. General-purpose software packages called *program generators* are being marketed to reduce even further the laborious task of translating (coding) a program specification into the language of the computer. These do not, however, eliminate the crucial stage of specifying the task to be performed by the application program completely and unambiguously.

A relatively recent development in the quest for making the production of software a more efficient process is *object-oriented programming*. Conventional methods of programming are based on specifying sequences of instructions (procedures) which manipulate a collection of data. By contrast, in object-oriented programming there is no distinction between procedures and data; there are only 'objects', corresponding to real-life objects, which perform specified actions. 'Objects' communicate by passing messages in standardised format. The advantage of this approach is that an object-oriented program can work with any other (or re-use parts of other programs) which employ the same message-passing conventions.

But efficiency in software production is not the only concern: quality and reliability are becoming increasingly important attributes of software. Computers are being introduced into more and more *safety-critical applications* from nuclear weapons systems or power stations, to the automatic braking systems of cars. As a rule of thumb, the bigger and more complex the program the larger is the probability that it contains errors. This is because the larger the program the greater is the chance of human error, and the longer it takes to test it – in some cases an impracticably long time – with present methods.

The general trend is to employ more sophisticated development tools, as illustrated in Fig 7.2. Software designers are beginning to exploit some of the design methodologies developed in other engineering disciplines and new tools have evolved under the general heading of computer aided software engineering or CASE.

Fig. 7.2 Evolution of software development tools

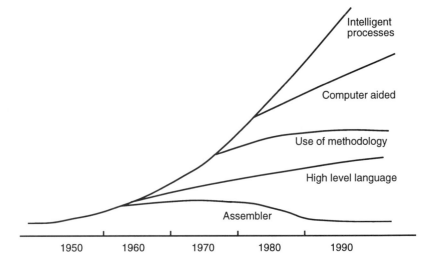

As the wisecrack says about computer 'standards', "the nice thing about them is that you can pick whichever you like". Progress in this area is being made through the gradual emergence of *open systems* – agreements between computer manufacturers providing a degree of standardisation. The rapid pace of progress of hardware and software, however, is likely to make even these 'industry standards' open to change.

Computer hardware   The relative lack of standardisation in the computer field afflicts hardware just as much as it does software. A processor developed by a particular manufacturer can work only with the input, output and memory devices which are compatible with it – usually a small fraction of products on the market. There is also rapid progress in hardware technology so that products are quickly outdated. For example, in the early 1970s a powerful processor, capable of operating in the time-sharing mode with 16 users, cost about $50,000. It needed a great deal of additional equipment to offer such a service, including 16 input-output terminals, such as video terminals. In the mid 1990s a processor, equivalent in power, is available for less than $300. Moreover, it has been reduced in size to the extent that each video terminal can contain its own processor and no time-sharing is necessary. Instead, the terminal can include functions hitherto provided by specialised devices – memory units, telecommunication interfaces, disc files, printers, etc.

The development of computer hardware is often discussed in terms of technology 'generations' corresponding to important advances in the reduction of size and increase in performance. (It is worth noting that the basic organisation of the digital computer has not changed over the 'generations'.) Table 7.1 charts the first four generations of computers.

Table 7.1 Generations of computer technology

Generation	First	Second	Third	Fourth
Year	1946–55	1956–63	1964–81	1982–
Computer hardware	Vacuum tube Magnetic drum	Transistor Magnetic core	Integrated circ. Semiconductor	VLSI Optical
Size of system (minimal)	Very large	Mainframe	Mini	Micro
Proc. speed	10 KIPS*	200 KIPS	5 MIPS	200 MIPS
Memory size	2 Kbytes+	32 Kbytes	2 Mbytes	250 Mbytes

*KIPS = 1000 instructions per second; MIPS = million instructions per second.
+Kbytes = 1024 x 8 bits.

From mainframe and mini-computers in the 60s and 70s, the trend of the 90s is towards microprocessor-based, self-contained personal computers and workstations on the one hand, and superfast, high-performance computers on the other.

At the smaller end, the desk-top machines of the 80s have developed into portables, 'laptops' and hand-held computers of equivalent or higher performance and at a fraction of the size and cost. At the other extreme, supercomputers may cost tens of millions of dollars and operate at speeds of thousands of millions of operations a second. Clearly, the number of such computers in use today is much smaller, perhaps a few hundred, but they play an important role in military applications, in weather forecasting and other scientific projects requiring fast, accurate calculations.

Processors
One way in which the performance of a computer is increased is by employing more than one processor, with the individual processors sharing out the overall task. This multi-processor, or *parallel computing*, approach lies at the heart of most supercomputers but is also being developed for use in lower-price computers of the future.

An example of a processor which can be used either as the only processor of a computer or as an element in a multi-processor configuration is the *transputer*, developed by Inmos, originally a British company. The current version performs over 60 million instructions per second. The transputer is also an example of the currently prevailing general-purpose processors, that is processors which can cope with any completely and unambiguously defined task.

A great deal of research and development work is going into the design of new types of processor which are more suited to specific information handling tasks, rather than being general-purpose, as today's processors are. For example, processors for data-base operations, for content-related search and data retrieval, for simultaneous rather than sequential steps in program operation, are being built and evaluated.

Another way in which processor performance is being improved is by reducing the number of elementary instructions which it can carry out. Such *reduced instruction set computers* (RISC) can perform only a small set of instructions; but they execute these at very high speeds.

Data storage

There is also rapid progress in data storage technology, in which a variety of physical effects is being exploited for the temporary or long-term storage of binary-coded data. Semiconductor-based storage devices include *random-access memory* (RAM) and *read-only memory* (ROM) integrated circuits. The first of these types can be used to store *or* retrieve data, under the control of the processor. The second type has data permanently or semi-permanently 'built' into it, and can only be retrieved from the processor.

Fig. 7.3 The number of electronic elements constructed on a single chip for various types of devices

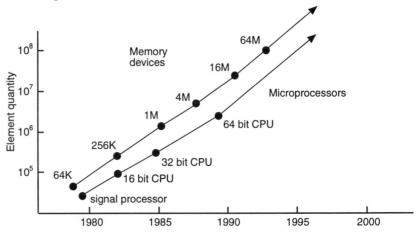

Figure 7.3 illustrates the trend towards more and more complex processor and memory elements (transistors and connections) packed into smaller and smaller circuits. This apparently limitless reduction in size is made possible, in a theoretical sense, by the independence of the informational value of a binary digit from its physical representation. In practice, however, limits are imposed by engineering considerations, such as the propagation time of signals within the computer, and the amount of heat generated by the operation of the circuits. The propagation time limits the number of operations achievable per second, while heat must be dissipated rapidly, otherwise it literally melts the components. At the time of writing, the 'state-of-the-art' in very large-scale integration (VLSI) is the 16 Mbit RAM which contains over 5 million transistors. Since 1975 the

number of transistors has at least doubled every two years and is expected to reach over 100 million by the year 2000. (A 16 Mbit RAM can store about two million characters, equivalent to the contents of a 64-page newspaper.) To gain an idea of the fineness of detail necessary to produce the circuit elements on the chip, imagine a map of the British Isles showing sufficient detail to identify even the narrowest side-street in London. At the currently achievable line thickness in integrated circuits, the entire map could be reproduced within the 5 cm square area of a 32-bit microprocessor.

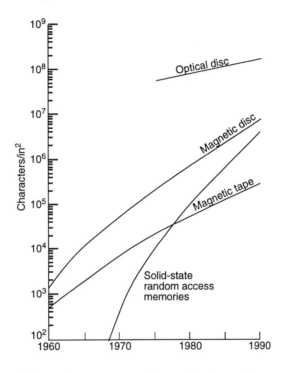

Fig. 7.4 Projections of the data-storage densities of various media. The units of characters/in^2 may be converted to bits/cm^2 by multiplying each value along the vertical axis by 50. (Source: *Report of the Committee on Data Protection*, HM Stationery Office)

Magnetic storage media are dominated by *magnetic tape* and *disc* devices. Tape and disc are able to store and present large quantities of data under the control of the processor (they are often called mass-storage devices). Tape units include cassette and reel-to-reel types, while discs are available either in flexible ('floppy disc') or rigid (fixed-head or moving-head) form. A comparison of the storage densities of electronic, magnetic and optical devices is shown in Fig 7.4.

Optical storage technology is now coming to the fore, utilising the technologies described in Chapter 6. A 35 cm disc can hold 4 gigabytes of data, equivalent to 4000 million characters, or 1 million closely typed sheets of A4 paper. The potential of optical discs as data storage media is promoted in terms of its "lower cost than the rental of the volume of office space necessary to store paper containing an equivalent amount of information", but with much faster access to an item of stored data in direct text or graphic form, readable by people or by machines, or as *holograms* which require laser-based recording and reading apparatus. Whilst all magnetic media are easily erased and over-written, the dominant optical medium is CD-ROM. The current production costs for a CD-ROM disc are claimed to be as low as $1 whereas the cost of re-writable (phase-change or magneto-optical) discs may exceed $15.

Kodak's Photo-CD is aimed at the domestic consumer and stores 100 35-mm colour photographic images for replay on a domestic TV. The player currently costs around £300 and processing costs about £15.

8   Digital networks

Introduction and fundamentals

The purpose of digital networks is to interconnect computers and other devices which work with computer-coded data, so that data can be transferred from one location to another. As far as the user of information technology is concerned, data networks operate 'behind the scenes', but they exert a profound influence on the application of information technology.

There are three obvious examples of this:

- access to remote information systems (see p. 137),
- the operation of electronic mail (see p. 131),
- and, to an increasing extent, the world's telecommunication services (see p. 78).

They are all dependent on the transmission of digital data.

The problems of setting up and operating data networks are essentially technical and economic ones, but the decisions being taken about these problems today are going to influence the progress of information technology for many years to come.

At first sight, there seems to be no good reason to distinguish between telecommunication networks and data networks. After all, they are both concerned with the transmission of signals representing information, and they both have the same origins: the public telephone and telex networks.

Indeed, it is important to bear in mind that the carriers which can be used to transmit digital (data) signals can also be adapted to communicate analogue signals of an appropriate bandwidth, and vice versa. The reason for making the distinction lies in the cost-effectiveness of different channels in dealing with the two signal types.

The signals which represent computer data are digital, or on-off pulses. The world's telecommunication network, prior to the need for data transmission, was built up to handle speech and telex signals, which reflect the information handling rates of people. As a result, a single speech link is allocated a bandwidth of about 3500 Hz on the public telephone network.

Bandwidth for data transmission

In theory, a telecommunication channel can be used to transmit twice as many pulses per second as the numerical value of its bandwidth, expressed in hertz. Thus, a telephone speech channel with its 3500 Hz bandwidth could carry, theoretically, up to 7 kbit/s (unencoded). In practice, the maximum data rate is about the same as the numerical value of the bandwidth, that is 3.5 kbit/s for the speech channel. This is due to the presence of noise and other interference affecting all transmission media.

It is important to bear in mind that the numerical equality of bandwidth and of the maximum data rate of a channel is not reflected in the bandwidth requirements of the signals which the channel carries. Table 8.1 shows the bit rates needed when certain analogue signals are converted into digital ones by sampling.

Type of signal	Analogue bandwidth	Required bit rate	Bits per sample
Telephone voice	3.5 kHz	49 kbit/s*	7
Hi-fi music (mono)	15 kHz	480 kbit/s	16
CD-Audio (stereo)	15 kHz	1.41 Mbit/s	16
DAT (stereo)	22 kHz	2.46 Mbit/s	16
Colour TV	5.5 MHz	11 Mbit/s	10
High-definition colour TV	40 MHz	800 Mbit/s	10

*In practice 56 kbit/s (US) and 64 kbit/s (UK) are normally used

Digital transmission is therefore more profligate in its use of bandwidth for the same information.

When the public switched telephone network is used for data transmissions, the situation is further complicated by part of the available bandwidth being taken up for telephone control signalling. This restricts data transmission rates of a public speech circuit to about 1.2 kbit/s. Considerable improvements on this figure - up to 19.2 kbit/s or more - are possible by employing data-encoding and echo cancellation techniques. The transmission of digital, i.e. pulse-coded signals, along a telecommunication channel offers several ways of increasing the channel's apparent bandwidth. This is achieved by coding the information so that its redundancy is reduced, and a larger number of information-bearing items is squeezed into a channel of a given capacity.

Conversion between analogue and digital signals

An analogue signal may be transmitted over a digital network in several ways, as illustrated in Fig. 8.1. The carrier waveform is assumed to be a regular sequence of pulses which is modulated by some characteristic of the analogue waveform to be transmitted - normally its amplitude.

The first method varies the amplitude of each pulse such that it is proportional to the amplitude of the analogue signal, and is known as *pulse-amplitude modulation*. The second method varies the width of each pulse in proportion to the amplitude of the analogue signal, and is known as *pulse-width modulation*. The third method varies the timing of the rising edge of each pulse in proportion to the amplitude of the analogue signal, and is referred to as *pulse-position modulation*.

The equipment which performs the conversion at one end of a digital link, and re-converts the encoded representation to an analogue signal is the codec (short for coder-decoder). A codec is thus the inverse of a modem (modulator-demodulator) which converts digital signals for analogue transmission. A codec can also be used to convert a digital signal to another, more redundant form. This is useful when the channel is subject to noise. A combined form of modem and codec is also available under the name of 'modec'

Fig. 8.1 Pulse-
modulation techniques:
(a) pulse-amplitude
    modulation (PAM)
(b) pulse-width
    modulation (PWM)
(c) pulse-position
    modulation (PPM)

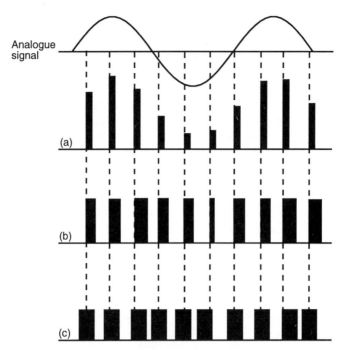

However, if the modulated pulse sequence is transmitted over a long distance it will be subject to distortion, and will be difficult to reconstruct at the far end - information may be lost. To combat this, *pulse-code modulation* is normally used.

The analogue signal is first quantised, that is converted to a signal that has a discrete number of amplitude values, as shown in Fig. 8.2. The figure shows a sinewave quantised to 8 discrete levels.

Fig. 8.2 Pulse-code
modulation (PCM):
(a) the analogue
    waveform is first
    'quantised' – made
    to occupy a discrete
    set of values (here
    8)
(b) it is then sampled at
    specific points – the
    approximate values
    are read at regular
    intervals of time.
    The PAM signal
    that results can be
    coded for PCM
(c) the coded pulse
    may be transmitted
    in a binary form with
    the longer pulse
    representing '1' and
    the shorter '0'

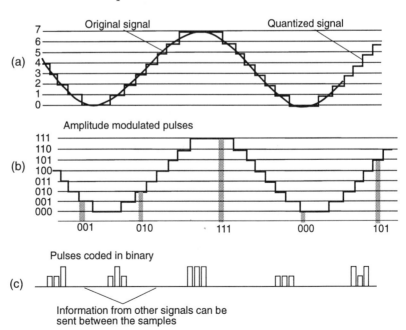

The quantised signal is then sampled at regular time intervals, normally at a minimum rate corresponding to twice the bandwidth of the analogue signal. In the case of 8 quantisation levels the coded values of the amplitude of the samples can be represented by three bits and it is the value of these three bits that are transmitted over the digital network.

The discontinuous variation of digital signals and the speed at which computers operate impose a completely different demand for bandwidth on the transmission channel. To illustrate this, consider the effect on common computer operations of sending data at two different rates, as shown in Table 8.2.

Table 8.2 Effect on common computer operations of sending data at two different rates (bit-by-bit transfer)

Data to be transferred (using serial transfer)	Approximate no. of bits	Transmission times At 1.2 kbit/s	At 64 kbit/s
Video screen full of text	$1–4 \times 10^4$	8–32 s	0.16–0.64 s
A4 page of text	6×10^4	50 s	1 s
Floppy disc, 9 cm	9.6×10^6	133 min	2.5 min
Computer tape, 720 m reel	1×10^9	230 h	4 h
Facsimile page, black and white	$2–6 \times 10^5$	2.5–8 min	3.2–9.6 s
Digitised speech, PCM, 1 sec	6.4×10^4	1 min	1 s

The first transmission rate shown in the table, 1.2 kbit/s, is what can be achieved, without resorting to complex and expensive encoding techniques, on an ordinary public telephone line. The second transmission rate is that of a single channel ISDN line of 64 kbit/s. Note, for example, that more than a few seconds wait for a screenful of text is considered to be undesirable in most applications, while the 1 minute transmission time of one second's worth of speech makes that transmission rate impracticable for speech.

Modern digital networks operate at hundreds of megabits per second and so are best used in combination with wide-band carriers, i.e. optical fibres and satellites. Furthermore, they carry a much greater variety of information, each with its own transmission rate requirements, as listed in Table 8.3.

Apart from the different bandwidth requirements, the transmission of data on the conventional telephone network is inconvenient because it takes up the available channels for longer times than the average conversation (thus causing congestion), and because it is easily corrupted by line noise and other transmission problems. A considerable amount of technical ingenuity has gone into alleviating these problems, so that the highly expensive national and global speech telephone networks could be exploited for data transmission. Simultaneously, a start has been made by several countries on the creation of new networks for the transmission of data only, including digitised speech and TV signals.

Thus digital networks may be based on the public telephone network, private telephone lines leased from a national telecommunication network operators, or on the new generation of public and private transmission and switching networks established specifically for data communication.

Table 8.3 Data rate
requirements for
different information

Data rate kbits/s	Information
10	ASCII text
20	Full screen photograph with JPEG compression
30	Telephone sound quality (300-3400Hz)
50	AM radio sound quality
64	ISDN single channel (Europe)
100	Animation (quarter screen at 10 frames/sec)
500	Full-screen motion-JPEG video at 20 frames/sec
1000	Animation (full-screen at 20 frames/sec)
1200	Stereo CD-Audio sound quality (20-20,000Hz)
2040	30 channel ISDN (Europe)
4000	Theoretical limit of *slow* Token-Ring LAN
8000	S-VHS compressed video
10,000	Theoretical limit of Ethernet LAN
15,000	Uncompressed VHS video
16,000	Theoretical limit of *fast* Token-Ring LAN
30,000	HDTV

Eventually, we can expect all data traffic to move completely to the new facilities. The main advantages of doing so are that all-digital networks can provide higher transmission rates and immunity to the kinds of electrical noise and interference which affect analogue circuits.

The simplest data network is one which interconnects a few pieces of computer equipment by lengths of wire. This works well provided:

(a) the distances involved are not large (a few hundred metres for a wire-pair, a few kilometres for a cable);

(b) the number of items of equipment is small (if each of them is to be able to communicate directly with all others);

(c) the transmission rates are relatively low (a few hundreds of kbit/s for wire, a few Mbit/s for cable);

(d) the items of equipment have all been produced by the same manufacturer (or are otherwise compatible).

The simple network is also constrained by the fact that, in many countries, legislation prevents the transmission of signals by other than the national telecommunication organisation, beyond the user's premises.

When any one of these assumptions proves too constraining, it is necessary to examine commercial alternatives. Depending on how they cope with these problems, commercial data networks can be categorised as shown in Table 8.4.

Table 8.4

Coverage	Wide area and local networks
Interlinking	Circuit-switched, message-switched and packet-switched networks
Data rates	Narrow-band and wide-band networks
Compatibility	Standardised and non-standard networks
Ownership	Public, private and value-added networks

Wide area networks

Wide area networks are operated in most countries by state-owned telecommunication authorities (exceptions to this are the United States and the UK, but the European Union has introduced legislation to enforce competition). To overcome the problem of signal deterioration with distance, national and international data networks include signal regeneration equipment (repeaters) in their long-distance segment (trunk network), but the link to this segment from/to subscribers' premises is often just a wire-pair. The installation and usage costs of long-distance links are quite high, so a great deal of effort goes into ways of transmitting the maximum amount of data through the smallest number of long-distance links.

One approach is to share a data link (line) among several different pieces of equipment. A commonly used, efficient technique for this is *multiplexing* (see also p. 71). If the bandwidth (data rate) of the link is higher than the requirements of the individual senders and receivers of data, the successive characters of messages can be interleaved at the sender's end of the line and unscrambled at the receiver's end, as shown in Fig. 8.3. Thus, multiplexing aims to ensure that the capacity of the link is fully utilised. The interleaving and disentangling of the data elements is performed automatically by multiplexers placed at each end of the line (Fig. 8.4).

Fig. 8.3 A time-division multiplexer interleaves parts of messages from several channels for transmission along a bi-directional link. Synchronising pulses at the end of each block of data ensure that the two multiplexers keep in step

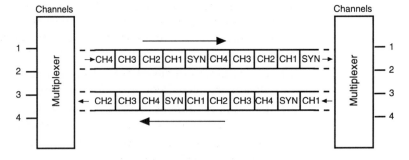

The current stage of development of such *time-division* techniques can ensure, for example, that a link operating at 9.6 kbit/s can be shared by over 100 pieces of equipment operating at 110 bit/s, or alternatively by a mixture of equipment using different data rates, and even a variety of computer codes.

A new generation of multiplexers has been recently introduced under the names of *data concentrators, network processors,* and *statistical multiplexers.* They include a mini- or microcomputer to improve the utilisation of a line even further. The computer in this type of multiplexer detects when a sender or receiver which could be using the line is in fact not active; this allows either additional or faster-operating equipment to be connected to the line. The computer is also useful in detecting and correcting transmission errors and, in some cases, allowing data and non-digitised speech to be multiplexed on a line designed to transmit speech only. The cost of such equipment, however, has to be balanced against the costs of operating without it.

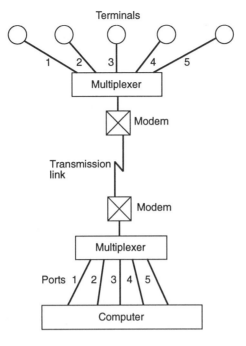

Fig. 8.4 In data transmission between a computer and distant terminals, the multiplexers ensure that the same link can be exploited by a cluster of terminals. Modems (modulator-demodulators) match the data signals to the link

A completely different approach to the transmission of data in both wide area and local area networks is to group short sequences of a data stream into standardised 'packets'. Each packet can then be sent by the best available route in a digital network, and the original full sequence re-assembled at the recipient's end. This packet-switching approach will be considered in greater detail on p. 115.

Local area networks

Local area data networks (LANs) aim at interconnecting large numbers of different types of data equipment in a single site, for example, in a factory, office or university. They also represent one of the fastest growing areas of IT. By the end of 1994 it is estimated that the number of installed PCs within the professional sector of the European Union will exceed 23,750,000 and that of these almost 13,700,000 will be connected to LANs. Furthermore, whilst the annual growth rate for PCs is about 8%, that for LAN equipment is over 25%.

An example of such a network is shown in Fig. 8.5. These networks are more recent in conception and execution than the speech-oriented telephone network. They have been developed to deal specifically with data, and are faster, cheaper and less prone to error than the long-distance telephone network.

Local networks can be constructed along the same principles as long-distance ones, but on a smaller scale, and under the complete control of the user organisation. Thus, the transmission media can be twisted pairs of insulated wire, coaxial cable, fibre optic cable, etc. The medium will, to some extent, determine the data transmission rate within a network, but as before, the use of repeaters will overcome inadequacies of the medium. Current designs of local area network employ a variety of data rates between 0.25 and 100 Mbit/s. What characterises LANs, however, is that all items of equipment connected to them share the same transmission

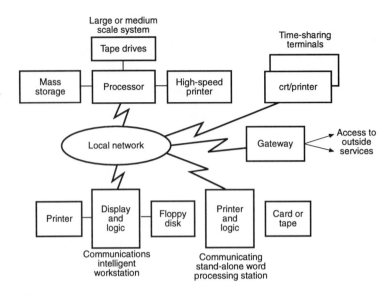

Fig. 8.5 A local network can interlink various items of computing and office equipment and can provide access to other public and private networks and computing and communication services

medium. In one of the main types of LAN, shown in Fig. 8.6, the medium is cable formed into a loop or *ring*. There can be many devices connected to the same ring, each capable of sending or receiving data, or both.

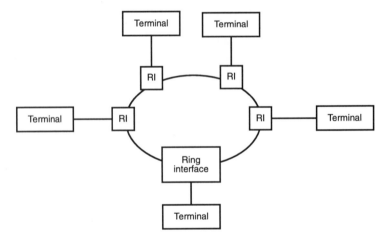

Fig. 8.6 In a ring-type local network, interface equipment is used to launch messages on the ring from terminals, to 'pick off' messages addressed to particular terminals, and to boost signals travelling in the ring

Data, in the form of messages, circulate around the ring from interface to interface. Each message is headed by an address which identifies one or more of the devices at which it is directed. An interface examines each message that passes it, accepts it only if it addressed to its associated device, and then re-transmits it – acting as a repeater. Messages can be launched into the ring by an interface only when the network is not in use by other senders. One widely used way of ensuring this is similar to that used in the early days of single-track railways to avoid collisions: *token-passing*. A train driver had to be in possession of the token (a metal disc) in order to use the line. For LANs the token is a special message circulating around the ring. If the token is marked as free, any interface receiving it can transmit a message. It marks the token as busy, and appends it to the message. After a complete circuit, the sender changes the token back to a free one.

The main strength of a ring network is its low error rate: less than one wrong received digit in 10 billion is claimed. Its weakness is that it needs a repeater, or signal booster, at each point of attachment, and that a simple fault or change in an interface halts the entire network.

Another widely used type of LAN is the *bus* or *broadcast* layout. This is analogous to a stretch of highway with access roads at junctions along the way. An example of the broadcast configuration is shown in Fig. 8.7. It was originally developed by the Xerox Corporation in the USA, under the name Ethernet. The transmission medium is coaxial cable operating at the data rate of usually 10Mbit/s. The network is extendible as it employs repeaters to regenerate the signals. Items of equipment link to the cable through a transmitter-receiver unit, an interface and controller. These serve to select from the data travelling along the network only that portion which has been addressed to them. They also launch into the network data destined for other specific pieces of equipment.

A disadvantage of broadcast-type networks is that, because they are open-ended rather than formed into a closed loop, there is no confirmation that a message has been received, and there is no easy way of correcting transmission errors. By contrast, in a ring network, a message is 'read' by the addressee and is returned in its received form to the sender. If the sender is satisfied with this acknowledgement, it removes the message from the ring, otherwise it repeats the message.

Fig. 8.7 In a broadcast-type local network, separate transmitter-receivers (transceivers) with repeaters are used to boost the signals

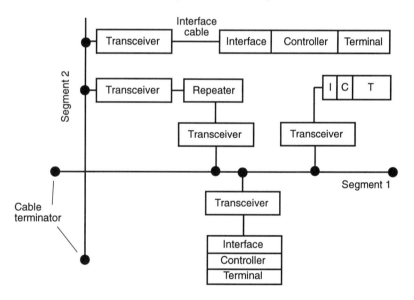

In addition to these two types of local network, operating at data rates of up to 10 Mbit/s, and aimed at interlinking terminals and computers, wider-band local networks are also being introduced. One such network has a 350 MHz bandwidth, split into three segments: one handles 32 channels at 9.6 kbit/s and 16 channels at 64 kbit/s; the next one can take up to seven television channels; the third is a single channel of 12 Mbit/s data rate. This allows simultaneous digital speech, terminal-to-computer, computer-to-computer and television communication on a single coaxial cable. It is also possible to interconnect individual LANs, for example by cable TV networks. As such networks are usually installed in urban areas, they have become known as MANs, or Metropolitan Area Networks.

Circuit-switched networks

When a large number of items of equipment is to be able to send and receive data, it becomes first uneconomical and then physically impracticable to provide a permanent direct connection from each piece of equipment to all others. This problem, of course, is not unique in data networks but arises in all telecommunication networks employing wires or cables. The traditional approach, in telephone and telex networks, is to link a limited number of items of equipment not to each other, but to a switching centre (exchange). There is only one connection from each item of equipment to the switch centre, resulting in a star-shaped network, called a *star-network*. The job of the switching centre is to establish a short-term link between any two lines connected to it. The existence of a temporary link between two (or more) parties is referred to as a call, while the path between the calling and called parties is known as the *circuit*.

In long-distance networks, switching centres themselves are interconnected, forming a *mesh-network*. In this way, a circuit can be established, on a temporary basis, between an increasing number of items of equipment around the world. While the call lasts, in circuit-switched networks, the circuit and some part of the switching equipment are completely dedicated to that call, i.e. they are unavailable for other calls, even though at some point in time there may not be any signals passing along the circuit. Circuit-switched networks are currently the most widely used means of data transmission.

The greatest advantage of circuit switching is that the customer is guaranteed the full bandwidth of the circuit for the duration of the connection; however, the circuit provider may not get the best utilisation of the network equipment. Another disadvantage is that each circuit takes time to set-up and in some cases set-up takes longer than the actual call. For this reason other forms of switching systems have been developed.

Message-switched networks

The idea of message switching has already been introduced when discussing the flow of messages in local area networks: messages are launched into a network, each headed by the address of the recipient. Within the network, the message is passed along from one switching point to the next until it reaches its destination. Message switching aims to overcome the problem of engaged lines (or expensive peak-rate call charges), by allowing messages to be sent to and stored temporarily at the switching centre. The messages are then 'delivered' automatically by a call from the switching centre to the called party. For these reasons, message switching is often referred to as *store-and-forward*.

Message switching is usually employed in star- and mesh-networks when some time delay between the origination and reception of a transmission can be tolerated. The switching centres in store-and-forward data networks are, in many cases, computers which can conveniently store data, monitor the availability of lines, initiate transmission according to pre-programmed rules, and so allow better utilisation of the network.

Message switching can provide faster overall transmission times than circuit switching, much depends on the loading of the network. Figure 8.8 shows a timing comparison between circuit and message switching for a network comprising four switching centres. All messages sent across a communications channel are subject to three types of delay:

Propagation delay: the time taken for the electrical or optical signal to propagate across the channel. This is generally negligible due to the speed of propagation of electromagnetic waves.

Transmission delay: the time taken by the transmitter to send a block of data. For example, it takes one second to transmit a block of 1000 bits if the transmission rate is 1000 bits per second.

Node delay: the time it takes the switching centre to route data from the incoming circuit to the outgoing circuit.

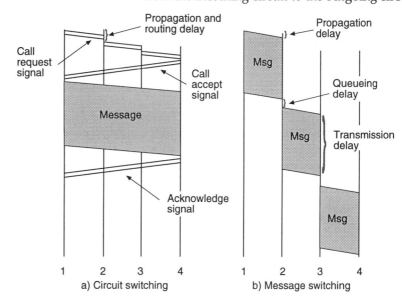

Fig. 8.8 Timing comparison of circuit and message switched networks

The slope of the lines represents the small propagation delay between switching centres. The small vertical displacements at each switching centre correspond to the node delays setting up the routing for the next segment of the network. The height of each message block represents the transmission delay for the message. The figure illustrates that message switching can actually be quicker for short-duration links, since there is no delay setting up the circuit. However, each switching centre must be capable of storing the entire message prior to onward transmission. Hence for long-distance messages, traversing many switching centres, message switching usually takes longer. Whilst posing some problems for speech and interactive terminal operations, it is ideal for off-peak data transfers.

Packet-switched networks

Packet switching is a relatively new technique in data networks, first proposed in 1964 in the USA, but now established world-wide. It is close to message switching in principle as it employs computers to control the flow of data and does not provide a dedicated physical path between the sender and recipient. The technique, however, does not operate with complete messages, but rather with segments of them, broken up into blocks with a given maximum size, called data *packets*, or data *segments*. Each packet carries the identification of the intended recipient and also data about the position of the packet in the sequence which makes up the complete message, as well as data which aid in the detection of transmission errors. A packet of data, together with such auxiliary control data, is called a *datagram*. The datagrams are formed and 'unpacked' by computers which are local to the sender and receiver. In the network, switching computers examine the addressing instructions of each packet and determine the appropriate route for it. If necessary, because of congestion, packets can be stored at such switching *nodes*. As a result, there may be some delay in transmission, just as in a message-switched network, but usually not more than a fraction of a second.

An important variant of packet switching is the *virtual circuit* in which a *logical* connection is established between the source and destination before any data packets are transferred. To all intents the user appears to have a dedicated circuit and hence all packets travel by the same route and arrive in the correct order. Setting up and closing down the virtual circuit takes time and can be a significant overhead for short messages. Figure 8.9 shows a timing comparison between the two forms of packet switching.

Fig. 8.9 Timing comparison of packet switching systems

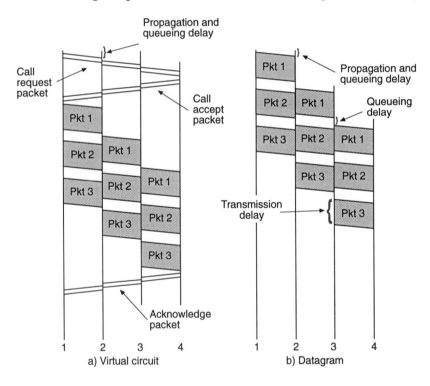

The virtual circuit option does provide a number of benefits, such as flow control of the packets to prevent overload at the receiver, error detection, and error correction by automatic requests for retransmission. The user is therefore provided with a guaranteed quality of service. Datagram systems on the other hand offer no such guarantees, unless they are provided at higher levels of network service.

An important advantage of packet switching is that the rate at which data are sent by a piece of equipment need not be fixed. In other words, a sender can generate packets of data at a rate appropriate to its purposes. Note, however, that the bit-rate of the packets is fixed. In this way, the available bandwidth of the transmission channel is continually re-allocated between users, to make the most of an expensive investment. This is in complete contrast to circuit switching, where a circuit with a fixed bandwidth is allocated to a call, whether it is carrying data or not. (Keyboard terminals are estimated to be active for only one-eighth of the time of a call.) But this is not all: the technique allows for the recipient accepting data at a rate which suits it, so that devices with very different data rates can communicate with one another. This is something that is not possible in circuit-switched networks unless the devices themselves contain adequate 'buffer' storage.

An example of a packet-switched network is Britain's PDN (public data network) which conforms to the CCITT X.25 standard for virtual circuits and forms the basis of most current WANs. This is the network, for example, which is used by the cashpoint machines around the country to communicate with the banks' central computers. PDN is a development of EPSS (the Experimental Packet Switched Service) introduced in 1976. The world's first experimental service, Arpanet, started operation in the United States in the early 1970s. EPSS was linked to Arpanet and other similar services by IPSS (International Packet Switched Service) in 1981.

PDN, like other national packet-switched networks, is separate from the public switched telephone network. The transmission paths along which the packets travel, and the digital exchanges where they are routed have been designed with the needs of data transmission in mind. There is, however, a linkage between the two: it is possible for a user with a modem to call from a PSTN station one of a set of public entry points (packet assemblers and disassemblers, or PADs). There the data stream from the modem is converted into packets, and is launched into the PDN. At the far end, a reverse process may be followed, depending on whether the addressee is a modem user. The alternative is for a private PAD to be located at the user's premises, and be connected to the PDN by a direct link. Both public and private PADs have unique network user identifier (NUI) numbers by which they can be addressed from any other PAD in the international packet-switched network.

Narrow-band and wide-band networks

The terms 'narrow-band' and 'wide-band' are ill-defined but they are usually taken to describe bandwidths below and above the telephone circuit bandwidth of 3500 Hz.

For transmission by the telephone network, data must be converted into signals in this band of frequencies, by means of *modems*. Practical considerations constrain the data rates on the existing public circuit-switched telephone network to an upper limit of 1.2 kbit/s, or 28.8 kbit/s with specialised data-encoding techniques. The use of non-switched telephone lines allows this limit to be raised to 48 kbit/s, but at considerable extra cost. Public packet-switched networks normally run at maximum data rates of 56 (US) or 64 kbits/s (UK and Europe).

Example of a digital network

The Integrated Services Digital Network (ISDN) is being installed in the UK, to replace gradually the present public switched telephone network (PSTN). Figure 8.10 shows the overall lay-out of the new network. It consists of System X digital exchanges interlinked by high capacity data channels. Customers' terminals are linked to the exchanges by Integrated Digital Access (IDA) lines.

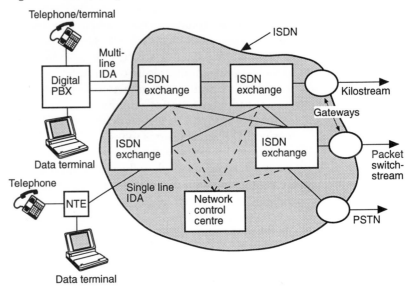

Fig. 8.10 Schematic view of the Integrated Services Digital Network, which is to replace the national telephone network. The new network employs digital transmission (at both trunk and local levels) and digital switching. (PBX=private branch exchange; NTE=network terminating equipment; ISDN=Integrated Services Digital Network; IDA=Integrated Digital Access; PSTN=public switched telephone network)

Each IDA line provides 3 channels, but one of these is reserved for signalling. The other two may be used simultaneously, for calls to different destinations. One of the channels is for data or voice (64 kbit/s), the other is a slower data-only channel (8 kbit/s). The connection of user equipment to the ISDN network is shown in Fig. 8.11.

Fig. 8.11 Connecting to the ISDN

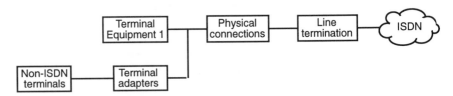

The ISDN will also be linked to other services, including the PSTN and the packet-switched network. The modecs mentioned earlier (see p. 106) will allow terminals on the ISDN to communicate with modems on the PSTN. Links are to be provided to the new digital networks of other countries.

Such international links have been made difficult by the slow pace of standardisation (see Chapter 18). Thus, the IDA just described may be viewed as an early form of the international standard. The latter will include two 64 kbit/s voice/data channels, a 16 kbit/s signalling channel for packet-switched data and a 48 kbit/s control channel. Further 384 kbit/s channels are to be provided for services such as digital audio broadcasting, facsimile, teleconferencing, etc.

Future developments

The current trend is to provide all levels of customer with ever-increasing data transmission capacity. Domestic premises can already opt for a dual channel ISDN service offering two 64 kbit/s lines and capable of supporting simultaneous voice and data or good quality video conferencing. Business premises can opt for 2 Mbit/s ISDN links capable of supporting 30 simultaneous voice calls, high-quality video conferencing, high-speed data transmission, or a combination of all three.

The eventual aim is to construct a world-wide Broadband Integrated Services Digital Network (B-ISDN), capable of supporting a mixture of voice, data, audio, and video transmission services. Such a service would probably utilise a combination of coaxial cables, optical-fibres and satellite transmission media and dynamically allocate the bandwidth required for the information being transmitted.

Ownership of data networks

The lack of widely accepted standards has been one of the main reasons for the proliferation of *private data networks*. The access to a private network is limited, and as a result greater security of data is possible than on a public network. However, private networks are expensive to set up and operate. The ownership of long-distance networks is, therefore, in the hands of national governments or large corporations. They then either market the transmission facilities of the network to the general public or lease some part of the network to those wishing to set up a private network. An interesting development is the interlinking of local private networks with long-distance public networks and through them, possibly, with other local networks.

In the early 1980s, a third type of network was started up in the United States, the *value-added network*. This is based on transmission facilities leased from public network operators but uses privately owned switching computers. This enables the operators of networks like Tymnet and Telenet to provide facilities not normally available on public data networks, such as an electronic mail service. Whether such value-added networks continue in the longer term depends on the willingness of the owners and operators of public networks to add the extra facilities to their own service. Value-added networks have now also been introduced in many countries.

Applications

The annual growth rate of the volume of data transmitted along networks in Europe is currently estimated at around 20 per cent. Most of this growth is attributed to the use of computer-based information systems via the public networks. Similar rates of growth have been reported in the US by the Electronic Messaging Association, especially by organisations which are themselves geographically distributed, for example, banks, large manufacturing, retail and administrative organisations, e.g. for bulk-data transfers.

In the longer term, we can expect the full range of current telecommunication applications to be taken over by data networks, including voice communication, teleconferencing, electronic mail, electronic funds transfer and videotex.

9 Satellite communications

Introduction and fundamentals

Communication satellites are spacecraft launched for the purpose of providing broadband communication channels. The carrier medium is microwaves, in the 1 to 30 GHz band (corresponding to electro-magnetic waves of 30 cm to 1 cm wavelength).

At their simplest, communication satellites can be thought of as repeaters or relay stations in a communication link. For example, the most important class of satellites, called *geostationary* satellites, are in an orbit 35,786 km directly above the equator which makes them appear fixed (i.e. stationary) relative to the rotating Earth, as illustrated in Fig 9.1. The original idea for using geostationary satellites was described by Arthur C. Clarke in his article *Extra Terrestrial Relays* in the October 1945 edition of *Wireless World*. Clarke determined that global radio coverage could be established with just three satellites.

Fig. 9.1 Geostationary satellite orbit

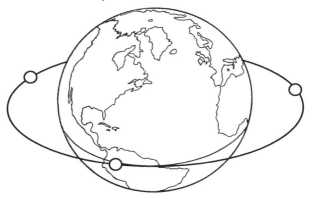

Unlike the Moon, which is Earth's natural satellite, these artificial satellites do not set and rise but remain in the same, predictable positions in the sky. They are therefore continuously available for the transmission of messages.

Transmitters on the ground can modulate message signals on the microwave carrier of a fixed frequency. These are received by the satellite, amplified (increased in power), and re-transmitted at a different frequency back to earth. A different frequency is chosen so as to avoid interference between the sent and transmitted signals. Since electromagnetic waves travel in a straight line, and the re-transmitted beam spreads, just as the beam of a searchlight would, the signal will be received within a circular area of the earth's surface. In practice, the size and even the shape of this 'footprint' can be adjusted to meet specific requirements. At its maximum, the footprint covers about 42% of the earth's surface, so three geostationary satellites between them can reach any geographical point.

Advantages of communication satellites

The launch and operation of a communication satellite represents a multi-million pound investment. There are a range of considerations which make this a worthwhile expenditure.

1 A transmission can originate from any point, and can be received at any *or all points* within the coverage of a satellite. This characteristic makes the communication satellite particularly attractive for broadcasting purposes. In effect, the satellite acts as a transmitter on top of a very tall mast. Because of its height, transmissions are not affected by mountains or any other obstructions, and are not subject to the terrain problems which affect terrestrial cables (e.g. crossing oceans or deserts).
2 The bandwidth of a satellite channel enables it to carry thousands of simultaneous telephone conversations, or 1–2 television programmes, or data at rates of several Mbit/s.
3 The cost of communication is distance-independent: it costs the same to send a message by satellite to another location 5000 miles away, as it does to cover 5 miles.
4 Satellites can just as easily be used as a link between mobile sending and receiving stations as fixed ones. This has led to their use as a means of communication with ocean-going ships, as well as alternative pathways to the international telephone network.
5 Because of their reach, they can deliver communication services directly to the users' premises, irrespective of whether these are in cities or in remote rural areas.

Limitations of communication satellites

1 The geostationary orbit can hold only a limited number of satellites. Current technology enables satellites to be placed at 2° intervals. To some extent, this limitation is countered by mounting several receiver-transmitter pairs (*transponders*) on each spacecraft, and by placing satellites into other than geostationary orbits (e.g. low-earth orbit). In addition, each position can be occupied by more than one satellite (operating at different frequencies and/or polarisations).
2 The large distance between the earth and satellite has two main consequences:

   (a) Messages take an appreciable time to arrive at their destination: it takes about a quarter of a second for a signal to travel via space. This poses a special problem in using a satellite link for telephone conversations.
   (b) The signal loses its strength, and becomes contaminated by noise. To overcome this, special, relatively high cost transmission and reception equipment is needed, both on the ground and on the spacecraft.

We shall now briefly look at the equipment which underlies communication satellite transmission and reception, and how it links to other networks.

Satellite networks

Signals for communication satellites may originate from telephones (voice), computers (data) or TV and radio studios (video/audio). In each case, the signals are sent to a ground station via cables or terrestrial microwave links. At the ground station, one or more *antennas* or *up-link stations* transmit the often multiplexed signals, modulated on to a microwave carrier to a chosen transponder on a satellite. Typical transmitter power is in the kilowatt range, and bandwidths (data rates) are of the order of tens of MHz (tens of Mbit/s).

Before up-linking, the transmitted signal may be coded, either to preserve its security (in the case of data) or for commercial purposes (in the case of TV transmissions). On reception, the reverse process occurs, that is signals are amplified, demodulated, de-multiplexed and de-coded. Depending on the strength of the signal transmitted from the satellite and the position of the receiver relative to the centre of the footprint, the receiving antenna (dish) may have dimensions in excess of 10 metres or as low as tens of centimetres.

The received signal may be fed directly into a TV set, as in the case of domestic DBS (*direct broadcasting by satellite*) systems, or linked to other distribution networks, such as the public or private telephone network, local area networks, cable TV networks, etc.

Satellite technology has developed rapidly, as shown in Table 9.1 below for the Intelsat series of satellites and the European Space Agency's experimental Olympus satellite.

Table 9.1

	Intelsat I	Intelsat V	Olympus
Year for first launch	1965	1986	1989
Weight (kg)	38	1670	3300
Electrical power (W)	40	2264	7500
Capacity (telephone circuits)	240	33000	
Designed lifetime (years)	1.5	7	10

Very small aperture terminals

The satellite telecommunications services provided by the national authorities (e.g. PTTs) are essentially point-to-point and are used to link the land-based networks of individual countries. The cost of the ground stations required for the up and down-links to the geostationary satellites are expensive and utilise very large dish antenna. They are therefore not best suited to meet the communications needs of the global information operators.

The very small aperture terminal (VSAT) services have been developed to overcome these limitations. Data from the user is transferred to a conventional ground station, via land lines, for transmission to the satellite. The satellite rebroadcasts the signal down to any number of VSAT dishes within the footprint of the satellite's transponder. A receiver-only terminal utilises a dish antenna of 0.9 m, small enough not to require planning permission in the UK. Two-way services require a larger 1.2 m dish in order to focus the beam to the geostationary satellite. Larger dishes also permit greater power output.

In 1992 VSAT accounted for 3% of the US long-haul tele-communications market. A typical installation for a hotel chain might support 200 - 300 sites with the VSAT equipment located on the roof. Average costs are about $400 per dish. Some networks are much larger, for example, the KMart retail chain utilises over 2000 VSATs to link each retail unit to corporate headquarters.

VSAT technology also provided the means for Western TV viewers to watch the bombing of Baghdad during the 1991 Gulf War. The Cable News Network (CNN) linked news gathering cameras to VSATs for live transmission to the US and thence on to customers via more satellites and cable networks.

The small size and relatively low cost of VSAT equipment (about £12,000) has provided a short-term solution to the lack of land-based services within Eastern Europe. General Electric Information Services, for example, has installed more than 50 VSAT transceivers in Russia, Hungary, Poland and Czechoslovakia to provide a combination of data and voice services.

Inmarsat provides global communications services for some 30,000 customers, be they ships, trucks or even explorers in undeveloped countries. These services include global paging, voice and data transmission, global positioning (for ships and yachts) and TV transmission. A pager costs around £300, a voice/data terminal £17,000 and a TV terminal about £25,000.

Satellite systems for mobile communications

The growth in demand for mobile global communications has encouraged a number of service providers to explore the use of satellites to implement a global cellular phone service. The main area of interest is in the deployment of low earth orbit satellites (LEOs), utilising some of the technology gained through the strategic defence initiative (SDI). The main advantage of LEOs is that the satellite orbit is only 200 to 1600 km above the earth, hence transmission delays are reduced to around 40 ms and signal loss to some 20dB. This would permit the use of a hand-held terminal, about the size of a modern cellular telephone, with an omni-directional antenna.

There are currently half a dozen proposals to create a global mobile satellite phone service and these can be subdivided between 'little' and 'big' LEOs. Little LEOs planned to start in 1995 are intended to provide data services across the US utilising the 140 MHz band. The satellites are small, about 120 kg, and can be launched with existing missile technology. It is envisaged that these services will be used by researchers wishing to transfer data from remote locations, aid agencies, and small boats.

Big LEOs will operate in the 1.6 and 2.5 GHz bands, but they will require enormous investment, anything from $2000 to 4000 million. The reason is that at the low altitudes employed the satellites appear to travel at a little more than 16,500 mph relative to the Earth's surface, so many satellites will be required to give global coverage.

Motorola's Iridium proposal is based on 66 satellites in 11 polar circular orbits at an altitude of 765 km. The satellites in alternate orbits would be positioned 'out of phase' to provide the continuity of coverage, as illustrated in Fig. 9.2.

Fig. 9.2 LEO satellites in polar circular orbits

Each Iridium satellite would provide 48 channels corresponding to an individual cell in a cellular array on the earth's surface. Each cell would be several hundred kilometres in diameter. The digital service would employ the same Time Division Multiple Access protocol used by the GSM cellular service. One of the unique features of Iridium is that it is proposed that calls intended for a remote user would be switched through the satellite network and not via an earth station. Hence each satellite will need to incorporate a complete cellular switching system.

Globalstar's LEO proposal is based on 48 satellites in circular orbits (non-polar) at an altitude of 1389 km and inclined at 52 degrees to the equator, as shown in Fig 9.3.

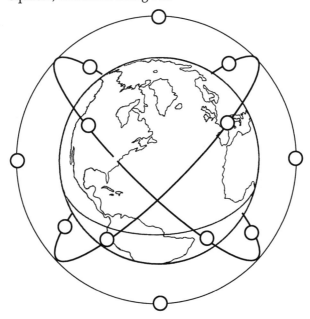

Fig. 9.3 Inclined circular orbits

In order to keep the system simple, calls will be switched via ground-based stations. Code-Division Multiple Access (CDMA) will be employed rather than TDMA. This technique, originally developed for the military, is inherently secure and overcomes many types of interference. The digital data stream is multiplied by a high bit-rate pseudo-random code and transmitted on a shared frequency band as other data streams. Recovery is achieved by applying the same pseudo-random code in reverse. The technique will permit several service providers to utilise the same frequency allocation. Unfortunately the CDMA signals cannot be switched until they are decoded and at present the decoding technology is too large to build into a satellite of 200 - 700 kg, hence ground-based switching.

Weight could well be a deciding factor in the financial viability of LEO systems, and current goals are aimed at satellites weighing between 150 - 700 kg. At these weights it is envisaged that between five and eight LEO satellites could be launched on a single delivery platform such as Ariane-4 or the Space Shuttle.

Applications

The main current applications of communication satellites are: telephony, data services, direct broadcasting and specialist applications.

Telephony includes both fixed and mobile services. In the first, satellites act as an alternative routing to international cable networks; in the latter, they can deliver signals to individual receivers. Data services primarily support business and financial applications, and are often point-to-point, that is used as a single broadband link.

Direct broadcasting initially made use of surplus or spare capacity of telephony applications, but is now increasingly based on national satellites launched specifically for the purpose. Finally, special applications cover a variety of uses, like weather monitoring, space research, radio-location, earth exploration, military surveillance, navigation and frequency beacons for ships and aircraft, etc.

Communication satellites thus represent an important building block of wide area, broadband communications, capable of carrying both analogue and digital signals. Their main competitors are optic communications systems to be considered in the next chapter.

10 Optical communication systems

Introduction and fundamentals

Optical communication systems are a recent addition to the armoury of telecommunication systems. (The first commercially viable systems appeared only in the 1970s.) Their main use so far has been in long-distance digital networks, and increasingly also in local area networks.

They exploit light as the carrier of information (in contrast to electrical signals in electronic communication systems), and optical fibres as the medium for transmitting the light signals (analogous to wires and cables in electrical transmission). Additionally, light waves can be used for the direct transmission of signals, just as radio waves are employed to transmit conventional broadcasts. However, the direct form of optical communication has limited use because of its short range (a few kilometres).

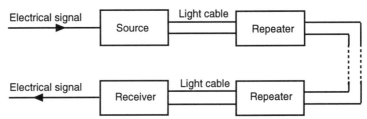

Fig. 10.1 An optical fibre tele-communication link requires equipment to convert between electrical signals and light, and repeaters to boost (electrically) the pulses travelling along the optical fibre cable

Most optical communication systems in current use are linked to established electronic communication networks and devices. The conversion of signals from one form to the other is carried out by special coupling components. Figure 10.1 shows the main parts of an optical-fibre communication system interfaced to an electronic system. Electronic signals are converted to pulses of light, in the infra-red range, by a *source* (e.g. a light-emitting diode or a laser). The light is picked up by one or more optical fibres which may be linked end-to-end. At the far end, light is reconverted to electronic signals by a *receiver* (a photodetector). Signals can be transmitted in either direction, provided, of course, that both ends of the fibre are equipped with a source and a receiver. If transmission is to take place over distances in excess of some 10 km, the light signals need regenerating in *repeaters*. This is because light is absorbed to some extent in the optical fibre. The fibre conducts light by virtue of its transparency (it is made of glass or, in some applications, clear plastic) and by not allowing light to escape from its walls. The pulses of light bounce along the fibre by a series of total internal reflections. This process is similar to the way jets of water in illuminated fountains trap the light from underwater light sources, and then release it as the individual jets disintegrate (the transmission path stops).

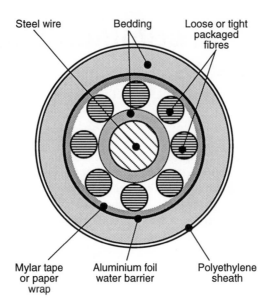

Fig. 10.2 Optical-fibre cable in cross-section

Steel wire   Bedding   Loose or tight packaged fibres

Mylar tape or paper wrap   Aluminium foil water barrier   Polyethylene sheath

Today's fibres are about 0.1 mm in diameter, with a central light-transmitting core of silica glass of about half that diameter. The rest of the fibre is cladding and filling, to aid transmission and to provide protection for the core. Several such fibres may be laid alongside to form an optical-fibre waveguide or cable, as shown in Fig. 10.2. Fibres and cables are light-weight, flexible, and of high strength. The bandwidth of an optical cable is greater than that of a metal coaxial cable. Data transmitted at the rate of about 140 million bit/s can be sent almost without distortion in an optical cable over about 30 km. A coaxial cable, at the same data rate, would produce unacceptable distortion after only a few kilometres. First-generation methods provided for 2000 telephone calls per fibre. British Telecom in 1988 demonstrated a technique based on frequency division multiplexing which made it possible to carry more than 75,000 simultaneous calls on a single fibre.

Example of an optical link

In Britain, the first optical-fibre communication link came into public use on 8 September 1980. By mid-1988, 58% of the total trunk network of the country (211,000 km) was based on fibre. The use of duplex (bi-directional) transmission methods increased the data rates from the initial 140 Mbit/s to 565 Mbit/s. Central London has a high concentration of fibre optic cabling, with the City of London being particularly well served with 60,000 km of fibre cabling.

Current estimates suggest that Mercury has already installed over 8000 km of fibre and that by 1997 BT will have installed 3,500,000 km. But there are new players in the market place. The National Grid Company has set up a telecommunications arm called Energis, to exploit the potential of offering optical fibre riding on its power distribution network. Special equipment has been developed to permit the optical fibres to be wound around the earth conductor on its overhead transmission lines. National Grid has some 7000 km of these lines and is currently wrapping optical fibres at the rate of 80 km a week.

In the US the first long-distance optic fibre link was put into service in February 1983 between New York and Washington. The transmission rate used was 90 Mbit/s, equivalent to 1344 voice circuits. Systems currently being installed will operate in excess of 650 Mbit/s.

The first transatlantic fibre-optic cable came into use at the end of 1988. The TAT-8 cable, with a total length of 6665 km, links the USA to the UK and then on to France. The cable can carry up to 40,000 simultaneous telephone calls. The latest generation (TAT-12) is due for installation in 1995 and will carry the equivalent of 600,000 simultaneous telephone calls.

An even longer distance is bridged by the first trans-pacific fibre-optic link between the USA and Japan. This is the first of about 10 such links planned to support the emerging Pacific Basin trading area.

The new optical network is able to make use of existing cable ducts and exchange buildings, so installation costs are lower. Moreover, optical-fibre cables can resist the ill-effects of sea-water much better than the metal cables of today, and due to their lighter weight can be suspended to form aerial cables in rugged countryside, e.g. of Wales, where the laying of ducts would be prohibitively expensive. These cost savings are offset, to some extent, by the cost of the cable itself and of the conversion equipment between optical and electronic signals.

Applications

The primary field of applications of optical communication systems is telecommunications, but it has potential uses wherever wires and cables are employed at the present time. In telecommunications, optical-fibre cables are well suited to the new range of computer-controlled telephone exchanges, to form a completely new all-digital data network (see p. 117). This will handle both speech and computer data in the form of pulses rather than as a continuous electrical signal, as in the present system. The advantage of such a mode of transmission is a better quality service, as digital transmission is less susceptible to interference. The optical-fibre cable contributes to this better performance by using a non-electrical mode of transmission, which leaves it unaffected by electromagnetic disturbances (induced voltages, clicks, atmospheric effects, etc.).

The high-bit-rate cables are currently economical only where the capacity of the cables is fully utilised, as in inter-city trunk routes and submarine cables. They are in competition, however, with radio and satellite transmission systems. But the bandwidth of even the lower-bit-rate optical-fibre cables makes them attractive as a possible alternative or supplement to the wire-pairs used in local networks (taking the telephone service to subscribers – see p. 72). A wide-band optical cable could supply not only the voice-grade service of the present but also the video services envisaged for the future: view-phone (Picturephone), videotex, advanced facsimile, etc. It can also fulfil, in a single entity, the role of present cable TV installations.

With these advantages, fibre cabling is now starting to replace conventional wiring in some office buildings. In the Broadgate office development in London 128 km of 12 mm diameter cable was used to serve some 800 users. However, the high cost of installation is likely to form an obstacle to the wholesale replacement of existing cabling with optic fibre for all UK subscribers. The cost of that operation was estimated (in 1988) at over £20 billion, or more than £1000 per connection, but more recent estimates (mid 1994) suggest £10 to £15 billion.

An encouraging development in this field is the emergence of standards for the connection of equipment to fibre optic cabling. For example, the Fibre Distributed Data Interface (FDDI) will provide for a local area network of computers communicating at 100 Mbit/s.

Apart from telecommunication applications, optical fibres are also used for transmitting signals in aircraft, in measuring instruments, in high-voltage installations, etc., where their value lies in their being unaffected by extraneous electromagnetic 'noise' and so providing more reliable transmission.

An important feature of optical-fibre cables in such applications is the difficulty of tapping into them. This results in more secure data transfer than with metal cables, because any attempt to interfere with optical transmission causes an immediate change in the received signal, which is easily detected.

Local networks may use optical communication without resorting to fibres for transmission. Signals may be carried over short distances by infra-red light. One such system, developed by IBM in Switzerland, consists of a source-receiver mounted on the ceiling of a large office, with corresponding source-receivers at each work-station in the office. The system can be used to link each work-station to a larger telecommunication or data network. The advantage it offers over wires is that it does not need re-connecting when the layout of the office is changed or when the work-stations are replaced by equipment requiring a higher bandwidth link. Infra-red communication systems have also been employed for personal location systems within offices. Individuals in the office wear a badge that communicates their location to a central controller. As they move around the office the controller redirects telephone calls to the nearest phone.

Optical communication is still in its infancy, but it is one of the major growth areas in the engineering substructure of information technology. With anticipated developments in optical sensor, switching and display technologies, it offers a wide-band, light-weight, low-cost and safe alternative to metal cable networks.

11 Electronic mail

Introduction

Electronic mail is primarily an alternative to the conventional postal mail service. Additionally, it offers a range of new features based on the storing and processing abilities of computers (see p. 100).

The concept of electronic mail covers a broad spectrum of systems and services whose main common feature is that the messages are converted to electronic signals for the purposes of transmission. Thus, the notion of paper as the medium of the message is discarded, and paper is not even considered to be necessary, in some systems, as the starting and final forms.

Input to, and output from, an electronic mail system can be via a video terminal, or word processor with printer, a facsimile machine, or indeed any data terminal, including computer vision (see p. 161) and voice communication systems (see p. 221). Transmission of electronic mail requires a *telecommunication network*. The vast majority of electronic mail is transmitted as computer-compatible data, and travels along data networks. Computerised switching systems may offer electronic mail as one of a range of services.

Electronic mail systems to be considered here include telex, facsimile, communicating text processors, message-switched networks and computer-based message systems.

Telex-based services

Telex (short for *tele*printer *ex*changes) is a text-orientated service. It is in many ways similar to the public telephone service, except that it carries teleprinter signals instead of speech signals. The signalling rate is 50 bit/s or 6.6 characters/s. Teleprinters, which are a combination of a keyboard and a printer, generate a paper record of both received and sent messages.

The telex network is well-established with over 1 million subscribers world-wide. It is also highly automated, standardised, and is under continuous development. There is also a 'super telex' service under the name *teletex* (not to be confused with teletext, which is a system for displaying broadcast text on modified television sets – see Chapter 13).

Teletex is faster than telex, working at 2400 bit/s with packet-switched data, or 1200 bits/s when using the switched telephone network. It also allows a larger possible set of characters than telex. Teletex effectively amounts to an international network of communicating text processors. A standard teletex page is A4 size (or 8.5 by 11 inches in North America), with 55 lines of up to 72 characters, or 38 lines of up to 100 characters.

In theory, any computer terminal or personal computer can use teletex, with an appropriate adapter. Additional advantages of teletex over telex are the possibility of using the terminal to compose or edit documents while it is automatically sending or receiving another document; and the detection and correction of transmission errors. In spite of its advantages, teletex got off to a slow start – only 2000 sets had been installed by the end of 1982, the year of its introduction. A reason for this may be the rather loosely formulated international standards which have been interpreted differently by various manufacturers.

Facsimile services

Whereas telex and teletex cater for text only, facsimile treats a document as a picture. Facsimile services can utilise either the telephone or the telex network for transmission of a faithful copy of an original document. The signal for transmission is generated by automatically scanning the page to be sent. Present standards provide for 3.85 scan lines/mm. An A4 page under these (Group 2) standards takes 3 min to transmit. An alternative digital standard, Group 3, offers higher resolution (200 lines per inch) and much reduced transmission times, with recent systems taking less than 30 seconds to transmit an A4 page. The incompatible Group 4 service is even faster, taking as little as 6 seconds for an A4 page, making use of the 64 kbit/s transmission of ISDN.

The main advantage of facsimile is that it transmits text and graphics, diagrams, handwriting etc. equally as easily because it treats them all as still pictures. Its transmission accuracy is of particular benefit in sending financial documents, engineering drawings, satellite photographs, newspaper pages, etc. International standards for facsimile are well-established.

In 1984 there were about 1 million terminals installed in 70 countries, with public bureau services in 44 countries. By 1991 there were 1.7 million new terminals installed in Europe alone. In the same year the UK's top companies sent an average of 40 documents a day, but one year later the average had more than doubled to 93 documents per day.

One serious limitation of facsimile systems is that the sender and receiver terminals are expected to operate simultaneously, one scanning, the other printing the page. But if the receiving terminal is busy or faulty the service comes to a halt.

Combining a facsimile with a computer overcomes this difficulty. The time-consuming process of converting the page to data signals can proceed continuously, and the messages batched for automatic transmission at the appropriate time. An obvious development, therefore, was the combination of the fax-modem. This often takes the form of an add-on 'card' inserted into the computer. The card takes care of sending and receiving computer-generated documents, when connected to the public telephone network. The current generation of hardware and software for PC-based services permits any document displayed on the screen to be transmitted via a dialled connection. A data-base stores individual phone numbers or permits the creation of groups for broadcasting and transmission can be timed to match local cheap-rate periods.

Computer-based services

The common feature of telex and facsimile is the need for paper as the input and output media. Paper-less electronic mail is usually associated with computer-based electronic mail systems. *Communicating text processors* are an example of these. Text processors are essentially computers, and so offer not only facilities of keyed input and printed output (as in telex), but also aids to editing messages prior to dispatch, and the accumulation of received messages. Some manufacturers provide for the linking of their text processors to a local computer network, or to the public telex network, as well as directly to other text processors. In such installations, a one-page letter can be transmitted from one text processor to another in a matter of seconds, depending on the transmission medium used, and also on whether the receiving terminal is ready to deal with the message.

However, when text processors are required to communicate with non-compatible computers or with ordinary computer terminals, a *message-switching*, or *store-and-forward* system can be used (see also p. 114). The message switch is an 'interface' computer, which accepts messages directed at some other terminal or computer, and performs any necessary conversions on data to compensate for speed or code incompatibilities between the sending and receiving equipment. It also stores any messages which it cannot forward because the receiving terminal is busy or which can be sent at off-peak times.

A recent development, *voice-mail*, allows the message to be spoken rather than keyed. The voice input is converted into computer-compatible form, and is forwarded, or stored by the message switch, as necessary. As a rule, a message-switching computer is not used to provide general computational or text processing facilities, it is more like a policeman directing traffic at a busy intersection of 'data highways'.

There is, however, but a short step from text processors, communicating via a message switch, to a *computer-based message system* (CBMS). The computer, or network of computers, at the centre of a CBMS, is now equipped to file and retrieve messages and offer text processing facilities. Therefore, it centralises many of the text processing functions, allowing less sophisticated terminals access to electronic mail services. Computer-based message services can be offered on an in-house network, or they can be rented from a public-access network. *Videotex networks*, with message facilities, are an example of this type of system (see p. 143). An important advantage of a CBMS is that it allows mail-box type, person-to-person, rather than terminal-to-terminal communication. This is achieved by means of identity codes which a person must use to retrieve mail from the system. The code may be entered from any terminal connected to the network, so a person is not constrained either by location or time from sending or receiving mail. Indeed, portable terminals connected through the public telecommunication network to a CBMS offer the same freedom as a radio-telephone but with the added convenience of storing a message if the recipient is not available at the time of the call.

Using the same analogy, messages can also be 'broadcast' on a CBMS to other users, or to a defined group, by providing the computer with a single 'copy' of the message and a list of addressees. Such facilities are provided by the 'listservers' of Internet. A 'registered mail' facility notifies the sender when his message has been received. Some CBMS also allow the computer to generate messages (announcements, reminders, etc.) to be read by people or by autonomous programs.

An example of an 'electronic mail-box' service is 'Compuserve', which currently supports 45,000 users in the UK and is expected to grow to

100,000 users by the end of 1995. The computer supporting the mail-boxes is actually located in the US, but local call rate access is provided in many UK cities. Users pay a monthly fee for their mailbox together with a small charge for each message sent and received.

Anyone with a microcomputer and modem can connect to Compuserve, provided the equipment has a standard RS232 socket and appropriate software installed. The sender on Compuserve has to start with the details of the recipient(s) and give a subject heading. The latter is displayed in a rapid scanning mode when the recipient next looks at the contents of his 'mail-box'. This allows the more urgent items to be picked out. All mail can be stored and later accessed by keywords (such as the name of the sender, the date, the subject, etc.).

Similar public mail-box services are offered in the UK by Compulink (also known as CIX), Tel-Me and New Prestel, but there are also numerous private systems operated by commercial, government and educational institutions. Most universities, for example, provide campus-wide e-mail services and by means of the Joint Academic Network (JANET) provide access to every other university. International mail services are provided via the Internet (p. 138).

As in other areas of information technology the rapid growth of electronic mail services gave rise to incompatibility between systems. In particular, the formats used to store and transfer messages varied from one service to the next. To overcome this, in 1984 a first attempt at standardisation at international level was made – X.400.

The *X.400* recommendation, updated in 1988, provides for the sending of messages, computer files and even telexes between computers. It relates to Layer 7, the application layer, of OSI (see p. 174). Among its features is a link to a global directory (the X.500 recommendation) which for each person lists the variety of ways in which they can send and receive messages, including both conventional and electronic mail.

Applications

The complete range of electronic mail is applicable to the office and business environments. Conversely, office and business applications currently represent the main thrust of marketing activities of the providers of electronic mail systems. Beyond that, and in the more distant future, the home user is likely to be the target of new electronic mail systems. In all these areas, there are three main applications where the initial impact of electronic mail is likely to be felt:

(a)   an alternative mail service;
(b)   a complement to the telephone service;
(c)   an optional medium for holding meetings and conferences.

Electronic mail can already claim advantages in speed, reliability and convenience over conventional postal services. It is, however, a long way behind them in cost, general availability and psychological acceptance, in particular as far as the data protection aspect of the messages is concerned (see p. 150). But electronic mail has one overwhelming advantage over paper-based mail which is likely to affect the balance in its favour over the next few decades: information is essentially a weightless, media-independent commodity. To transfer conventional mail, it is necessary to produce and move vast quantities of paper. To transfer the equivalent amount of information by electronic mail, no physical material needs to be moved from one place to another, and the energy requirements are vastly smaller.

In relation to the telephone service, electronic mail does not depend on the simultaneous availability of both parties. Messages can be stored and then forwarded to the recipients, or retrieved by them, from any location as long as they have access to the network. In some cases, there is also an advantage in there being a written record or follow-up to otherwise ephemeral telephone conversations.

Lastly, electronic mail is being promoted, particularly in the United States, as an alternative to travel for certain types of face-to-face business meetings or small conferences. Provided that the participants already know each other, and also when it is difficult to find a mutually acceptable time or place for a meeting, it is possible for them to make written contributions via a computer-based message system. These contributions are then instantaneously available to the other participants. The 'computer conference', or collaborative project, may then go on over a period of time. People may address their remarks to all others for interaction and rapid dissemination and publication of ideas, with opportunities for immediate feedback.

12 Information services

Introduction

'Information services' is a non-standard term covering computer-based services which provide information in response to specific requests from users. There are two types of input to such systems: the data which they store in anticipation of requests, and the requests themselves. The data may be stored as references to documents, microforms, or computer-coded text, graphics, etc. The service may be offered on a local basis or via a telecommunication network. Here, we are not concerned with the communication aspects; they are largely covered in the chapter on digital networks, p. 105.

Information systems may be operated by organisations for their own benefit or offered to the public on a subscription basis. An example of the latter is videotex (see p. 143). The output from an information service is either a document, or computer data presented, say, on a video display or as voice output (see p. 223).

The main purpose of an information service is to satisfy users' information needs. The way in which these needs are expressed largely determines the principles of operation of a particular information system.

Document and data retrieval

Perhaps the most straightforward request for information is when the user supplies a complete reference for a document. The job of the service then is to locate a copy of the document and deliver it to the user. This is usually referred to as a *document retrieval* service. It may be aided by computers in compiling the index to the documents in store, and in physically locating a required document (as in a computerised warehouse). More often than not, however, information needs are expressed in terms of a request for data, such as,

"How many computers are installed currently world-wide?",

or

"What books have been published about information technology?"

To answer such questions, reference must be made to records stored either in printed form or as computer-coded data. The first of these is often referred to as *information retrieval,* the latter as *data-base search.* Information retrieval itself may be preceded by a data-base search, when the index to the printed records is computerised.

The distinction between document retrieval and information retrieval, then, is whether the object of the search is a completely specified document, or whether it is either part of the contents of a document (e.g. a telephone number retrieved from a directory) or one or more documents satisfying a content-related inquiry.

Differences in systems

Computer-based information systems differ from one another in a number of important respects:

(a) the range of subjects or documents covered;
(b) the assumptions made about the users of the service;
(c) the input-output interface;
(d) the equipment used to store the data;
(e) the programs which assist in the input, indexing, storage, identification and output of data.

Example: Euronet-Diane

Euronet-Diane is an information service which was inaugurated in 1979 by the telecommunication authorities of the member countries of the European Economic Community. It is used to provide users in those countries with access to the information system Diane (Direct Information Access Network in Europe).

The information available through the network is aimed at researchers, engineers, scientists, managers, economists, the legal and medical professions. The subject coverage is correspondingly broad, embracing bibliographical data in these areas (publications, documents, etc.), reference and handbook material (catalogues, directories, statistics, case-law, etc.), patents, compilations, from lists of research projects in Britain to lists of national defaulters in Italy. The data are held on the computers of various participating organisations which originally compiled the data-banks for their own use, or as a free-standing service. The network essentially acts as a publishing medium for these organisations.

Users are assumed by the system to be able to formulate and carry out their own searches, while on-line to one of the participating data-bases. (These users may be, of course, the people with information needs, or they may be intermediaries who are specially trained information workers.)

The hardware interface to the system is the computer terminal, operating at speeds from 110 to 9600 bit/s. To specify a request, a user must formulate it in a 'command language' (this may be proprietary for older established data-bases, or a standardised version for new ones). One of the commands causes a display on the terminal of the allowed search terms. These terms can be combined so as to narrow the field of search. The outcome of the search may be one or more titles or abstracts of publications, or some factual information. The data which can be accessed through this service is stored in conventional computer data storage devices – magnetic disc units.

Example: Internet services

Internet is a network of computer networks and not an information service, but it provides access to so many information services that it is more appropriate to consider it under this heading.

Internet's origins go back to 1969 when the US Defense Department's Advanced Research Projects Agency (DARPA) initiated a project to link various research groups throughout the US. In 1972 Arpanet was demonstrated to the public. By 1980 the networking protocols were developed to permit other computer networks to interconnect. The name

Internet was coined in 1983 when ARPANET was split into a military network (Milnet) and a civilian network (ARPANET).

In 1984 the National Science Foundation (NSF) of the US launched a programme to enable non-DARPA funded institutions to become interconnected. Since 1986 the NSF have announced various developments towards NSFnet, a high-speed communications link between the NSF super-computers. In 1988 the service offered 1.5 Mbit/s and was handling 85 million packets per month, but by 1992 the service was up to 45 Mbit/s. Current developments are towards NREN, the national research and education network capable of 1000 Mbit/s and due to enter service in 1996.

As of 1994 there were some 1.5 million computers connected to the Internet, supporting over 20 million users and message traffic is increasing at around 20% a month.

The information accessible over this network of networks includes major university libraries, abstracting services, commercial data-bases of company accounts and performance, and news services (e.g. Press Association).

The Internet protocols permit a user to remotely log-in to the host computer, initiate file-transfers, remotely search a data-base and automatically transfer the information, interact in computer conferences, or more recently send faxes to remote destinations.

At present individuals cannot connect to the Internet directly from their PC, but must access the service via an institutional host. In part this is due to the way the addressing system operates, which is based on a hierarchy of domains. At the highest level is the country. Next is a split between education, government, commercial and military. The third level corresponds to the institution and the fourth (if it exists) the name of the host computer. The final part of the address is the user's name. So John Smith with an account on Compulink's CIX service in the UK would have an e-mail address of jsmith@cix.compulink.com.uk.

Example: Commercial services

Compuserve, New Prestel and Tel-Me offer access to numerous information services via a single host, including e-mail. For a monthly (between £6 and £12) or annual (around £300) fee users can access news services - including press-cuttings options, share prices and share dealings services, home banking, company records data-bases, UK and European rail time-tables, hotel listings, weather services, Ordnance Survey maps, and road traffic information. New Prestel boasts some 300 different services and the only real-time stock market quotation service.

Blackwells, the book publisher, has launched an on-line literary service called Uncover which provides access to over 5 million articles from 15,000 journals and magazines dating back to 1988. An on-line search system enables the user to locate articles of interest which is then faxed back within a guaranteed 24 hours. Charges run out to about £9 per article.

Type and range of inquiries

Although most information systems are effectively sophisticated filing systems, the use of computers contributes a range of features not normally found in manual filing systems. These features are based on the processing abilities of computers, which in this case are exploited alongside their capacity for data storage. Perhaps the most important of these features is the type and range of inquiries with which they are able to cope. This, in turn, is largely determined by the *search strategy* adopted in the system.

Some systems are specifically aimed at giving rapid response to anticipated types of inquiry. These include, for example, airline reservation systems, where inquiries may relate, say, to the availability of seats on specific flights. Current videotex systems, such as New Prestel, are also of this type, although this may not be apparent at first glance. For example, a user may wish to know about restaurants in a certain part of London. Information is organised in the data-base in the form of a search tree (see the section on videotex, p. 143 for more detail), and in making choices at various points (e.g. which part of London?) the *system* tells the *user* what questions it is able to answer. That is, the inquiry has been subtly transformed from the one which the user had in mind, to the one which the suppliers of information anticipated as being of general interest. By this 'sacrifice' such systems can give rapid service to a large number of inquiries.

At the other extreme, certain information systems allow for inquiries formulated in natural or slightly constrained language (the latter is usually referred to as a *query language*). The first task of the system is to convert the user's way of expressing an information need to one which the computer can handle. In some cases, this involves the language processing program asking questions of the user to remove ambiguities from the original formulation of the question. The program also warns the user if a particular question would require a lengthy search. The response is put together by the system after examining a very large number of stored records and extracting from them the relevant information – a time-consuming process for even well-structured storage systems. In most systems of this type the search is performed by software, although ICL in Britain have introduced the *content-addressable file store* (CAFS) which searches by hardware, and therefore potentially more rapidly.

With the increasing capacity of computer storage devices, the amount of data stored is also on the increase. To find any particular item of data within a reasonable amount of time will remain a challenge for information services. A development in this area is *hypermedia*. Instead of the *tree-like* organisation of information mentioned earlier, hypermedia references the stored information through a *mesh* or network of cross-references. In some implementations the user of a hypermedia information service is allowed to add his or her own linkages, so that the data-base becomes personalised.

Programs are used also to assist with the original entry of data into the data-base – a vital process since it determines the ease with which the data can be later retrieved. Some of these programs automatically scan the text, looking for certain keywords and recording them, together with the context in which they occur; others automatically classify new data in terms of the keywords or other attributes. Yet others check users' authority to make use of the system.

Although the general-purpose electronic digital computer is at the heart of the current generation of information systems, a considerable amount of research is going into new developments, such as the design of computer structures specially aimed at dealing with data structure and retrieval (data-base machines), and devices which are optical, rather than electronic, methods for recording and searching for data (e.g. holographic stores and optical computers).

Applications

Information systems aimed at dealing with inquiries in anticipated form are employed in many operational situations. These include, for example, in communication, telephone directory inquiries; in finance and commerce, bank balance inquiry systems; in industry, production control and parts storage systems; in administration, police emergency systems. The common feature of these applications is the need for rapid response from the system. There is another set of applications, where the response time is measured not in seconds, but in minutes, and possibly in hours. These information systems aid in strategic decision-making, planning (e.g. management and government information systems), non-time-critical research and investigative work, statistical, archival and reference applications, where inquiries are random and unanticipated in form.

A recent example is the emergence of environment-related and geographical information services. These include digitised maps, such as the Ordnance Survey, possibly linked to Land Registry data, possibly linked to data on underground utility supply networks, to assist for example, housing developers or potential house buyers. On much larger scale, the Global Resource Information Data-base includes satellite photographs, weather data, agricultural and industrial information, etc. aimed at exploring the consequences of various proposed schemes on the global environment.

13 Videotex and teletext

Introduction and fundamentals

Videotex or *viewdata,* as generic terms, apply to interactive (two-way) systems for transmitting text or graphics stored in computer data-bases, via the telephone network, for display on a television screen. This description, however, can equally well apply to the use of a time-sharing computer or a specialist information service (see p. 137) via a data network, or indeed to some forms of electronic mail (see p. 131). What distinguishes videotex from these systems is that it is specially intended as a simple-to-use, low-cost information service, catering for large numbers of users.

Teletext is a non-interactive (one-way) form of videotex, that is, a method of transmitting text or graphics stored in a computer data-base, as part of broadcast transmissions, for display on a television screen. Again, it is intended for wide public use, carrying information of broad public interest. (It is technically quite feasible to operate teletext services for a small number of users. However, the economics of such a service may not be sufficiently attractive to make it viable. With videotex, it is both technically and economically possible to cater for special-interest groups in a larger system.)

Fig. 13.1 The main components of videotex and teletext. User terminals link to the data-base computers via the telephone network for videotext, and via broadcast channels for teletext. Only videotex has the reverse link allowing direct communication with the computer

Videotex and teletext systems have a similar structure, as indicated in Fig. 13.1. The hardware of each consists of a central data-base computer (or several such computers), linked to a large number of television displays via a telecommunication network. The software for both includes a data-base storage and retrieval program operating on an organised set of textual and/or graphic data. The data are organised as 'frames', each containing a screenful of alphabetic, numeric and graphic symbols. The format of the frame, and the transmission codes for the characters are virtually the same for the two systems, at least for systems used in any one country.

The human element also tends to divide into the same groups for both systems: on the one hand, the users (the general public) and, on the other, the 'information providers' (organisations or individuals who supply the contents of the data-base). Other interested parties include the operators of the systems, and the suppliers of the various technical components.

Videotext and teletext differ, however, in the way they transmit the data and also in the way the user controls what data are to be displayed.

Videotex systems

Videotex systems assume that the user has a telephone, to which a TV monitor or television set can be connected, via an electronic interface internal or external to the set. The interface usually includes a control keyboard, a modem (for converting data signals to and from the form used for telephone transmission), an auto-dialler (for calling the data-base computer and identifying the calling terminal at the press of a button) and circuitry for generating the displayed picture from the received data. There may also be provision for connecting a printer and/or some recording device so that received frames may be stored by the user. Other videotex systems, such as the Prodigy system described below, assume that a personal computer is being used instead of a basic terminal or TV set.

The user selects a frame to be displayed by pressing keys on the keyboard. Each frame is identified by a unique code and this can be keyed in directly, if the code is known to the user. Alternatively, a set of choices, in terms of subject break-down, lead the user to a particular information frame. Various indices, presented as frames in the system, also help in selecting an information frame. In some systems, the keyboard may be used to gain access to the data-base by typing in a keyword, to discover what data are being stored on a particular subject.

Teletext systems

Unlike videotex, teletext systems do not employ sound-coded signals travelling within the relatively narrow bandwidth of telephone circuits. Instead, the coded character signals are sent as part of television picture signals. On a 625-line TV system, the data transmission rate is just under 7 Mbit/s. However, this rate is not sustained: in most teletext systems, data transmission occurs only in bursts. The duration of the burst is some fraction of the time it takes to transmit one TV picture. For example, the Ceefax and Oracle teletext systems in use in Britain transmit data at this rate for about one ten-thousandth of a second, 50 times a second. The full data rate would be available only if no TV picture were transmitted simultaneously with the teletext transmission, as it could be, for example, if a complete TV channel was devoted to teletext, e.g. in a cable TV network ('cabletext').

In the British teletext systems, different sets of frames are transmitted on a 'carousel' basis. This means that each complete set of frames, held in the data-base, is transmitted, one frame after another, in a continuous cycle, just as a carousel-type slide projector would show slides if placed under automatic control. Each set of frames, or 'carousel', is transmitted on a different broadcast channel.

The reason for this mode of operation is that a user cannot signal to the computer which frame he or she wants to view, since the broadcast channel is one-way – from the central transmitter to the receivers. As in videotex, each frame is identified by a code, and the user is supplied with an index which briefly describes the content of each frame. Combined television-teletext receivers offer the user a set of switches or keys which can be set to the code designating a particular frame. When that frame is transmitted in the sequence frames, electronic circuitry in the set identifies its code and stores the data which make up the frame. It also converts the data signals into a viewable picture which is retained on the screen until the computer changes the contents of that frame. In order to reduce the waiting time for a particular frame, the number of frames in the 'carousel' must be rather limited. An alternative approach allows more frames in the 'carousel' and yet keeps the average waiting time acceptably low by inserting the more popular frames several times into the cycle. The use of sub-pages is yet another way of increasing the total amount of information available to viewers while making the system reasonably fast.

The current generation of television receivers in Britain is often available with a teletext option, some providing advanced features like pre-selection and local storage of preferred frames, direct access to information related to the one being displayed, etc. Another recent development is the use of additional TV bandwidth for the transmission of coded information for closed user groups (e.g. financial data) as part of a commercial information service.

Frame content

In both videotex and teletext systems, the content of any particular frame can be changed while the system is in operation. In videotex, a user will receive the contents as they exist at the instant when the user's selection is made. In teletext, a fixed selection setting will present the new contents of a selected frame when that frame next comes around in the 'carousel'. In this way, for example, news flashes and other 'instant' information can be received as it is keyed into the computer's data-base, or 'sub-titles' to a TV program can be produced, super-imposed on the TV picture.

Developments and compatibility

Videotex and teletext systems are under continuous development. Moreover, there are several different, technically incompatible systems being developed in different countries, with no clear standard emerging at the time of writing.

Prestel (British videotex system)

Prestel, the world's first public videotex service, started its market trials in 1978. Public service began in 1979, followed in 1981 by an international service.

A Prestel frame is made up of 960 character positions in a 24 row, 40 column array. Each position may be filled by a text character or a graphic rectangle. The graphic rectangles in turn are broken down into 3 rows of 2 smaller squares, each of which may be either dark or coloured. Low-resolution graphics can be made up from combinations of such rectangles. For obvious reasons, this is referred to as a 'mosaic graphic' facility. A character or graphic rectangle may take any one of seven colours, with a different coloured background, if required. Characters may also be doubled in height and made to flash. The coded frames are held in magnetic-disc stores in a network of computers distributed around Britain. Data are transmitted from the computers to the users at 1200 bit/s, from the users to the computers at 75 bit/s.

Although initial expectations of take-up of Prestel were very high (of the order of millions of users, i.e. the numbers who now have access to teletext), in 1989 there were less than 100 000 terminals attached to Prestel. In 1994 the service was bought and re-launched as New Prestel with 30,000 subscribers.

There are many lessons that can be drawn from this slow growth: as usual in information technology, they represent a mix of economic, social and technological considerations.

The presentation of pictorial information in Prestel has been 'traded off' against a lower cost of the adapter needed in all videotex sets. However, a planned feature would allow a sub-area of each frame to be occupied by a higher-resolution graphic.

Another useful facility enables users of Prestel to gain access to a wide range of computer-held data-bases and information services via a 'gateway' – a standardised computer-communication link controlling the flow of data between the 'host' computers and the videotex network. Alternatively, videotex searching can be made part of an integrated services digital network.

Antiope (French videotex and teletext standard)

Antiope[*] is a combined videotex and teletext standard. A videotex service based on it, called Teletel, came into operation in 1981. It is in many ways similar to Prestel, with the following main exceptions:

(a) a larger set of possible text and graphic character attributes is used (each character being defined by 16 bits rather than by 7 bits as in Prestel), in a 40-row 25-line mosaic;
(b) the use of packet-switched data transmission in the videotex mode, and the broadcast transmission of selected frames from a common data-base in teletext mode (the common data-base may include a range of public or private information systems).

The Teletel service started in 1984, and by the end of 1988 there were about 3 million attached terminals. The eventual number is projected at 8 million, or 1 in 3 telephone subscribers. Telecom France, the operator of the service, has encouraged this development by providing users with a free terminal, worth about £80 each.

Prodigy (US videotex service)

The Prodigy service in the United States has taken a different approach to Prestel and Teletel: it assumes that users already have personal computers (IBM-compatible at present, although support is being planned for some other machines as well). Prodigy supplies the software which fulfils two main functions:

1   it allows the user to communicate with a regional data-base, via a 2400 bit/s modem;
2   it contains some frequently used graphical images (such as a map of the United States) so that they do not have to be transmitted each time, say, the user asks for weather information. In that case, only the

---

[*] Antiope stands for Acquisition Numerique et Televisualisation d'Images Organisees en Pages d'Ecriture (digital acquisition and tele-display of pictures organized as written pages)

specific weather data would be sent and superimposed by the computer on the stored map.

The regional data-base holds only a limited amount of information. Similarly to a local library, it can request information from a central data-base, if it cannot supply a user request from its own holdings.

Prodigy started in 1984, and by 1989 it had about 75 000 users, concentrated around 4 cities. It is being extended to eventually cover the entire United States.

Captain (Japanese videotex system)

Captain (Character and Pattern Telephone Access Information Network) is one of several experimental public information systems for Japan, and one that has operated as a service from 1983. Its pictures are made up of an array of dots (192 rows by 240 columns). This caters for the display in any one frame of up to 480 of the 3000 to 4000 possible Kanji, Hiragana and Katakana characters of written Japanese. The relatively high resolution picture requires an increased data rate compared with other systems – up to 4800 bit/s. Captain is intended for operation via the public telephone network.

Applications

Apart from their role as information services, teletext and videotex can be considered as potential distribution media for all kinds of digitally coded data. One natural candidate for this type of application is *computer software* (see p. 98). After successful tests, there are now regular services offering, from a central 'computer program repository', packaged programs via videotex. These can be stored in a user's computer, and then used in a self-contained mode. This application has been referred to as *telesoftware*. Other data so transmitted into people's homes could include electronic mail, electronically published newspapers, books, educational materials, etc.

Videotex, being a two-way medium, is particularly suited to electronic mail (message sending) applications. These account for the largest proportion of users of the Teletel system, which was initially introduced for a completely different purpose: directory inquiries. In Britain, the largest user of videotex, over its first 10 years, was the travel industry. An estimated 70% of package holiday bookings in 1988 had been made through a videotex-based system with terminals located at travel agencies.

At the present stage of development of computer, telecommunication and data-network technology, a truly large-scale person-to-person electronic mail service involving millions of subscribers is not a realistic proposition.

On a smaller scale, though, within large organisations or on a limited subscription basis, an electronic mail videotex network is quite feasible. Private videotex services have been built to demonstrate this feasibility and to explore the potential of this medium. The British 'Campus 2000' service, linking together schools in Britain and other countries is an example of such a network. A line of future development, linking the smaller networks via data 'gateways', offers an evolutionary way towards an international electronic mail and information system. In some countries, particularly in North America, a different line of development is possible.

There, significant investment is being made into cable TV, including two-way cable. This may provide an alternative data pathway to the traditional telephone network. Thus, a combination of teletext and cable TV systems can lead to a competitive range of facilities for the users, including, for example, mail order or 'yellow pages' directory information and simple access to information-retrieval systems.

In the final analysis, the method of delivery of the data (whether by telephone, broadcast, cable or satellite) is less important than the quality of information and the services which become available to very large numbers of people in a cost-effective way. As noted in earlier chapters, some possible services are already being explored on a smaller scale as 'add-on' options to the telephone service: electronic mail, banking, publishing, etc. As to the quality, range and cost of the information, these are likely to be the main determinants of the pace at which this new communication medium develops.

14 Data protection

Introduction

"The increasing use of computers and sophisticated information technology, while essential to the efficient operations of government, has greatly magnified the harm to individual privacy that can occur from any collection, maintenance, use or dissemination of personal information." (From the Preface to the *US Privacy Act, 1974, Public Law 93-579*.)

In its strictest sense data protection is the set of legislative and technical measures taken to ensure the privacy of personal information. The legislative aspects are very much bound up with the notion of 'privacy', and differ from country to country. Thus, legislation in many European countries (Sweden, Denmark, Norway, Luxembourg, West Germany and France) covers the use of data about the individual by both the public and private sectors, and is legally enforceable. In the United States and Canada, it applies only to the public sector and compliance with it is voluntary. In some countries, not only the individual but 'legal persons' (companies, etc.) are also protected by data laws.

Taken in its broader sense, data protection also covers the maintenance of the integrity, quality and ownership of data handled by information technology systems. The main threats in this context are:

- the *loss of information*, e.g. its destruction or falling into unauthorised hands;
- the *corruption of information*, e.g. the alteration of its representation, whether accidental or deliberate;
- the *misuse of information*, e.g. the exploitation of information for other than legitimate purposes.

With the increasing use of information technology, the potential consequences are also increasingly serious. Reported cases of computer fraud, which may involve all three types of threat listed above, result in losses amounting to tens of millions of pounds a year, but many cases go undetected or unreported. There may be threat to life when the systems are involved in, say, nuclear transport or health care applications.

Privacy and security

It is important to distinguish between the *privacy* and *security* aspects of data protection. Privacy is concerned with avoiding the misuse of information relating to people or corporate bodies. In practice, it is expressed by laws, principles or codes of practice. Security is concerned with the implementation of these expressions of privacy. Without security, privacy cannot be ensured, but even with security, privacy cannot be guaranteed.

The advent of information technology has not created the problems of privacy and security of information. Rather, it has thrown them in a new light, and provided new means of both protecting and breaching the security of data. Before, the cost of obtaining personal data from manual filing systems was relatively high. Now, with computerised data-bases and vast amounts of data in transit, access to it – authorised and unauthorised – is more practicable. Unauthorised access to data can be accidental or deliberate.

Accidental disclosures may result from a system error (both hardware and software) or a human operational error, such as an authorised user not signalling to the system the end of an access transaction, and leaving the system open to an unauthorised inquiry. *Deliberate unauthorised access* is possible while the data are being processed, stored or transmitted. The methods can include legitimate access to the data-base to obtain unauthorised information, obtaining legitimate access by improper means, theft of storage media, wire-tapping, the insertion of misleading information, the initiation of bogus transactions to the advantage of the perpetrator, etc.

These methods may threaten the data while they are processed, stored or transmitted. For example, so-called *computer viruses*, i.e. mischievously introduced rogue programs, can affect system software or application programs. A computer 'worm', a special form of virus, is a program which replicates itself inside the memory of the computer, displacing other stored information. Transmitted data can be intercepted while it passes through switching exchanges, wire or broadcast links. Computer systems interconnected by networks may also provide an unwitting way for the spread of computer viruses. Electro-magnetic radiation emitted by computing equipment can be picked up at a distance to yield a view of the data being processed.

Security measures against unauthorised access need to be effective and they also must be *seen* to be effective. Both accidental and deliberate disclosures of confidential information can be countered by administrative measures, such as the control of access by passwords, auditing and monitoring, or technical measures. These latter may include control of access to stored data by, say, automatic finger-print or voice-print identification, or protection of data while in transit through a privacy transformation, better known as cryptography.

Scrambling and unscrambling

The transformation (scrambling) of data can take place prior to its storage or transmission, and can guard against accidental disclosures and wire-tapping or other electronic 'snooping'. Although no code or cipher has been theoretically proved to be unbreakable, the aim of security measures is to make the cost of breaking them greater than the value of the information which they protect.

The scrambling and unscrambling of data are processes which are readily performed by computers, but they are, of course, available also to those who deliberately seek unauthorised access. Moreover, the use of a computer for privacy transformation leaves open the question of how to protect the code (key) used in the scrambling process, as well as the need to convince the non-technical individual of the effectiveness of the method.

To cover some of these points, a Data Encryption Standard was introduced in the United States in 1975. It may appear, at first sight, unwise to establish standards for encypherment as any publication of methods is likely to assist the intruder. However, once one recognises that data are transmitted from one organisation to another, the technical compatibility of message formats needs to be ensured. The Data Encryption Standard (DES) is based on multiplication of the already digitally coded message by a randomly generated 'key' – a string of 56 binary digits. It has been estimated that, secure as this standard may appear, advances in parallel-processing computers will make unauthorised decoding of DES-coded messages feasible. This factor, and the relative expense of equipment to perform the scrambling and unscrambling of data, made DES relatively unpopular.

A new development came with the idea of using different keys for the scrambling and the unscrambling of data (the Hellman-Diffie method). Moreover, the method allowed for the scrambling key to be made public. If a directory, similar to the telephone directory, is published listing personal keys it becomes possible for a scrambled message to be sent to anyone, which only the intended recipient can unscramble. (The scrambling and unscrambling keys are mathematically related.)

An alternative use of the same method demonstrates another advantage of privacy transformation – the authentication of messages, also known as an *electronic signature.* It works by reversing the roles of scrambling and unscrambling keys. Suppose, for example, that A wants to send a message to B. He first scrambles it with his own *unscrambling* key. The resulting code is then further scrambled with B's published scrambling key. On receipt, B uses his own unscrambling key, but of course still cannot read the message because of the *double scrambling.* Only by applying A's (and only A's) public key can the message be finally unscrambled and simultaneously the identity of the sender verified. Only A could have sent that specific double-scrambled message, so it carries his electronic signature. Fortunately for ordinary users, the method does not require the scrambling and unscrambling to be done by hand, but rather by special microcomputer-based devices, which can be portable and very rapid in operation. Unfortunately, this entrusts security to a device which can be lost, stolen or become faulty.

A less secure alternative (because it uses a much shorter key) is to issue everyone with just a single personal key they can remember – not necessarily a number, but possibly a combination of letters and/or numbers which are chosen by a person for its private memorability. This is known as the personal identity number, or PIN. Such numbers are already in use for the authorisation of electronic funds transfers.

One way to increase the security of PINs is through *dynamic passwords.* These are generated for each individual by a 'smart card' – a combination of a microprocessor, liquid crystal display and battery, all packaged into a credit-card size device. This generates and displays a new password at regular intervals, say once a minute. This is related to and is synchronised with the computer to which the user seeks access. To become a legitimate user of the computer he or she needs to key in the password currently displayed by the smart card together with the PIN.

The whole topic of encryption and security is alive with debate as many governments become increasingly concerned about the improper use of electronic messaging systems, the growth of computer 'hacking' and malicious damage. The US government has argued very strongly for tight controls over encryption technology and currently restricts the sale outside the US of the basic hardware and software tools.

The National Security Agency of the US is currently (1994) trying to get approval for its own encryption technology (the Clipper chip) to be installed in telephone systems and computer networks, but industrial support has not been forthcoming for two reasons. Firstly opponents argue that the system is too slow for the next generation of high speed networks. Secondly, there is some concern that the encryption algorithm has a 'trapdoor' that would enable government agencies to decrypt phone calls and electronic messages. Although there is much lobbying against the NSA proposals, observers suggest that fear of loss of Government sales will force manufacturers to implement Clipper.

Legal protection

Apart from the purely physical methods of protecting data, there have been also recent developments on the legal front. Most of the threats mentioned earlier are covered by legislation and attract stiff penalties:

- Computer fraud is covered by the Theft Act, and by the 1981 Forgery and Counterfeiting Act.
- Illegal copying of software and of computer-generated material falls under the 1988 Copyright, Designs and Patents Act.
- Legal protection of the privacy of the individual is provided by the 1984 Data Protection Act.
- Unlawful access and disruption to computer systems is covered by the 1990 Computer Misuse Act.

Briefly, the Data Protection Act requires all those who process personal (name-linked) data to register this fact and the purpose for which they do so with a Data Registrar. The Act says that data should not be used or disclosed in a way incompatible with the declared purpose. Any person can find out from the Registrar whether a particular company holds data about them, and obtain a copy of the data. Persons, or 'legal persons', to whom the information is disclosed will also be registered, and their identity stored together with the data. The final sanction for breach of the rules is deregistration. However, even before the Act had a chance to become law, there were serious objections raised to it:

1   A major objection is that it specifically excludes the very large area of manual records (paper files and card indices, as opposed to computer data banks).
2   Another objection relates to the various exemptions to the provisions of the Act, where protection "would be likely to prejudice the assessment or collection of any tax or duty", national security, the prevention of crime, etc.
3   The important question of who decides when prejudice is likely is not answered in the Act.
4   Lastly, the Act does not deal with the privacy of electronic mail.

Of the estimated 250,000 organisations collecting or storing personal data on computer in the UK in 1993, only 150,000 were registered. It has been estimated that one in three small companies and nearly one in six large companies are unaware of their statutory obligation to register their use of personal information. Registration costs £75 for three years and those failing to keep within the terms of their registration face fines of up to £5000 in a magistrates court or unlimited fines in higher courts.

So far there have been 100 prosecutions under the act.

Applications

Other application areas of data security techniques, apart from data-banks and electronic banking and shopping, include electronic mail, the use of computing facilities from remote terminals, satellite communications, defence and police work. Indeed, any use of data transmission and storage is a potential area of application as shown in Table 14.1.

Table 14.1 Some applications of data-base technology

Application	Use (examples)
Sales	Statements Credit control Electronic payment
Staff	Wages/salaries Personnel records
Other commercial	Banking Insurance Information retrieval
Education	Administration
Medical	Patient records and statistics
Statistics	Survey and statistical data
On-line	Information systems Reservation systems
Other	Electronic mail

15 Advanced systems

Introduction

Here and in the last few chapters we shall look at some of the main directions of research and development which are aiming to create the 'next generation' of information technologies. There are several major national and international projects under way in this area:

- the Japanese 'fifth generation' project;
- the European Commission's IT programme;
- the American and other state- and industry-sponsored initiatives;

all recognising information technology as a major area of economic activity and strategic significance for the coming decades.

The Japanese 'fifth generation' project

The first of the large-scale national research and development projects in information technology, the Japanese initiative, has been inspired by a view of what the needs of the post-industrial society will be, and how information technology can contribute to meeting these needs. Specifically, the project has envisaged the main role of advanced information processing machines in:

1 the enhancement of productivity in areas of traditionally low productivity (e.g. the office, small-batch manufacture, etc.);
2 the conservation of natural resources and energy by optimisation of their use;
3 the support of medical, educational and other services in solving complex social problems;
4 the bettering of international relations through the machine translation of languages.

These aims are taken to give rise to the following functional requirements for information processing machines:

1 input and output of information by speech, graphics, images and documents;
2 conversational processing of information using natural language;
3 the ability to put stored knowledge to practical use;
4 the ability to learn, infer, form associations;
5 better cost-performance than current computers;
6 light, compact, high-speed, large-capacity, highly reliable computers;
7 built-in data protection;
8 reduced burden of software production.

As an approach to satisfying these objectives the Japanese have proposed to develop computers which are organised differently from the general-purpose 'von Neumann' structure employed in computers hitherto. The particular aspect of the current structure is that it reflects the technical and cost constraints of the 1940s: highly expensive and unreliable hardware and an abundance of willing programmers. By contrast, the 1990s will offer virtually zero-cost, highly reliable hardware but expensive software, unless a different approach to information processing is found.

Fig. 15.1 Conceptual view of the Japanese 'fifth generation' computer design. (Source: Japan Information Processing Development Centre)

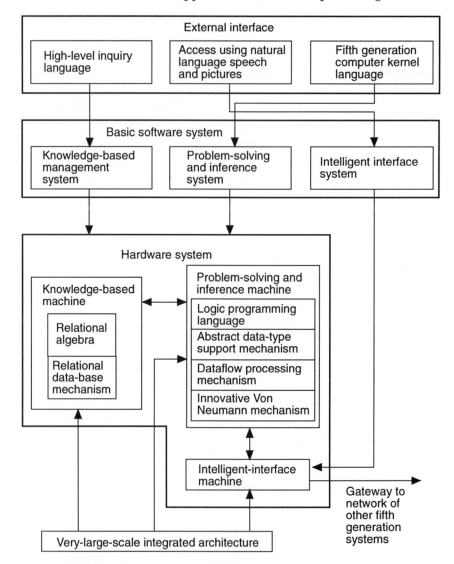

Figure 15.1 shows the conceptual organisation of the Japanese 'fifth generation' design. The 'intelligent interface machines' replace the input-output devices of the fourth-generation computer; the 'problem-solving and inference machine' is put in place of today's processor, and the 'knowledge-base machine' extends the role of current internal and external memory devices. Provision is also made for communication with other information processing machines via a digital network.

The project started in 1982, and was aiming to reach its objectives within 10 years. By the end of 1988, the project had made most of its advances in the area of 'problem solving and inference', creating both prototype hardware and corresponding system software. The resulting 'parallel inference machine' is made up of 'sequential inference units', working in parallel deriving logical conclusions (inferences) from input data. Initially 64 such units were connected together, but the project aims to interconnect up to 1000 units, producing over 100 million logic inferences per second.

The two related areas of software effort, the problem-solving and inference system and the knowledge-base management system, ultimately aim to accept a problem specification from a user (by means of speech, text, graphics, etc.), without requiring the user to also provide a complete and unambiguous solution to that problem, i.e. to write a program.

The European IT programme

The European Strategic Programme for Research and Development in Information Technologies (ESPRIT) started in 1984, with the following main areas of activity:

- advanced micro-electronics (VLSI and very-high performance micro-circuits, their computer-aided design, opto-electronics, etc.);
- software technology (efficient software development environments);
- advanced information processing ('knowledge engineering', 'knowledge storage', computer vision and speech interfaces, etc.);
- office systems (advanced office work-stations, communications, filing and retrieval systems, design of 'integrated offices');
- computer-integrated manufacture (CAD, CAM, CAE, FMS, robotics).

The latter two application areas again rely on the first three (enabling) technologies for their success. Figure 15.2 shows this inter-relation for the case of office systems projects.

Fig. 15.2 Relations of office systems to other ESPRIT subprograms and office environments. (Source: *Official Journal of the European Communities*)

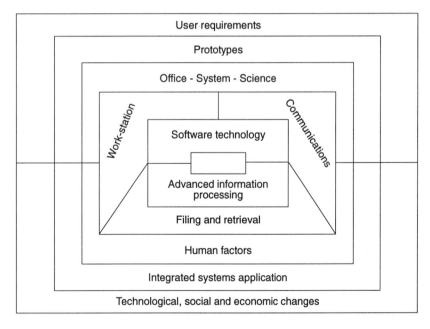

By 1989, there were more than 100 active projects in these areas. In the advanced micro-electronics area, ESPRIT aims to bring together computer manufacturers to produce microprocessors with the same design, so that software becomes more easily transferable, and based on sub-micron technology also being developed under ESPRIT (i.e. with a fineness of detail of silicon-based micro-circuits below 1 micron). In the software area, development is towards a Portable Common (Software) Tool Environment, which provides software producers with a 'standard' set of tools. Indeed, standardisation is a major objective of ESPRIT, and, in the office systems area, this has led to an agreed way of processing and transferring documents in electronic form between computers from different manufacturers. This way, Office Document Architecture (ODA) has been adopted as an international standard.

Another European programme, Research and development in Advanced Communication technologies in Europe (RACE), aims towards the introduction and commercial use by 1995 of broad-band telecommunication networks. The project started in 1988 and includes planning, technology development and application trials. A subsequent European Commission programme, approved in 1989, aims to create a 'European Nervous System' linking all the electronic networks and information services of Europe. This would make governmental, medical, police, transport, educational and other data available across national frontiers, and so involves issues of *data protection* (see p. 149).

The final example of a European programme aimed to advance information technology is in the field of language translation. It was prompted by the requirement of producing every official document of the European Community in languages of all of its members. However, the problem of translation from one language to another is much wider: there is a world-wide requirement for the translation of scientific papers, patents, business correspondence and marketing literature, etc. The 'Eurotra' project aims to develop machine translation for seven major European languages within the 1990s.

In spite of their apparent differences these initiatives have a number of elements in common:

– the further development of the 'enabling technologies' of computer hardware and software engineering, including micro-electronics, new computer structures, optical computing and data transmission (more on hardware/software developments later in this chapter);
– the introduction of 'intelligent' features into information handling machines: learning, problem solving, natural communication, etc.;
– the exploitation of these developments in many spheres of human activity, primarily in military and aero-space systems, industrial and office automation, financial and other services, etc.

Hardware developments

Two main areas of work emerge from the various advanced IT programmes: micro-electronics and new computer structures.

Virtually all advanced systems assume the availability of highly complex yet very cheap (effectively zero-cost) micro-circuits. As we saw in Chapter 7, an improvement by a factor of 1000 in performance and capacity is thought to be necessary for the building blocks of the next generation of computers, compared with what is available today. However, to go beyond the present half-million transistor chip requires major advances in fabrication and design aids. Current techniques can produce line-widths and other features on silicon chips down to 1 micrometer. Advanced systems will require the reduction of the size of the detail to below 0.5 micrometer.

This means that it will become possible to fabricate many complete processors on one chip. This, in turn, implies that the present 'one processor per computer' structure is likely to be superseded by multiprocessor ('parallel' or 'concurrent') computers. The resulting systems will be able to perform a large number of simultaneous operations.

The main research problem at the present time is how to organise and control the processors so as to make them contribute to a common goal. It is possible that no single solution to this problem will be universally efficient, but that different types of task will require different structures.

Software developments

The production of software is likely to become one of the main bottlenecks in the development of advanced information handling systems. While the performance of hardware has increased by several orders of magnitude over the last 30 years, the productivity of programmers has probably not even doubled. An important reason for this is that virtually every program is written afresh – there is very little re-usability of existing design and program segments.

Improvements may come from making existing programming methods more efficient (e.g. by rapid prototyping so that it can be quickly seen whether the program satisfies its specifications, by the modularisation of programs, by standardisation of computer languages and documentation, etc.). Much effort is devoted, in addition, to completely new approaches to software production. These include logic programming (emphasising and exploiting the relationships or constraints linking various data items), object-oriented programming (the possible responses to commands are built into, or associated with each of the data items), and the automatic generation of software from task specifications expressed in natural language. The major challenge, though, is the efficient programming of the new multi-processor computer structures mentioned above.

16 Computer vision

Introduction

'Computer vision' is a term applied, in the first instance, to the input of images into computer-based systems. The term is often extended to include the processing (enhancement, interpretation, 'perception', etc.) of images. Work in this field is still largely at the research and development stage. It links closely with work on robotics (see p. 28), expert systems (see p. 165) and voice communication with computers (see p. 221).

Considering computer vision in its wider sense, there are three distinct processes in evidence in the majority of working systems:

(a) input, or image acquisition;
(b) processing, or analysis of the data;
(c) output, or interfacing the system to a human or machine user.

Image input

The input of images is handled by specialised sensors. These may be a video scanner (a form of television camera), or an array of photodetectors. Both types of device convert the intensity of light representing an image into electronic signals. The representation, just as in the eye, is only a limited part of the visual world at any one time. Early work was mainly concerned with two-dimensional images and two intensity levels (black and white). More recently, work has concentrated on grey-scale and colour images and three-dimensional views, which require several, co-ordinated sensors.

Perhaps the best known examples of computer 'vision' are *magnetic ink character recognition* (MICR) used by banks in the processing of cheques, and *optical character recognition* (OCR) used on gas, electricity and rates bills. In each case, specially designed letter and number shapes are used which can be read by people, but are also conveniently distinguished by computers. More advanced OCR programs can handle a range of standard typefaces, and a few even simple images. Both MICR and OCR operations require the scanning of the document by an array of sensors.

The image is 'handed over' from the input to the processing stage as an array or grid of picture elements, often abbreviated as *pixels*. Each pixel represents the intensity, and in some systems the colour, of a small part of the image.

Robotics applications typically require a minimum pixel grid of 256 by 256, with 256 levels of grey for each pixel. This corresponds to approximately 500 kbit of data for a single image. For moving images at, say, 25 frames/s this would give rise to a data rate of over 1.5 Mbit/s. To process this amount of data 'in real time' requires expensive and complex equipment at present. So, reasonably-priced systems sacrifice either space- or time-resolution, i.e. make do with fewer pixels or grey levels, or a lower frame rate.

Scanners for text recognition and photographic input operate at anything between 150 and 2500 pixels per inch (or dots per inch) and are capable of providing 24-bit colour representation for each pixel. This corresponds to 8 bits for each of the red, green, and blue primary colours and a palette of 16.7 million colours. However, such scanners do not normally form part of a vision system, they are simply a means of entering data into a computer system. Nevertheless, they rely on the many techniques learnt from computer vision research.

Image processing

The processing of the array of picture elements is in most systems based on the assumption that the original image is made up of one or more objects. These may be objects in the usual sense of the word (such as parts which an industrial robot has to assemble or unknown structures on the surface of a distant planet), or they may be finger-prints or hand-written characters, etc. In applications where only the overall shape or outline of objects is of importance, two-level (black-and-white, or binary) processing is used. Current technology is capable of handling this well, by employing three stages of processing:

1   segmentation, or breakdown of the image into the objects contained in it;
2   recognition, or 'naming' of each object;
3   interpretation, or the analysis of the interrelations among objects.

There is a similarity of approach here to the processing of speech by computers (see p. 221) to the extent that it is usually referred to as the *linguistic approach* to computer vision.

Segmentation
In the segmentation process, objects are frequently characterised by their outlines or overall shape, as this represents a reduction of the amount of data that needs to be handled during processing. (The processing stages, particularly of complex, rapidly changing images, put a sometimes impossible burden on the present generation of computers.) In some cases, additional features, like the texture or surface properties of objects, are included in their overall descriptions.

The recognition of hand-written text by computers cannot, as yet, be performed reliably, mainly because of the difficulty of segmenting the text into individual characters.

One of the techniques used to pick out specific objects from their background is 'light striping'. Here, two very intense, laser-generated beams illuminate the background (say, a conveyor belt) from different points. A video scanner is focused at the point of convergence of the beams. When an object passes under the scanner it makes the beams diverge, and this shows up as a dark silhouette on the light background. The 'light stripe' method, with a mobile camera, can also be used to track an object or some feature of it (e.g. welding seams).

Recognition
During recognition, the computer's task is to match either the whole image or each object to a stored set of patterns or templates. In template

matching, the computer tries to find the closest digital representation in its data-base, and informs the operator of the discrepancies. In feature matching, the computer uses certain attributes, e.g. the number of edges, corners, enclosed spaces, etc. to overcome problems of variability of size and orientation of objects which should belong to the same category. It is the choice of the features used for recognition that is perhaps the most important distinction between the various systems employing the linguistic approach. The choice of features is indeed a crucial one since they must be efficient in distinguishing objects from one another, few in number to speed up processing, and invariant to changes in position, orientation and size of the object, and to minor errors in its representation. After all, a letter A, for example, must be identified as such, irrespective of where it occurs or who writes it.

Recent systems make the recognition process more efficient by employing context information, that is knowledge of the likelihood that certain shapes or objects occur jointly with other shapes. For example, a computer containing a dictionary of commonly used words in its memory can refer to this in the processing of text, to confirm (or reject) hypotheses about what letter a 'difficult' shape may represent.

In some situations, e.g. in automatic inspection of printed-circuit boards to detect production faults, the 'object' to be recognised is a fault. Thus, the computer is provided with a list of fault descriptions (such as the minimum distance between tracks) which it then applies to each part of the scene.

Where the scene is inherently three-dimensional, the problem is even more difficult. 'Light striping' can be taken a step further, by looking at the specific distortions of the stripe to identify a 3-D shape. By flashing the beams, the 3-D motion of an object can be tracked. Colour images are usually handled by breaking them up (optionally) into three constituent colours (red, green and blue) and analysing the resulting images separately.

Interpretation

The interpretation process involves the complete image. It is equivalent to building up a descriptive sentence from a set of words. This process is necessary in the analysis of complex scenes, and it is also helpful in identifying those objects which were missed at the recognition stage, from information supplied by the context.

Other methods

Variants of the approach just described include those which start the processing by looking at the overall image and then proceed to specific objects or sub-areas rather than the other way round. Computer-vision systems also differ in the relative extent of processing performed by software and by hardware. Programmed systems are more convenient to modify, which is an asset in the development process. Hardware implementations are faster and can perform a number of different processes simultaneously.

The output stage of computer vision is governed by the use to which the system is put. An automatic reading machine, for example, would produce an output as it processes each character, but an automatic surveillance system would generate a response only after identifying changes in the scene under observation. An industrial inspection machine would alert its operator only when it detects an out-of-the-ordinary image.

Applications

Perhaps the greatest impetus for computer vision at the present time is provided by industrial automation (robotics). Applications there include:

- automatic inspection and measurement;
- 'robot eyes' to monitor and guide robot actions;
- sorting, etc.

Their usefulness is evident in repetitive, boring but exacting tasks, such as looking for faults in woven cloth or mis-shaped plastic mouldings, or in dangerous environments, like radio-active and chemically hazardous work.

Other areas of current application include military and space technology, earth remote sensing (e.g. mineral exploration), atmospheric weather and climate analysis, medical image analysis, fingerprint and handwriting analysis, etc.

Many of the techniques learnt about hand-written character recognition have been applied to pen-computers, which permit the user to write commands on a small screen, rather than key in commands. The user is required to train the software so that it can build up a reference data-base of characters and words. Apple Computer have used this technology in its Newton pen-computer.

Speeding cars and dangerous drivers are likely to find it more difficult to escape prosecution following the introduction of infra-red cameras and neural computing software on the M1 motorway in Leicestershire. The infra-red capability permits 24 hour operation of the cameras and the neural software enables recognition of characters even if the numberplate is dirty. The six month experiment, which commenced in June 1994, will flash up the number of speeding cars, in the hope of encouraging drivers to slow down, but the long-term option may be a fully automatic speed trap. The technology will also be used to support a European-wide effort to reduce the transport of stolen cars. The Inca project will link the automatic recognition system with police data-bases in the UK, Sweden, Spain, Portugal and Greece. France and Germany will join the system once their central data-bases come on-line.

17 'Intelligent' systems

Introduction and fundamentals

'Intelligent' systems are capable of exhibiting some aspects of human intelligence. They currently include expert systems and neural computers. Expert systems, or knowledge-based systems, are computer programs aimed at providing expert 'consultancy' advice and assistance with problem-solving in limited specialist fields of science, engineering, mathematics, medicine, education, etc.

Expert systems represent one of the most advanced facets of information technology, in the sense introduced in Part 1. That is, they aid people in some of the most complex and least understood human information handling tasks: decision-making, problem-solving, diagnosis and learning. They do this by storing a large amount of factual information on a subject area, together with lines of reasoning employed by human experts in that area. Most of this material is supplied to the program at the time that it is written, but it also has facilities for adding to this base of information as it is applied in new situations. The subject expertise is provided initially by interviews and observations of successful practitioners of the subject.

Expert systems represent an attempt to harness, as an intellectual tool, those features of the computer where it excels in the handling of data:

(a) its ability for storing a very large amount of data;

(b) the retention of these data for an arbitrarily long time in a prescribed form;

(c) its ability for making precise calculations and exhaustive searches of stored data at high speed.

As a result, expert systems are able to

(a) answer a range of questions within their area of expertise;

(b) present, if required, the assumptions and line of reasoning used to arrive at the answer;

(c) add new facts, rules and lines of valid reasoning to their knowledge base.

Practical expert systems

The basic structure of practical expert systems is similar to that shown in Fig. 15.1. As explained in the chapter on 'Advanced Systems' the hardware components shown in that figure are still under development, so current implementations still use third- and fourth-generation machines.

The basic software consists of the *knowledge base* and *the inference system*. The former is more than just a factual data-base – it also includes rules, relationships and procedures which have been found to work in real life.

The latter works with the knowledge base, applying the rules of formal logic and making inferences (deductions) relating to the situation on hand.

A third software component, the *interface system*, links the first two to the outside worlds, in some cases via computer vision and speech systems (see Chapters 16 and 24).

Although there is not, as yet, a standard approach to the production and operation of expert systems, most of them work on the principle of guiding the user from some 'current situation' to a goal or solution of a stated problem. For this, the programs can employ either 'brute force' or a more 'intelligent' strategy. The 'brute force' approach amounts to searching through the knowledge base which lists all possible contingencies (steps of reasoning, actions, etc.) needed to go from the current situation to the goal. Clearly, this approach is highly intensive of storage space (assuming that such exhaustive information is available in the first place), time and cost. In some cases, such as fault tracing in cars and other equipment, or even in the medical diagnosis of certain conditions, the cost may not be prohibitive.

However, an example of the problems which arise from the 'brute force' approach comes from the game of chess. Ideally, one would ask the computer to supply the 'winning line' at any stage in the game. To give this advice, the computer would have to store an astronomically large number of possible positions on the board. Instead, the programs usually use a more intelligent approach and *generate* a limited number of possible 'next moves' and *examine* the implications of following each of these paths in terms of their leading to the eventual goal, or even a local sub-goal.

Thus, expert knowledge is effectively stored by the computer as a set of empirical rules which help in selecting plausible paths to the goal and in evaluating the situations which then result. Any situation may suggest a possible action or it may lead to a request for further information. The latter would be the case, for example, if in seeking a medical diagnosis the program would suggest that some specific test be carried out in order to distinguish among several possible conclusions.

Although effective in highly specific areas, this assemblage of task-related 'rules-of-thumb' also means that the program does not have 'common sense' and exhibits no creative leaps of imagination. This, of itself, is not necessarily a disadvantage in some situations, provided the limitations of the system are realised. However, it demonstrates clearly the present lack of detailed understanding of human intelligence.

Artificial intelligence

Expert systems form a major area of research in a hybrid field known as *artificial intelligence*, or AI. Artificial intelligence brings together computer scientists and engineers, psychologists, and linguists with workers in various areas of its potential application. Such a convergence of many backgrounds and viewpoints is necessary to grapple with three of the main unsolved problems of expert-systems research:

1. How can the user of such a system communicate the problem to the computer in a natural way (rather than having to fall in with the quirks of the computer)?

The problems of making computers deal with everyday ('natural') language in spoken or even written form are enormous. As discussed in Chapter 24, a very large amount of implicit knowledge is needed for speech understanding. Pending fundamental developments in natural language understanding, current expert systems assume perfect understanding and a willingness on the user's part to 'play the computer's game'.

2.   How should the computer deal with the stated problem?

This is also a fundamental question – it leads to further questions of the internal representation of knowledge, the organisation of the selected representation to facilitate the search for a particular item and the addition of new items, and the use of common-sense general rules for reasoning, deduction and problem-solving. These are, of course, the questions that psychologists have been asking themselves in relation to human thinking, planning and learning. One aspect of artificial intelligence research is the mutual benefit that can result from psychological research and work on 'knowledgeable' computers.

3.   How can people control and check the operation of an expert system?

This is also a crucial question – if the user is presented only with a recommendation, without knowing the reason for that advice, then the system is not really functioning as an aid, but more like a dictator. On the other hand, if the computer automatically presents all the decision points and subsidiary information used to produce the recommendation, this may be too tedious. The program, therefore, needs to adapt itself to the routine needs of its current user, but have the facilities to give a complete account of its 'reasoning' if required.

In addition to these three basic questions, research on expert systems also links to work on computer vision (see p. 161) and speech input and output (see p. 221), as means of acquiring data and providing a response to requests; on data-base design, as ways of organising and interrogating collections of data; and on the general development of computer systems, as the embodiments of working prototypes.

These requirements reinforce the search for new computer structures and software methods that underlie the current work on 'future generations' of information systems.

Neural computing
One such approach is *neural computing*. Although the term is new, the idea behind it has been around since the early days of computers. The idea is that the notion of intelligence can be approached not only from a psychological but also from a physiological point of view. In other words, if models of nerve cells and of the interactions between them can be produced, this may lead to networks of such model neurons, exhibiting some form of intelligence.

Developments in the hardware of computers have made the idea more practicable than it was 30–40 years ago. Large numbers of specialist processors can now be produced and formed into parallel, distributed neural computers, at relatively low cost.

Applications   One of the earliest expert systems was concerned with organic chemistry: the Dendral system. This originated at Stanford University (USA) in 1965, and is still in use as an aid to finding plausible new molecular structures. The program is based on analytical data and on practical constraints, supplied by the user. A later program in the same field, Simulation and Evaluation of Chemical Syntheses (Secs), is being used in pharmaceutical laboratories for suggesting to chemists new compounds which are chemically sound. Among its achievements is the deduction of 8 of the 11 known ways of making a pesticide called Grandisol.

In the field of medicine, the task of the Mycin system is to diagnose blood infections and meningitis infections, and to recommend an appropriate drug. Mycin operates by a set of empirical rules which have an associated degree of confidence or reliability. The rules are 'acquired' by another system, by the following procedure: a diagnosis is presented to a medical expert on the basis of the facts of a specific case. If the expert does not agree with the diagnosis, he is shown the line of reasoning of Mycin, and is led back along the logical chain to the point where he finds a fault. The rule there is either changed or a new one is introduced. The 'consultation' is then repeated, until the expert agrees.

The recent generation of neural computers has been applied primarily to pattern recognition and voice communication tasks. For example, the German company Siemens uses a neural computer to identify faults in noisy electrical motors. Ford employs them to check for faults in car-paint finishes. A text-to-speech conversion computer 'learned' to produce intelligible speech after 10 hours of operation.

All these systems are essentially research tools, of increasing sophistication. There are also some commercially available systems which make use of some of the better-established features of laboratory systems. A particular successful area of application of expert systems is to advise on the selection of a combination of components from a large number of possibilities, to form a customised system.

For example, a computer company uses a commercial expert system to put together and price configurations of hardware and software to suit the requirements of its would-be customers. This is claimed to save the company £10 million a year. The same 'shell', or basic approach was used to produce a product selection adviser system for an engineering components company, bridging the roles of its technical and marketing departments. The system is said to save hundreds of thousands of pounds a year by reducing the time spent by people on tedious searches.

A relatively recent development is the use of expert systems in education and industrial training. A system at the Stanford Research Institute International trains operators in the assembly of an air compressor. A spoken dialogue between the system and the trainee would proceed as follows:

System: Try to assemble the air compressor.
Trainee: How?
System: Install pump, install pump brace, install pulley, install belt housing cover. Ready for questions.

Trainee:	None.
System:	Install pump.
Trainee:	How?
System:	Get four 1/4 inch long 5/16 inch hexagonal bolts, and four 9/16 inch flat washers, and four 5/16 inch hexagonal nuts.
Trainee:	OK.

:
:
etc.

The system can start at any point in a logical sequence of assembly steps and take the trainee to the desired objective – a fully assembled compressor.

Superficially, and in limited areas of application, some expert systems may appear to be highly intelligent. Indeed, there is good reason for this since their knowledge base is derived from recognised human experts.

At the deeper level, the reasons for these shortcomings are clear: they are the three problems listed earlier. Expert systems are essentially computer models of human thought and they are only as good at *being original* as the psychological models employed by their programmers. They are never more than advice-givers. In the final count, it should be the responsibility of people to take decisions and actions in vital areas like defence and medicine, and to remain fully accountable for those decisions and actions.

18 Open systems and standards

Introduction and background

The main reason for standardisation is the existence of a wide range of products and services in the market place which are available as separate entities but need to work together in specific applications. For example, a non-standard fax machine may not be able to communicate with another, this becoming evident only after some wasted attempts to connect and a resulting loss of time and money. In addition, standardisation aims to define and ensure performance and quality attributes of products and systems, safety and reliability features, as well as clear methods of testing and measuring these attributes and features. Effective standards which have gained wide acceptance can *reduce uncertainties*, e.g. in relation to purchasing decisions, and in this way *encourage the development of a market place*. This, in turn, will stimulate the entry of new producers and system providers into the market and so *increase the choice* available to the users.

Standards and their role

A *standard* is a technical specification approved by a recognised standardising body for repeated or continuous application, with which compliance is not compulsory. It takes the form of a document, drawn up with the involvement and agreement of all interested parties, e.g. by representatives of users, manufacturers, government agencies, etc.

A standard is to be distinguished from a *technical specification* which is issued by a manufacturer or producer organisation, rather than a standardising body. Although such technical specifications form the 'raw material' of standards, they may never become a standard unless put forward for adoption by a standardisation body. A standard is also different from a *technical regulation* which is usually drawn up by the public authorities of a state, and is binding within that state.

A standard is thus a convention which is applied on a voluntary basis. Compliance with standards, nevertheless, is the best way of meeting essential requirements relating to safety, health and environmental or consumer protection.

Since standards can be issued by a variety of bodies, they do not necessarily interwork smoothly or cover a particular domain in a consistent manner. It is necessary, therefore, in some cases to produce a set of *harmonised standards*. One field where harmonisation is being attempted is information technology, and in particular under the banner of 'open systems'.

Open systems

In the general sense of the term, an *open system* is independent of its manufacturer or supplier and is capable of working together with other open systems. This would mean, for example, that the same programs can be run in a variety of computers (*software portability*), and even when the subsystems of the computers are physically separated (*open distributed processing, or ODP*). Because of the wide range of proprietary systems and products on the market this simple-sounding objective is difficult to reach in practice.

The first step in the creation of open system standards is to draw a framework into which the detailed standards fit. A framework for open systems standards is currently under development. The framework includes *architectural standards, base standards and functional standards*.

Architectural standards define the structure linking the standards for a particular area. For example, one such area is information system interconnection where the *OSI Basic Reference Model* (see below) is an architectural standard.

Base standards provide a full specification of each of the functionalities included in the architectural standard. For example, in the field of open systems, base standards are being developed to cover the areas of system interconnection, user interfaces, data structures, data management, distributed applications and basic operating system functions.

Functional standards, or *functional profiles*, specify the use of the base standards or the joint use of base standards where this is necessary to satisfy specific application needs. An example is the set of standards which cover various aspects of open systems interconnection (OSI).

Let us now look at some examples of the standardisation work which being undertaken within the open systems framework.

Layered architectures: the OSI Reference Model

A frequently used approach to coping with the complexity of modern information technology systems is to organise (partition) them into a set of functionally specialised but interconnected parts. In this way, the various parts of the system can be designed, produced and maintained in a relatively simpler way than a 'monolithic' system. One organisational principle often used with computer networks is *layering*. In this approach each successive layer builds upon its predecessor(s). In other words, each layer provides services, or functionality, to its successors, but the successor need not take into account *how* these services are provided. What is of importance, however, is the exact description of the services provided, and of the way in which the corresponding layers in different systems interact or communicate. The rules governing the interaction (mutual communication) between corresponding layers are the *protocols*. A specific set of layers and protocols forms a *layered architecture*.

In developing the Open Systems Interconnection architecture the International Standardisation Organisation (ISO) group evolved the following guiding principles:

- do not create so many layers as to make the engineering task of describing and integrating the layers too difficult;
- create a boundary at a point where the description of services can be small and the number of interactions across the boundary is minimised;
- create separate layers to handle functions that are manifestly different in the process performed or the technology involved;

- collect similar functions into the same layer;
- select boundaries at a point which past experience has demonstrated to be successful;
- create a layer of easily localised functions so that the layer could be totally redesigned and its protocols changed in a major way to take advantage of new advances in architectural, hardware or software technology without changing the services expected from and provided to the adjacent layers;
- create a boundary where it may be useful at some point in time to have the corresponding interface standardised;
- create a layer where there is a need for a different level of abstraction in the handling of the data;
- allow changes of functions or protocols to be made within a layer without affecting other layers;
- create, for a layer, boundaries with its upper and lower layer only.

The resulting OSI reference model comprises seven layers but to start it may be more convenient to envisage these seven layers reduced to the three layers shown in Fig. 18.1.

Fig. 18.1 A layered architecture

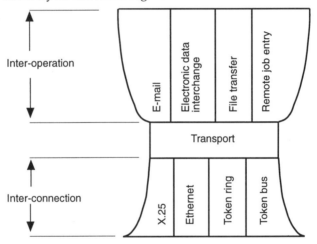

The upper layer provides for inter-operation between computers, permitting file transfers, electronic mail, remote job entry, etc. The bottom layer provides for the inter-connection between systems and permits use of existing network standards. The middle layer hides from the upper layer the differences between the various types of network, enabling standard applications to be used with non-standard networks.

The divisions within the figure also indicate something of the progress made to date, in that inter-connection standards are well developed and widely adopted, whereas inter-operation is proving more difficult to standardise. Applications such as electronic mail, file transfer and document exchange require their own standards and these are only now beginning to mature and to be adopted.

The generic architecture is more precisely defined by the *OSI Reference Model*, published in 1984, as the seven-layer model shown in Fig. 18.2.

Fig. 18.2 OSI seven-layer reference model

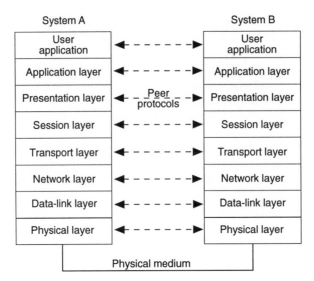

When two computers employ the OSI model, each system will have its own operating system and applications software, together with an OSI interface. It is through this interface that each application gains access to the network services. Messages from a user's application go to the top of the seven layers, the Application layer, which acts as the entry point to the OSI services. The messages are then passed successively down through the layers to the lowest one, as illustrated in Fig. 18.2.

At the destination system the messages pass up through the layers until they reach the top layer, where they are passed to the user application. Each layer engages in a peer-to-peer protocol, represented by the horizontal arrows, but the only physical connection between the systems is at the lowest layer. The basic function of each of the seven layers is described briefly below.

Application layer: provides access to the OSI environment for users and also provides distributed information services.

Presentation layer: provides independence to the application processes from differences in data representation (syntax).

Session layer: provides the control structure for communication between applications; establishes, manages, and terminates connections (sessions) between co-operating applications.

Transport layer: provides reliable, transparent transfer of data between end points; provides end-to-end error recovering and flow control.

Network layer: provides the upper layers with independence from the data transmission technologies used to connect systems; responsible for establishing, maintaining, and terminating connections.

Data-link layer: provides for the reliable transfer of information across the physical link; sends blocks of data (frames) with the necessary synchronisation, error control and flow control.

Physical layer: concerned with the transmission of unstructured bit stream over a physical medium; deals with the mechanical, electrical, functional and procedural characteristics to access the physical medium.

The OSI model also provides for the situation where the source and destination systems cannot be linked directly, but are connected by way of an intermediate node of the network (e.g. packet switched networks). In such cases the intermediate node must provide the services of the lowest three layers, as illustrated in Fig. 18.3.

Fig. 18.3 Network with an intermediate node

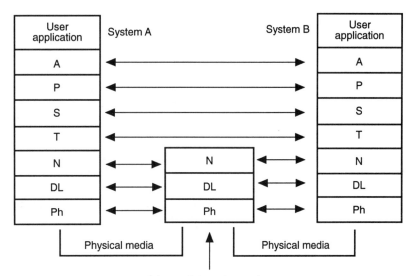

Messages from System A are passed to the intermediate node where a decision is made on a suitable routing to reach System B which may involve another exchange. The routing function resides within the Network layer, hence the intermediate system (or relay) must provide the full functionality of the Network, Data-link and Physical layers. Since the physical connections of the two sides of the intermediate node are totally separate, it may be used to perform a communications protocol conversion between Systems A and B (e.g. between token ring and Ethernet protocols).

Base standards

Base standards provide a full specification of the functionalities identified by an architectural standard. At present there are six major areas of base standards development.

Basic operating system functions standards are addressed by the POSIX (portable operating system interface) standards work of the IEEE and includes elements to define: i) multi-tasking and multi-user operation; ii) hierarchical file directory structures and shared file access; and iii) an element of control over the variable characteristics of operating systems.

Data management standards cover : i) basic facilities provided by the data-base language (e.g. standard query language SQL) in terms of the declaration of structures and operations; ii) the services for creating, maintaining and accessing a dictionary of information definitions; and iii) the distributed operations which define communication procedures for operations on remote data-bases.

Interconnection standards support the networking infrastructure defined by the OSI reference model and include: i) the functions providing the transport services of the lower four layers of the reference model; ii) the functions of the presentation service defined by the presentation and session layers; and iii) the functions of the basic tools for communication in the application layer.

Data structures standards define the structure of the data to be exchanged and include: tools for specification such as the *Abstract Syntax Notation* (ANS.1 and ASN.2); document interchange standards such as ODA (office document architecture) and SGML (standard generalised mark-up language); and registered specifications of *document types* and *body parts* for distributed applications.

Distributed applications standards define inter-working between applications running on different networks and cover: i) generic facilities such as file transfer, access and management (FTAM) and transaction processing (TP); and ii) general and specific distributed applications such as the distributed directory service, for example the Comité Consultatif International Téléphonique et Télégraphique (CCITT) X.500 and message handling system (CCITT X.400) and message oriented text interchange standard (MOTIS).

User interface standards embrace: i) the communication functions as represented by the virtual terminal (VT) standard, the X-Windows system and the terminal management system and; ii) the display functions represented by the graphical kernel system (GKS) and the programmers hierarchical interactive graphics system (PHIGS) standards

Functional standards
The OSI base standards provide a wide range of options to meet the various requirements of specific applications, but in some cases the possible combinations permitted actually becomes a barrier to successful inter-operation. To minimise potential difficulties a number of groups have drawn up functional profiles which identify a set of one or more base standards which can be applied throughout an organisation.

The UK Government is a large purchaser of IT and requires that all large purchases conform to OSI standards, but since many areas are not yet covered, procurement personnel have found it difficult to conform. To assist with this task the Government Centre for Information Systems has developed a functional profile known as the UK government open system interconnection profile, but more commonly referred to as UK GOSIP. The goals of GOSIP are to simplify procurement and acceptance testing, ensure that departmental systems can inter-operate at an assured level of functionality, and provide clear guidance to manufacturers.

The European Union has established the European Procurement

Handbook for Open Systems (EPHOS) project to produce a harmonised OSI-based procurement profile for use by all member states. The outcome from the project will be a series of procurement handbooks providing guidance for purchasing and testing. The first of these was published in 1992 and is intended to:

"provide all those involved in European public administration procurement with definitive information and guidance on the standards and specifications to be used in the acquisition of OSI conformant goods and services in the field of Information Technology communications."

The World Federation of MAP/TOP User Groups is another organisation developing standardised profiles. The manufacturing automation protocol (MAP) originated from work carried out by General Motors Corporation with the goal of improving inventory and work-in-progress systems. The technical office protocol (TOP) was the outcome of a task force established by the Boeing Corporation to define the inter-operation of management information systems with production and design systems. The work of these two groups has now been drawn together into the single profile shown in Fig. 18.4.

Fig. 18.4 MAP/TOP profile

Layer	File services	Messaging services		Directory services	Terminal services
7	ISO 8521 FTAM	ISO 9506 MMS	ISO 10021 MOTIS	ISO 9594 DS	ISO 9041 VT
6		ISO 8823			
5		ISO 8327			
4		ISO 8073 Class 4			
3		CLNS ISO 8473			
2		ISO 8802-2			
1	ISO 8802-3	ISO 8802-5		ISO 8802-4	

The profile shows each of the seven layers of the OSI reference model together with the specific base standards employed for each layer. With the exception of the application and physical layers single standards are specified. The profile embraces multiple applications at the top layer and hence multiple standards, but the individual applications employ single standards.

The physical layer of the profile includes three different standards. MAP users normally specify the Token bus option because of its guaranteed response time and immunity to the electrical environment of the factory floor. TOP users can choose either Token ring or Ethernet protocols, which have gained greater acceptance in office environments.

The standard makers

World IT standards bodies

The two principal international standards bodies dealing with information technology and telecommunications are ISO and CCITT. Within ISO, the principal body responsible for IT standards is a joint technical committee, JTC 1, which covers most areas of IT, other than those related to public communications, and some specific applications.

European standards bodies

In addition to these two world-wide standards bodies, there are also a number of European bodies established by the Commission of the European Communities in order to remove technical barriers to a single internal market. Directive 83/189/EEC requires all member states to notify the Commission with respect to all national standardisation activities, and may require them to call a halt to such activities which may then be substituted at a European level.

The principal European standards and recommendations-making bodies are:

- CEN (European Committee for Standardisation)
- CENELEC (European Committee for Electrotechnical Standardisation)
- CEPT (Conference Europeenne des Postes et Telecommunications)
- ETSI (European Telecommunications Standards Institute, which has taken over the function of preparing draft technical specifications from CEPT).
- EWOS (European Workshop on Open Systems which provides a workshop function for users' and manufacturers' organisations with the CEC/CENLEC framework)

In addition to these formal bodies, there are also a number of interest groups and associations, which, in some cases, issue their own standard recommendations, and exert an influence on the formal bodies through direct or indirect membership. These include, among others:

- SPAG (Standards Promotion and Application Group)
- ECMA (European Computer Manufacturers' Association)
- ECTEL (European Telecommunications and Professional Electronics Industry)
- EMUG (European MAP Users' Group)
- CECUA (Confederation of European Computer User Associations)
- X/OPEN (Standardisation group for UNIX operating systems)

It is not possible to leave the subject of IT standardisation even in such a brief overview without noting that the standardisation process itself is highly time consuming and complex. The resulting standards and in particular sets of standards themselves may be too cumbersome, and/or too expensive to implement and a long time coming. This vacuum may be filled by successful products or product ranges becoming *de facto* standards, at least until overtaken by another 'proprietary standard'.

As noted in the Introduction, compliance with standards is not compulsory, either for users or manufacturers. They get accepted in practice, as opposed to on paper, only if they are seen to be useful to both 'sides'. In information technology, technical developments have taken place with such rapidity in the recent past that the formal standardisation process has been unable to put forward a coherent, up-to-date set of generally acceptable standards. It is likely that this state of affairs will continue until IT, or some branches of it, stop evolving as rapidly as in the past.

Part 3

Part 9

19 Introduction to Part 3

Introduction

Information Technology embraces a very wide range of products and systems, supported by a variety of techniques and technologies - all aimed at processing and transferring information. For many years the whole IT industry appeared to be driven by the need for greater processing capability, bigger storage devices, and faster transmission speeds. But as the technical capabilities of IT systems have expanded, prices have fallen to the point where radical changes have occurred in both the uses and users of the technology.

IT systems have burst out of the protective domain of the specialist computer department and now sit on the majority of desks of information workers. In order to gain the acceptance of these non-programmers and to be effective within an organisation, system designs needed to be changed so that they are both more flexible and easier to use. Given the diversity of potential users and the range of their applications, new design strategies were required which strived to make the operational characteristics of the hardware and software transparent to users, allowing them to concentrate on executing the task in hand.

Achieving such transparency requires designers to think beyond technical considerations and to focus on the interaction that takes place between the user and the system. Drawing on engineering analogies, it was believed this interaction could be defined in terms of a *user interface*.

During the latter part of the 1970s and early 1980s the user interface became a general concern to designers and researchers. For Moran (Moran, 'The command language grammar: a representation for the user interface of interactive systems' *International Journal of Man-Machine Studies*, 1981,Vol 15, No 1, p 3-50) the user interface was "those aspects of the system that the user comes into contact with", whereas for Chi (Chi, H.U.,'Formal specifications of user interfaces: a comparison and evaluation of four axiomatic approaches', *IEEE Transactions on Software Engineering*, Vol. SE-11, No 8, 1987 pp 671-85) the user interface could be defined in terms of "an input language for the user, an output language for the machine and a protocol for interaction".

Hardware and software vendors quickly coined the phrase "user friendly" to imply a better quality of design, when in fact all that had been achieved was tidier and more consistent display screen designs.

Researchers on the other hand, were investigating how computers might enrich the working environment and facilitate the exploitation of the new generation of information systems. The key was to understand the capabilities and limitation of human users, that is the physical and psychological processes necessary to interact with computers. Hence the term human computer interaction (or HCI) was adopted to describe a new field of study. HCI has been defined as the "set of processes, dialogues and actions through which a human user employs and interacts with a computer" (Baecker, R.M. and Buxton, W.A.S. (1987 p 40) *Readings in Human-Computer Interaction*, Morgan Kaufman, San Mateo, CA.).

It quickly became apparent that there was more to HCI than just the physical aspects of the interface, equally important were a users cognitive processes and actual working practices, together with the potential health hazards.

HCI is very much an interdisciplinary field of study, as can be seen from Fig. 19.1. Each of these areas has contributed much to the recent developments in HCI, but it is not possible within this text to embrace them all, nor would it be appropriate.

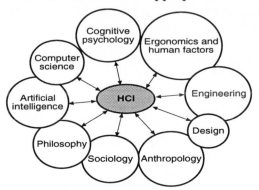

Fig. 19.1 Areas of study that contribute to HCI

Parts 1 and 2 focus very much on the technical aspects of information and information systems and in keeping with that trend this Part takes a more technological view of HCI, as indicated by Fig. 19.2. Chapter 20 introduces some basic ideas about users and in particular explores the notion of modelling the user in terms of their functional characteristics. Chapter 21 provides an overview of the operating environments that have evolved to permit a dialogue between user and machine. Chapters 22 - 24 review the characteristics of the numerous devices and techniques available to enter and extract information from a system. Finally, Chapter 25 explores some of the emerging issues of the health and safety of users of information systems.

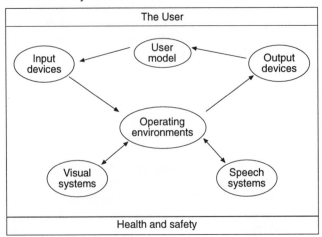

Fig. 19.2 Areas of study covered in Part 3

20 Designing for the user

Introduction

Designing any form of human interface to modern technology requires a good understanding of how users perceive and interpret instructions, co-ordinate their responses, and carry forward what they have learnt for future use. But humans are highly variable, have large mood swings, forget a sequence of operations, lose concentration, exhibit fears and prejudices, and so on. Nevertheless, they are capable of remarkable feats of problem solving, respond rapidly to external stimuli, and can create artistic masterpieces. The combination of reasoning power and physical adaptability makes the human the most successful life form known.

Unfortunately information system designers have paid scant attention to the capabilities and limitations of human users. Historically this might have been excused on the basis of the relative costs of humans and information systems. Computers were expensive and difficult to program, so the flexible human was forced to adapt to the constraints of the computer.

The availability of low cost processing power has caused a dramatic change in attitudes. Information systems are no longer kept within the domain of the computer specialist, but sit on top of everyone's desk. Users have rejected the poorly designed and difficult-to-operate systems of earlier decades.

Current strategies place the user at the focus of the design of an information system and that requires application of the lessons of psychology - our understanding of the way people act and react to their environment - and in particular of cognitive psychology.

The overall aims are to gain a greater understanding of what users can and cannot be expected to do, to identify and explain the nature and causes of the problems encountered by users, and to create modelling tools to help develop more compatible interfaces.

The keys areas of human modelling are perception, attention, information processing, memory, learning, and cognitive models.

Perception
In the context of computers the primary perception mechanisms are the visual and auditory systems. The visual system interprets the images on the display screen (including text, graphics and photographs) utilising luminance, colour and contrast. The auditory system is of increasing importance as multimedia databases and speech synthesis provide alternatives to text-based information systems.

Attention
Our perceptory system is continually processing the sights, sounds, and smells of everyday life and in order to cope the cognitive processes limit

the amount of information that can be handled at any one time. This act of filtering is know as *selective attention* and requires that human interfaces focus the user's attention on the important information, regain their attention after a distraction and permit switching between various tasks as efficiently as possible.

Information processing

Interaction with an information system requires the user to perceive a stimulus (an item of information) and respond (select one of several options). Cognitive psychologists have modelled this behaviour as a series of information processing stages, analogous to those of a computer-based information system. A simple sequence for responding to an instruction for input could be defined as:

i)   encode the element of information displayed (the question);

ii) compare this encoded representation with previously stored representations;

iii) decide on an appropriate response;

iv) enact the response.

Although such analogies can be flawed they have provided a theoretical basis with which to develop design and evaluation tools.

Memory

Memory plays a crucial role in all human activities, for without it even simple actions of opening a door, brushing teeth, reading a paper, or listening to a radio programme would become impossible. Memory permits us to recall how to undertake the simplest of tasks. The ability to recall is very variable and is linked to the amount of time and effort associated with storing the information in the first place.

Learning

Learning how to use technology is an active process and the effort required is strongly linked to success. Strategies adopted include learning: through doing; by active thinking; through setting goals and creating plans; through analogy; and from errors.

Models

Models provide designers and users of information systems with a means to predict and explain behaviour. The *design model* defines how the system should work and seeks to be complete and consistent. Users create *mental models* from experience, interaction, and documentation. The goal of human computer interaction is to draw the design and user models closer together.

Psychologists also create cognitive and perceptual models of humans from which are built the design and evaluative tools for developing user interfaces.

The model human processor

One of the most influential of such models is that developed by Card, Moran and Newell and known as the Model Human Processor. This model draws an analogy between the processing and storage units of a computer and the perceptual, cognitive, motor and memory activities of humans. The main units are shown schematically in Fig. 20.1. Perception, cognition and motor actions are controlled by independent processors that have a certain degree of parallelism, so the motor processor can be initiating movement of the hand whilst the cognitive processor is decoding images. Associated with each processor is a cycle time, analogous to the *fetch-execute* cycle of a computer's processing unit.

Fig. 20.1 Block representation of the processors and memories of the human processor. The figures in square brackets indicate the range of the parameters as deduced from experimental observations.

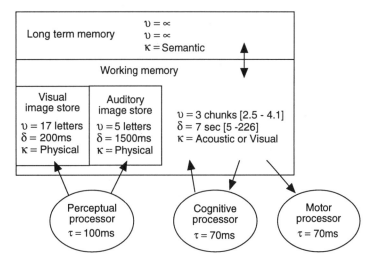

At the simplest level the model works as follows: a visual or audible stimulus is captured, the physical attributes of the stimulus are decoded (e.g. black and white space on the screen is interpreted as a question), and finally a motor response is initiated (e.g. click the OK button with the mouse). The processing and memory elements of the human processor work together to produce the desired result. But to see the consequences of this model for user interface design we need to explore the elements in a little more detail.

The memory model

The human processor is modelled as comprising four memories. The first of these are the two image stores, one for visual data, the other for auditory data, which hold the unprocessed data prior to interpretation. Both of these memories can be described in terms of their capacity (denoted by υ items), their decay time (denoted by δ ms) and the type of coding employed (denoted by κ), which may be physical, visual, acoustic, or semantic.

The capacities of these two memories are difficult to fix, but for working purposes can be assumed to be about 17 letters for the visual store and 5 letters for the auditory store. The reduced capacity of the auditory store is consistent with the fact that auditory signals can only be interpreted over time.

The image stores have limited capacity and the contents fade quickly. The measure used for this is the *half-life*, the time after which retrieval of the data has a probability of less than 50%. Experimental determination of these half-lives suggest about 200 ms for the visual store and about 1500 ms for the auditory store.

The coding employed within the visual store representation of a single letter would relate to its physical properties - the height and width, black and white spaces, but not the recognised letter. The auditory store would contain the data relating to frequency and temporal variations, not a recognised sound or word, once again relating to the physical properties of the data. Hence both coding schemes are referred to as physical.

Shortly after the physical characteristics of an acoustic or visual stimulus appears in an image store, a recognised symbolic, acoustically (or visually) coded representation (or at least part of one) appears in working memory, which is where all the intermediate results of thinking are held. This memory has a much longer decay time and a greater storage capacity than either of the image stores.

The fourth memory unit is long-term memory, which as its name implies is where all a user's knowledge is stored. As such it has infinite capacity and an infinite decay time. The implication here is that we don't forget something we've learned, we just can't find it. All items stored in long-term memory are semantically coded.

Working and long-term memory are said to store information as symbols or *chunks*, and these chunks are crucial to locating stored information. In fact one model of long-term storage is that it is a network of chunks. A simple example of how chunks operate can be shown as follows. Suppose you were asked to look at this list of nine letters for 10 seconds then try to recall them.

I B Y C V K B T S

Most people would fail. However, if we rearrange the letters of the list into three-letter mnemonics, say BBC ITV SKY, its quite easy to recall all nine letters. Each three letter group is referred to as a chunk.

Another example shows how networked chunks enable us to recall items of information. So I might use the chunk *HCI* as a means to recall various aspects about *menu*-based user interfaces, but it could also take me to *mouse* or *speech recognition*, as illustrated in Fig. 20.2. Of course I could also arrive at *menus* by starting out with the chunk *restaurant*, but the contextual differences would enable me to distinguish between the two types of meanings of menu.

Fig. 20.2 Chunks used to recall items from long-term memory

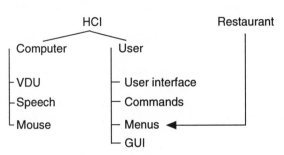

The associations fired off by the first chunk (in this case HCI) are transferred from long-term to working memory, where they will stay until displaced by new input from the images stores or new associations extracted from long-term memory. There is a good analogy between data held in a computer's RAM and that held on disk. RAM capacity is limited by access but is much faster, whereas a disk's capacity is greater but the access time much longer. These differences have important implications for the design of user interfaces.

There appears to be no consensus about the capacity and retention of long-term memory, hence the reference to infinite capacity and infinite decay time. The difficulty is actually locating the desired information, and that is why the notion of linked associations is so important. The more associations to an item of information the greater the chances of locating it over a long period of time.

This result is also demonstrated by the fact that humans are much better at recognising items than they are at recalling them. So we can recognise places we have visited, or faces and long lost relatives, much better than we can write down a list of the same items. One experiment showed that subjects who viewed 2500 photographs over a period of four days were able to recognise 90% of the images they had seen. Imagine trying to write a descriptive list of those same images. This result has important implications for user interface design (see under Applications).

The perceptual processor
The perceptual processor is somewhat analogous to a dedicated input processor in a computer, since it controls the transfer of the stimulus to the image store. It is characterised by its cycle time, which averages about 100 ms, but covers the range 50 - 200 ms. The more intense the stimulus the shorter the cycle time. So for the average human, a stimulus received on the retina of the eye will appear in the image store about 100 ms later.

Should two similar stimuli occur within a single cycle they are likely to be combined into a single event. Hence if two different audible events occur too rapidly they will tend to blur into fewer longer events. Similarly, if two different lights at nearby locations flash separately, but within one cycle time, will be perceived as a single light in motion. This latter phenomenon is what gives rise to the perception of moving pictures on cinema and TV screens. Normally such images are refreshed at a rate of either 24 (cinema) or 25 (TV) frames per second, but it is possible to produce usable animations on a PC at between 10 and 15 frames per second.

The cognitive processor
The cognitive processor performs a recognise-act cycle, akin to the fetch-execute cycle of the computer. At the start of each cycle the contents of the working memory initiate the linked associations into the long-term memory (recognise) which in turn modifies the contents of working memory (act) ready for the next cycle.

The average cycle time of this processor is about 70 ms, but may be as short as 25 ms or as long as 170 ms. Some illustrative examples of experimental data quoted by Card et al is shown in Table 20.1.

Table 20.1 Cognitive
processing rates

Matching items against working memory	
Digits	33 ms/item
Colours	38 ms/item
Letters	40 ms/item
Words	47 ms/item
Nonsense syllables	73 ms/item
Counting four or fewer objects	
Dot patterns	46 ms/item
3-D shapes	94 ms/item
Choice reaction time	
	93 ms/inspection
Silent counting	
	167 ms/digit

The motor processor

The final part of the human processor model is the motor processor which controls the muscular reactions in response to the input stimuli. In the case of HCI the two most important groups of muscles are the arm-hand-finger system and the eye-head system. The motion of these two groups of muscles is not continuous but comprises small discrete movements each requiring an average cycle time of about 70 ms, but covering the range 30 - 100 ms. The maximum observed repetition rate for hand, foot or tongue is about 10 movements per second.

Another aspect of the motor processor is motor skill, that is how well the user can control or co-ordinate muscle groups to produce a desired reaction. Particularly important are the combined movements of hand-arm muscle group, such as come into play when moving a mouse pointer across the screen to click on a response box, and the repetitive finger movements for rapid typing.

The model processor provides some guidelines as to how quickly such tasks can be undertaken. For example, repetitive keying requires two motor actions, lifting the finger up in preparation of striking the key, and pushing the finger down to strike the key. This combined action requires two cycles of the motor processor, each lasting 70 ms, for a total of 140 ms. If the keying uses both hands the operations can occur in parallel and the duration would be 70 ms. The model predicts that a *skilled typist* should operate within this range of 70 - 140 ms, less experienced typists will operate more slowly.

Touch pads or keypads are frequently used for computer-based public services (e.g. ATMs) and involve the user moving their finger over a distance **D** units to hit a target (or key) **S** units wide. Empirical evidence has shown that the time required to hit the target is determined by the ratio of the distance moved to the target width. Table 20.2 shows the action times predicted using the average response times of the human processor model for three ratios of D/S.

Table 20.2 Action time required to hit a screen target of width **S** at distance **D**	

Ratio of D/S	Action time
2	63 ms
4	126 ms
8	189 ms

Olson and Olson provide experimental data with which to compare the predictions for repetitive keying and targeting. The results are listed in Table 20.3.

Table 20.3 Motor response times for finger-hand-arm actions

Keystrokes

	Average non-secretary	280 ms
	Best typist	80 ms
	Worst typist	1200 ms
	Random letters	500 ms
	Complex codes	750 ms
	Spreadsheet formulas	220 - 330 ms

Pointing with mouse

	Small screen, menu target	1100 - 1900 ms

Movement of hands from keyboard

	To mouse	360 ms
	To joystick	260 ms
	To cursor keys	210 ms
	To function keys	320 ms

Applications of the model

The human processor model has provided user interface designers with a valuable tool with which to assess new interface designs. However it has to be remembered that it is a tool, not a precise model.

A number of useful design goals have emerged from the development and refinement of the processor model which are summarised briefly below.

Menus versus commands: command-based interfaces (e.g. Microsoft's MS-DOS) place a great load on the user to remember the commands and their associated optional *switches*. This arises from the fact that the user has to find a means of locating the command in long-term memory, that is it has to fire-up appropriate links to the desired command. Some of these associations will lead in the wrong direction and so have to be eliminated from the search. Eventually we find the right links and locate the appropriate command, but it all takes time. So command-based systems which require the user to *recall* items take longer to operate and place greater demands on the user.

Menus systems, on the other hand, provide a list of the optional commands and so the user is presented with a starting point in the chain of associations that lead towards locating the desired item of information. This process is described as *recognition* of the desired item. Hence with menu-based systems there is a much smaller chance of the user going off in the wrong direction, less time wasted searching long-term memory and a reduced load placed on the user.

Target size and distance: many functions of graphic user interface systems require the user to click a pointer within a specific target, perhaps an item from a menu or an *OK* box. The human processor model shows that the smaller the target, relative to the distance moved, the longer the time to hit the target. One solution to this problem has been to vary the size of elements in a menu, so that distant elements have a larger target size than closer elements. Another is to ensure that dialogue boxes appear close to the middle of the screen, thereby reducing target distance. A more recent addition to Microsoft's Windows has been a software utility which ensures that the pointer's cursor (the arrow head) is automatically placed on the default option box, so that there is no mouse movement at all.

Reduce hand movement: switching between keyboard and mouse takes a good secretary four and a half times as long as entering a keystroke. Even moving to function keys is equivalent to four keystrokes. So there is much to be gained by reducing the need to move hands from one form of input device to another. Many interface designs try to reduce such movement by providing shift and control key-combinations to replace mouse movements.

Keyboard designs: the human processor model and experimental evidence both indicate that the current QWERTY, or Scholes, keyboard layout is not conducive to rapid keyboard entry. In fact it is well known that the design emerged as a means of slowing down typists operating mechanical keyboards. Various alternative keyboard layouts have been developed, notably the Dvorak, alphabetic and chord. The Dvorak design (patented in 1932) has the keys arranged such that the most frequently used keys are placed on the *home* row. Chord keyboards are used by stenographers following speech.

Whilst both the Dvorak and chord keyboards offer faster input and place a smaller demand on the human motor system, they have never gained commercial acceptance, primarily due to the cost of replacing current keyboards and the cost of retraining all the users.

Validity of the model

The human processor model provides designers with a means to evaluate new designs and in particular to: constrain the design parameters, provide a balance between recall and recognition activities, estimate workloads for individuals, plan the training requirements for a new task, and provide directions for new research.

There are also many limitations of the model. In general the results are only applicable to skilled users and unskilled users will take longer to complete tasks. There is no indication of the learning requirements or the retention of the skills once acquired. The model ignores the errors that arise even with skilled operators and does not address the mental workload entailed or the fatigue users experience.

Human modelling should therefore be seen as a design tool not as a design solution. There are many other factors that play an important part in HCI.

21 Interactions and dialogues

Introduction

Modern information systems are capable of performing various and numerous processing tasks at very high speeds, but in general they remain slavish and rather stupid assistants to the human user. It is the user who decides what the processes are and when they should be performed. In order to do this the user must be able to *interact* with the information system and establish a *dialogue* for communicating the necessary instructions. What form the interaction takes and the nature of the dialogue are determined by the designers of the system.

Historically the early forms of interaction with computers were dominated by electro-mechanical keyboards and printers, and dialogues were limited to discrete commands that performed single tasks. Errors introduced into the syntax of such commands were greeted by cryptic messages which did little to help the user identify their mistake. For the majority of users the situation was bleak: learn the commands and the syntax or look for alternative employment.

Change was on the way. Early in the 1970s Xerox established a major research centre at Palo Alto, California, soon be to known throughout the world as Xerox PARC (Palo Alto Research Centre), and it was here that much of the early research on user-centred design and alternative user interfaces was conducted. One outcome was the development of the Alto computer system, complete with an integrated high quality graphical display and high capacity local area network.

Equally important in this evolutionary process was the development of Apple Computer's LISA, a microprocessor-based combination of hardware and software designed for use by executives.

Today designers can draw on a variety of techniques to facilitate the human-computer interaction and whilst the trend is towards graphical systems there remain numerous non-computing applications where simpler more cost-effective designs are appropriate.

Interactions and dialogues

A dialogue is an exchange of instructions and information between a user and a computer system. The instructions may be specified by typing, pointing, speaking, gesturing and so on, and are then translated by the computer to be followed by execution. The user trusts that their intentions were correctly identified and executed by the computer. The computer should provide some feedback, either confirming success or an intelligible message explaining what went wrong.

As the variety of communications between humans and computers has expanded, the use of the term dialogue has come to be regarded as too limiting, because of its verbal connotations. Many authors now tend to view the exchanges more generally and describe them as interactions.

Looking at a variety of different user interfaces it is clear that some interactions have a distinctive style whereas others are mixtures of several styles. Technically competent, or knowledgeable, users could quickly adapt to the style of command-based applications which matched the user and task requirements quite well. Furthermore, such users were more likely to overcome difficulties by sheer perseverance. Form-fill modes of interaction were aimed at clerical workers with little experience of computers, hence the user interface replicated the paper forms with which they were familiar. The goal was to retain as far as possible the characteristics of the manual task, while benefiting from the speed of processing of the computer. So these interfaces were aimed at somewhat different groups of users and tasks. Command-based interactions were sufficiently flexible they could be employed by experienced users across a range of applications, whereas the form-fill mode was aimed at a more limited type of task and less experienced users.

As general applications (e.g. word processing and spread-sheets) gained dominance over specialist applications, so software designers found themselves having to cope with a much more diverse range of user skills and experience. The result was the development of more supportive interaction styles such as menus. However, experienced users often found these more supportive designs impeded their work, they wanted the speed and flexibility of command-based systems. Hence, the emergence of hybrid systems to satisfy the different user skill-levels and preferences.

This chapter examines a number of interaction styles as though they were separate entities, but many modern interface designs combine the best features of several types of interaction. The goal is to integrate the most important elements of each into a single system.

Command-based systems

Commands provide a direct way of conveying instructions to the computer and may take the form of characters, function key combinations, multiple letter abbreviations, whole words or a combination of these (for example, using the 'Shift' key together with the letter 'c' to mean COPY a marked selection of text). Using single characters or function keys reduces the number of keystrokes required to execute the command compared with a word or an abbreviation (for example, having to type out COPY).

The disadvantage is that the user may find it more difficult to remember the single letter or key rather than a purposefully chosen name or abbreviation, especially if there are many such commands. The English alphabet also imposes a limitation; in that there are only 26 letters and a letter used for one command cannot be used for another command at the same hierarchical level. For example, if D is used as the abbreviation for directory it cannot be used to represent the delete (a file) command.

Short words, or abbreviations of longer ones, often make it easier for the user to recall the command than a single letter. So, for example, ERASE, TYPE, and DATE are to be preferred over E, T, and D. A typical command-based interaction is illustrated in Fig. 21.1, which shows the dialogue from the MS-DOS operating system for listing the contents of a disk directory. The '>' symbol indicates that the system is waiting to receive a command to tell it what to do next. The user then enters the command DIR to list the file directory, followed by the control key

Fig. 21.1 MS-DOS
dialogue for listing the
contents of a disk

```
>
>DIR<ret>
Volume in drive E is SCSI-2
Volume Serial Number is 1B70-61E5
Directory of E:\SNDZIPS

               <DIR>                11/11/93    1:42
               <DIR>                11/11/93    1:42
   AC33MUSC       ZIP 276,475  11/11/93   13:46
   CWB135         ZIP 76,288   11/11/93   13:46
   DMPLA231       ZIP 69,204   11/11/93   13:49
   JINGLE         ZIP 90,445   11/11/93   13:46
   MODED301       ZIP 376,328  11/11/93   13:47
   NOHISS10       ZIP 97,422   11/11/93   13:49
   NUSND102       ZIP 223,104  11/11/93   13:49
   PCTALK21       ZIP 139,748  11/11/93   13:50
   PLAY410        ZIP 74,964   11/11/93   13:51
   PLAYBWC        ZIP 133,342  11/11/93   13:52
   REPLA101       ZIP 137,100  11/11/93   13:50
   VM1088         ZIP 14,146   11/11/93   13:47
   VOCPAK20       ZIP 80,133   11/11/93   13:51
   WINPLAY        ZIP 22,197   11/11/93   13:47
        17 file(s) 1,810,896 bytes
                   42,782,720 bytes free
>
```

<return> to terminate the entry and execute the command. Once the
files have been listed the '>' symbol is displayed once again to indicate
readiness for the next command.

The choice of appropriate commands names can be crucial to the success
of the interface design, since it helps users to remember what processes the
commands refer to. However, command name choices should not be
viewed in isolation since this may be detrimental to the overall design. A
better strategy is to examine all the relevant factors of these complex user
interactions, including the application itself, and how users set about
mastering it.

Menu-based systems

A menu is a set of options displayed on the screen (see Fig. 21.2) as a
horizontal or vertical list. Selection of one of the options causes the
execution of one (or more) processes and may result in a change in the
state of the interface, that is new elements may appear or some may be
removed. A user is not required to remember the name or abbreviation of
a command; only recognise it from the list of options presented on the
screen. This can be of particular benefit to new users of the software. To be
effective the names of the options displayed in the menu have to be
self-explanatory and this can be difficult to achieve for complex processes
and large groups of users.

Options may also be displayed as *icons*, that is pictographic
representations of tools and processes. So, for example, the sequence of
interactions necessary to print a document may be represented by a printer
icon. To print the document the user simply points the cursor at the icon
and activates selection.

Menus do unfortunately take up a lot of screen space and so techniques
have been devised to maximise the usable area. The general solution is to
create a hierarchy of menus, the highest level of which is permanently

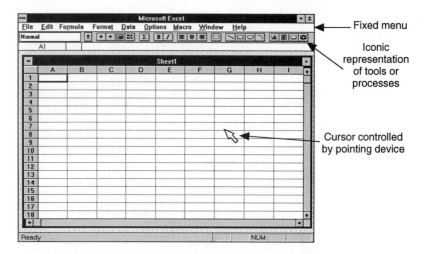

Fig. 21.2 Menu-based interface. User options are displayed as text and icons

Fixed menu

Iconic representation of tools or processes

Cursor controlled by pointing device

visible whilst the lower levels only appear after an initial selection. The 'Permanently' visible menu is typically displayed as a horizontal list of options and is referred to as the fixed-matrix menu. The lower level options are provided by means of pull-down or pop-up menus. In the former the secondary menu drops down from below the selected option in the fixed-matrix. An option is then selected from this secondary menu, at which point it disappears to leave just the fixed matrix (see Fig. 21.3). Pop-up menus are more commonly used in conjunction with icons. When the icon is selected a secondary menu, or list, pops-up and remains in position until the user completes the selection or chooses the 'close'option in the menu's window.

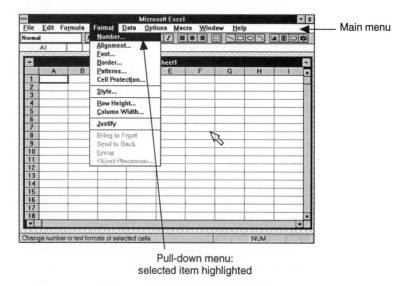

Fig 21.3 Pull-down menus extend the options available but without consuming too much screen space

Main menu

Pull-down menu: selected item highlighted

In situations where an even larger number of options are required a fixed menu can be combined with multiple levels of pull-down menu to provide a cascading menu (see Fig. 21.4). When an option is selected on the first pull-down menu, another, lower level, menu opens directly adjacent to it. The pull-down menu becomes in effect a fixed menu. This

Fig. 21.4 The cascading menu

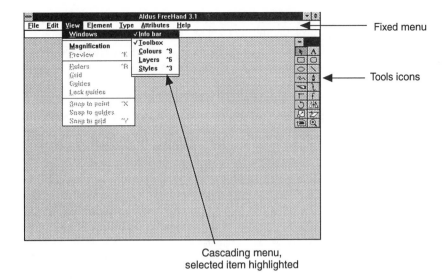

Fixed menu

Tools icons

Cascading menu,
selected item highlighted

progression through menus can continue for several levels; hence the name cascading. The cascade also provides a visual record of the selections made. However, it can be physically difficult to manipulate a pointing device to navigate through the different levels of menus.

Multiple menus, each with its own set of options, require that a user search through each menu to find the desired option. The fastest and simplest form of search occurs when the desired task matches one of the options displayed. An example of this is when the user wants to save a document and an option called SAVE appears on the menu. Other types of search require the user to evaluate the relationship between the job they want to do and the menu options available. For example, a user must decide whether the option to insert an index entry will be located in an EDIT or INSERT sub-menu.

Designers must therefore determine the most appropriate way to display the menus so that they are comprehensible and natural to users and they correspond to the way users carry out tasks. In the majority of cases this means some form of hierarchical organisation of the commands.

The main priority is that options should be organised in a way which is meaningful to users. Experimental evidence suggests that the four most favoured are: *alphabetical, categorical, conventional* and *frequency*.

Alphabetical should be self-explanatory, the options are listed according to the first letter of the name (e.g. COPY, CUT, PASTE, REPLACE). *Categorical* organization assumes that the options can be grouped into suitably distinct categories. This can be difficult to implement since it is more than likely that some of the options could fit into several categories whilst others will not fit in well with any of the categories. *Conventional* menus are those that follow existing conventions, such as the days of the week or the months of the year, or perhaps lie on a graded scale such as small, medium, large. Few applications lend themselves to such conventionally arranged menus. *Frequency* of use organises the menu options such that the most frequently used command appears first, then the next most frequently used, and so on.

Navigating through a series of menus should be as simple as possible, especially for systems employing hierarchically structured menus or a number of different menus that are displayed sequentially. Particularly important is a means of backtracking from an erroneous selection.

Natural language dialogue

The use of every-day language as a means of interacting with information systems is considered highly desirable because of its naturalness to the user. However, numerous difficulties arise in terms of imprecision, ambiguity and ungrammatical constructions. Although input via a keyboard does eliminate problems of accent and intonation, there remain the problems of spelling and keying errors.

Designing systems to cope with all aspects of natural language may not be possible, but it may be feasible to develop systems that understand a limited sub-set. Such techniques have been applied to the development of several expert systems and an intelligent tutoring system. The user has to learn how to use the language sub-set unambiguously and to construct the sentences in a way that can be comprehended by the target system.

The INTELLECT business and sales database application employs a natural language interface. The system has been designed so that after each user submission, the system rephrases the request to ensure it has understood exactly what the user wants. However, it has been observed that after a while users get tired of reviewing rephrased responses and start to write queries in the specific format that the system understands. Although this defeats the objective of using natural language it is still helpful to users who are prepared to learn the language, but less so for anyone who lacks this expertise.

As yet natural language interfaces are still dominated by keyboard entry and the amount of typing required should not be ignored, especially for novice users, who may find a menu much quicker and easier to use. Expert users may find a command-based interface faster.

Voice recognition systems have improved considerably in recent years (see p. 224) and whilst this may reduce the need for fast accurate typing, they pose their own problems in terms of the restrictions imposed on the delivery of speech by the user.

Form-fills

Many commercial data-processing applications involve the repetitive entry of alphanumeric items, such as for example invoice preparation or insurance applications. In such cases it can be helpful to the operator to design the screen as though it were a paper form (form-fill). The screen-based form can help a user position data correctly, thereby reducing the need to watch the screen too carefully. As each entry on the form is completed the user can simply 'tab' automatically to the position of the next item, and so on. The user is therefore saved both the physical and mental effort of having to locate each item, increasing their attention span. Of course poor design of the screen form can actually increase the effort required. Forms should be designed so as to help users recall which kinds of data are permissible in each field. It goes without saying that the design should ensure that users know how to make corrections. One way of making forms easy to use is to design them so that they are similar to well-designed paper forms in the way they look and are filled in.

Spreadsheet programs are another example of computer-based applications designed to imitate familiar paper-based activities, but with much greater functionality. In particular, they enable numerous types of complex calculation, such as standard deviations, net present values and internal rates of return, to be performed automatically on rows or columns of data that appear on the screen. A user can try out a wide range of alternative mathematical models and see the results displayed almost instantly.

VISICALC, the first successfully marketed spreadsheet program, was developed by a student at the Harvard Business School. The student apparently became frustrated at having to perform and type out the numerous calculations associated with his studies. So he built an 'instantly calculating electronic worksheet' that permitted computation and displays of results across 254 rows and 63 columns. Complicated calculations could be carried out involving any combination of single cells, rows or columns.

A notable feature of the design of VISICALC was that, by imitating an accountant's spreadsheet, it enabled anyone, regardless of their computing experience, to use VISICALC with minimal training - provided they knew how the paper versions of a spreadsheet worked. However, setting up the electronic version of the spreadsheet is not a simple task, since it involves learning the various commands and knowing how best to employ them.

Direct manipulation

The final class of interaction is that based on the direct manipulation of objects and elements displayed on the screen. In general such systems provide:

- visibility of the objects of interest
- incremental and reversible actions
- replacement of a complex command language syntax by actual manipulation of the object.

Users should therefore be able to move and transform objects as if they were real objects and undo actions so as to return to a previous state. The tasks to be performed should be broken down into a suitable sequence of actions so that the user retains control and understands what the system is doing. The objects themselves should be represented on the screen so as to resemble their real-life counterparts. Fig. 21.5 illustrates the display screen for a 'painting' application. The various tools required by the painter are represented by the pen, paintbrush, and eraser icons. Selecting a tool and directing it over the 'paper' permits freehand drawing, painting with a selectable colour, or erasure of ink and paint.

Direct manipulation can also be applied at the operating system level, where icons representing objects can be moved around the screen and manipulated by controlling a cursor. For example, opening a file may be done by pointing at a file name or its iconic equivalent. The cursor acts like an electronic hand, in that it can point at, select and manipulate objects on the display. Various types of visual and auditory cues can be used to inform users that operations are proceeding as expected.

The Apple Macintosh was one of the first commercial systems to include direct manipulation features. The basic analogy employed is that of a desktop on which are displayed icons representing objects commonly

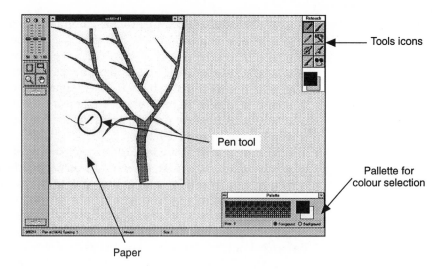

Fig. 21.5 Display screen of a direct manipulation application

Tools icons

Pen tool

Pallette for colour selection

Paper

found on the top of a desk. Documents, for example, are displayed as small sheets of paper and can be grouped together into another icon representing a folder. A 'clipboard' is available for temporarily storing pieces of documents for use by other applications and there is a 'waste basket' for disposing of dated or amended documents (that is, erasing files from a disk).

CAD systems for engineering, electronic circuitry, and architecture use some of the principles of direct manipulation. An electronic circuit CAD system might employ an interface that enables the user to design a printed circuit on the screen by placing and removing integrated circuits, resistors or capacitors with a pointing device.

Industrial robots can be programmed using another form of direct manipulation. The operator holds the robot's 'hand' and guides it through a spraying or welding task while the controlling computer records every movement. The computer then manipulates the robot automatically by repeating the movements that have been recorded.

Arcade games also employ direct manipulation with the player scoring points by directing the 'hero' through the labyrinth to the pot of gold.

The main advantages claimed for direct manipulation systems are:

- New users quickly learn the basic functionality.

- Experts can work extremely rapidly to carry out a wide range of tasks, even defining new functions and features.

- Knowledgeable intermittent users can retain operational concepts and error messages are rarely needed.

- Users can immediately see if their actions are furthering their goals and, if they are not, can simply change the direction of their activity.

- Users experience less anxiety because the system is comprehensible and because actions are so easily reversible.

- Users gain confidence and mastery because they initiate an action, feel in control and can predict system responses.

One of the major problems with direct manipulation is that not all processes can be described by objects and not all actions can be performed directly.

Graphical user interfaces

The dominant mode of interaction of the current generation of information systems is undoubtedly through a graphical user interface (GUI) of some form which combines the features of menus and direct manipulation. In addition most of these interfaces permit several applications to be displayed simultaneously, each within their own window, that is a segment of the screen devoted to the application. Some applications may require several windows to be active simultaneously.

The windowing facility itself introduces a number of special considerations, for example actions to move, size and collapse the window. A mechanism is also required to permit switching between running applications. Coupled with these are further actions which permit data to be exchanged between applications. Fig. 21.6 shows a user screen captured from Microsoft's Windows 3.1 with three active windows. On the left of the figure is a drawing application with a main window and one subsidiary window for the current drawing. The latter shows the vertical and horizontal scroll-bars used to pan horizontally or vertically over the drawing area. On the right of the figure is a window for the File Manager application. The elements used to collapse, maximise, and close the window are indicated, together with that used to switch between applications.

Fig. 21.6 Graphical user interface screen with multiple windows

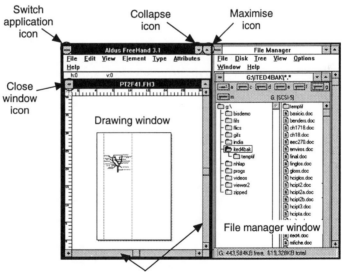

Switch application icon

Collapse icon

Maximise icon

Close window icon

Drawing window

File manager window

Horizontal and vertical scroll bars

One of the most important attributes of a graphical user interface is a high degree of consistency between different applications, since this facilitates the user to learn how best to operate with the interface. Apple and Microsoft have established guidelines for software developers which ensure menu layouts, keyboard options, icon representations and the general look and feel of any application are familiar to the user.

GUIs are available for all the major computer platforms. The predominant product, with over 15 million licences sold (1994), is Microsoft's Windows for the PC. IBM have developed a competitive product known as Presentation Manager. For the Apple Macintosh the current generation of GUI is simply referred to as System 7. GUIs also exist within the open systems framework, for example, the Open Software Foundation's Motif product.

Summary

This review of interactions and dialogues has highlighted a number of facets of user interface design. Menus are generally considered to be more useful for novices, because they operate by recognition rather than recall. Users do not have to remember so much detail and menus can guide users step-by-step through a sequence of operations. Command-based systems require users to be able to remember command names, characters or abbreviations, which commands correspond to which process and the correct syntax for each command. However, they tend to be faster and offer greater flexibility and are therefore best suited to experienced users.

Menus do tend to take up considerable display space and so hierarchical systems have been evolved using pull-down, pop-up and cascading menus, but these increase the complexity of locating the desired option. Ordering of options is therefore an important aspect of menu design and may be based on alphabetic, categorical, conventional and by frequency of command use.

Natural language dialogues, while promising the greatest flexibility and ease of use, are in practice quite restrictive. In many cases it is necessary for users to conform to a vocabulary and sentence construction imposed by the system.

Form-fills and spreadsheets also require a prescribed form of input, but such constraints serve to guide a user as to where to place data and also what data are permissible. Both applications are designed to be electronic counterparts of their paper predecessors. This makes it easier for people to become familiar with them and use them since users can apply their prior knowledge of these tasks.

Direct manipulation provides for an interaction based on representations of real objects. Actions are clearly visible to the user and may be reversed at will. Most direct manipulation systems, however, also use indirect manipulation techniques such as menus and form-fills. In addition it is possible to carry out a number of operations by keying in commands. This provides flexibility so that users can choose interaction methods.

Applications

Although this chapter has concentrated on user interfaces for computers, there are nevertheless numerous other applications which have benefited from the same basic research. These include many domestic products, such as games consoles, video recorders and microwave cookers.

The games console is a prime example of a direct manipulation interface. The characters of the game are directly controlled by the user through the operation of various buttons or a joystick. Menus may also be employed to facilitate the selection of characters, degree of difficulty and so on.

Video recorders have developed a notorious reputation for their interfaces and several surveys have indicated that over 60% of adults cannot set their machines to record a programme unattended. In an attempt to address the problem a new form of programmer has been developed and marketed as VideoPlus. In place of individual entries for on and off times, date, and channel, all the user has to enter is a numeric code which uniquely identifies the programme parameters. These codes are published alongside the programme listing in weekly television magazines and daily newspapers.

Some manufacturers have opted for a menu style interaction which guides the user through each parameter. Alternatively, for recorders with a teletext decoder, the programme timer may be set-up by picking the programme off the teletext page containing the TV viewing guide. Start and stop times are automatically determined by decoding the information stored in the teletext memory.

A final example of the everyday application of user interface design principles is the ATM, which employs menu selections to guide the user through a series of questions and answers. Surveys conducted by the financial institutions that provide the ATMs suggest that very few users encounter difficulties using these systems.

22 Input devices

Introduction

The first prerequisite to any interaction with computer systems is some means to enter commands or selection options from a menu. Currently the dominant input entry device is the alphanumeric keyboard, having originated with the earliest versions of the typewriter, but now used with almost any form of microprocessor-based system including computers, cash registers, ATMs, video games and home security devices. The basic function of the keyboard is to translate the alphanumeric character keys hit by the user into digital codes that can be interpreted by the computer.

Whilst keyboards may be adequate for alphanumeric data they are not well suited to modern user interface designs and the ever increasing demand for faster processing of a wider range of input data. Accuracy and speed are also far too dependent on the skills of individual operators.

A wide variety of devices have been developed to satisfy these other needs including: optical and magnetic document readers (scanners); bar-code readers; graphic tablets and digitisers; voice recognition; touch screens; analogue to digital signal converters etc.

The optimum device for any application will be that which best matches the physical and psychological attributes of the user to the task in hand, thereby enabling the user to perform efficiently and effectively. In many cases this requires more than one input device, such as, for example, the combination of keyboard and mouse used with many GUIs.

Input devices must also provide the user with feedback, either directly in the form of the resistance to motion of a key or mouse, or indirectly by way of a visible or audible warning. The feedback provides a means to reassure and inform the user and to identify errors that need correction.

Graphical user interfaces provide for a rich variety of feedback and most modern systems employ visual and audible warnings in addition to the tactile feedback associated with the physical data entry device. Selecting an icon with a mouse provides the immediate response of the button depression, to be followed by a colour or shape change to the icon or the appearance of a new selection window on screen.

This chapter describes some of the common characteristics of different input devices together with some of the factors that need to be considered when selecting an input device.

Types of input device

Input devices fall into several broad categories based on the motor actions needed to control them. The majority of devices utilise movement of the arm, hand and finger (e.g. keyboard and mouse), whilst a few employ sensors to detect eye or head movement. More specialist devices have been developed for physically disabled users, such as the foot-mouse and the puff-suck switch, and the eye-typer.

Touch and limb motion

The vast majority of user-centred input devices utilise a combination of touch together with wrist and arm motion. Everyday examples include the keyboard and mouse, but even bar-code and magnetic card readers at a supermarket check-out require a swiping motion during data entry.

When designing a user interface it is therefore essential to consider the physical demands the input devices place on the user. Precision movement depends primarily on the number of muscles and nerves employed, the quality of the sensory feedback and the type of action required. Muscle fatigue can arise from repetitive motion or unsupported limbs and will reduce control and accuracy. A further consideration is the static load, mostly on the back and shoulder muscles, arising from having to maintain an operating position. A user's manipulative ability may also be affected by the need to wear protective clothing or operating in unusual conditions where there are vibrations, extreme dampness or poor light.

Input devices can be conveniently subdivided into two groups: those that record continuous movement, such as drawing with a stylus or controlling a joystick, and those devices that record discrete movement such as pressing keys or a touch screen. A few devices combine both types of movement, for example, a mouse uses both continuous movement for positioning and discrete movement to activate one or more buttons.

No matter what form the motion takes tactile feedback is essential to ensure an acceptable degree of accuracy. This feedback is derived from sensors in the skin and within the muscles and tendons. It provides the user with information about how the muscles are being stretched or contracted, thereby providing feedback about the position of objects in space. When used efficiently, feedback enables a user to determine the position of a hand or finger and correct for errors. A skilled touch typist, for example, can usually tell when the wrong key has been hit without having to look at either the keyboard or the display.

Discrete entry devices

The simplest example of a discrete entry device is the on-off push-button switch which generates a simple binary input of 0 or 1. However, single switches are not much use for data entry applications and so switches are built up into groups or sets. Typical examples include calculator and telephone keypads and keyboards. The arrangement of the keys, both as individual components and as a group, is an important design factor, since even a simple alteration in the layout, the number or the physical characteristics of the keys will affect a user's speed and accuracy. The small, closely spaced keys of calculators and some telephones can cause some users considerable difficulty in locating and hitting single keys accurately.

Various studies have shown that typing involves a great deal of anticipation, with fingers hovering over the keys that are to be struck next. A trained typist does not perform a series of individual keystrokes, but looks ahead and processes text in 'chunks' (see p. 186), and then types it in chunks. A typical alphabetic chunk might be two to three words long whilst a numerical chunk is only three to four characters long. The effect of processing chunks is to increase the typing speed significantly.

Keyboards provide a very flexible form of input device capable of fulfilling the requirements of many different tasks. The most commonly employed is the alphanumeric keyboard associated with typewriters and personal computers, which contain a mixture of alphabetic, numeric, and punctuation keys. In addition to these are the function keys, such as the shift key of a typewriter, that when pressed in conjunction with another key modify the digital output code. Programmable function keys are also common and can be programmed either by the user or through the applications software.

Numeric data entry is most effectively processed with a separate numeric keypad combining the digits 0 to 9 together with a limited set of keys for arithmetical operators (that is, plus, minus and so on). Other specialist designs include the chord keyboard in which alphanumeric information is entered by pressing groups of keys rather than single keys.

Most computer users are familiar with the layout of the standard English alphanumeric keyboard - often called the QWERTY keyboard because of the arrangement of the letters in the top character row. This layout first became a commercial success in the USA around 1874 and was designed to reduce the incidence of jammed keys in manual typewriters, rather than as any optimal arrangement for typing. Although mechanical keyboards have been replaced by faster electronic keyboards the QWERTY layout remains dominant. The possible gain in input speed of more efficient layouts has to be weighed against the cost of replacing existing keyboards and retraining millions of people who have learned the QWERTY keyboard.

Alternative and more efficient keyboards do exist, such as the Dvorak and Alphabetic boards. The Dvorak keyboard, first patented in 1932, was designed using the following principles.

- The key layout is derived on the basis of frequency of usage of letters, letter patterns and sequences in the English language.
- All vowels and the most frequently used consonants are on the second (or 'home') row, permitting 70 per cent of common words to be typed from this row alone.
- Vowels and the common consonants are split between the left and right hands. This enables faster operation because there is a much higher probability that consecutive letters of words will require use of the fingers on alternate hands (particularly the index fingers).

The improvements made by the ergonomic design of the Dvorak keyboard are a significant reduction in finger travel and thereby a consequent reduction in fatigue, leading to an increase in accuracy. Dvorak also claimed that his keyboard arrangement reduces the between-row movement by some 90 per cent and allows about 35 per cent of everyday words to be typed on the home row. Despite these apparent benefits the Dvorak layout has never been commercially successful, once again because of the high costs associated with the changeover from QWERTY.

Touch screens are growing in popularity, partly as a result of falling costs, but also because they can be operated in environments where a keyboard is inappropriate. Typical applications include public information services and on the factory floor. The user inputs information into the computer simply by touching an appropriate part of the screen or some representation of the screen. In this way a computer screen doubles as both the input and output device of the system. The touch screen itself is an array of contact switches actuated by the pressure of a finger. Although there are numerous proprietary designs, the most common touch screen switch consists of two layers of electrically conductive polyester film separated by an insulator and each switch acts like a capacitor. The outer layer of the operating surface is protected by a tough abrasion and chemical resistant coating.

Using appropriate software, different parts of a touch screen can represent different responses as different displays are presented to a user. For example, a system giving directions to visitors at a large exhibition may first present an overview of the exhibition layout in the form of a general map. A user may then be requested to touch the hall that he wishes to visit and the system will present a list of exhibits. Having selected the exhibit of his choice by touching it, the user may then be presented with a more detailed map of the chosen hall.

The advantages of touch screens are that they are easy and fast to use, which makes them ideal for applications involving casual users who cannot be expected to spend time learning to use the system. However, some less favourable reports claim that touch screens may cause physical fatigue from reaching to the screen and that an operator's hand may sometimes block the line of vision. These problems can be eased by the use of a remote off-screen touch pad which can be positioned horizontally.

Touch screens can be combined with all current display technologies, such as cathode-ray-tube (CRT), liquid-crystal and plasma. In the case of CRTs the touch screen element is positioned between the glass screen and the case bezel. A waterproof seal can be incorporated for industrial environments. Recent improvements in the brightness and response of liquid crystal displays has made them popular for point-of-sale, medical diagnostics and test equipment applications. Plasma, electro-luminescent, and vacuum fluorescent displays provide high contrast and speed and so are favoured for military and aerospace applications. The flatness of the display allows use of an unsupported touch screen, installed directly on the surface of the glass.

Continuous entry devices

The second category of touch and limb motion input devices are those that permit the recording of variable motion, these are commonly referred to as continuous entry devices and include: joysticks, light-pens, stylus, tracker-balls and mice (see Fig. 22.1). In place of a binary on-off signal, these devices produce a continuously varying signal representing motion and position. Some devices generate an analogue voltage which must be converted to a digital representation, whilst others generate a digital signal or a stream of binary pulses. Buttons or switches are normally incorporated to permit the user to initiate some action once the device has been positioned. All these devices (also known as pointers) operate in two dimensions, typically moved over a flat horizontal surface, the exception being the light-pen which is moved across the display screen.

Joysticks are often used for cursor-positioning tasks where precision is required, such as CAD. The mechanical mouse contains a spherical ball in its underside which is rotated as the mouse is dragged across the surface.

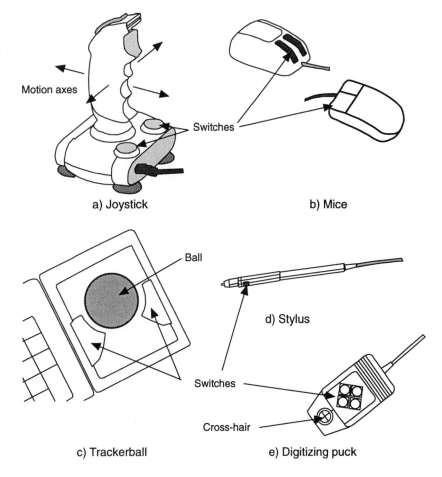

Fig. 22.1 Continuous input devices a) joystick, b) old and new mice designs, c) tracker-ball attached to keyboard, d) stylus, and e) puck with digitising cross-hair

Motion axes

Switches

a) Joystick

b) Mice

Ball

d) Stylus

Switches

Cross-hair

c) Trackerball

e) Digitizing puck

A tracker-ball is somewhat like an upturned mouse and the ball is rotated by movement of the fingers or palm. The stylus and puck are normally used in conjunction with a digitising tablet and operate by inductive pick-up. The puck has a visible cross-hair to facilitate tracing existing artwork. The light-pen is held against the surface of the screen and a sensor in the tip detects the passage of the scanning electron beam as it refreshes the display.

One advantage of a carefully designed pointer is that it can be used for moving objects around the screen, something quite difficult to accomplish using keys. The user gains a sense of manipulating selected objects, an important principle in the design of many of today's interfaces.

Movement of a pointer involves two types of motion. The first is gross motor movement to the general vicinity of the target. The second is the finer movement to hit the target. The designer must therefore consider how sensitive to make the motion translation. Mechanical resistance and gearing can be built in to joysticks and mice, but many software packages now incorporate variable acceleration. Fast hand movements of the device translate to large transitions on screen, whereas slow hand movements produce small transitions.

The foot-mouse is another form of continuous entry device, but operated by the feet, leaving hands free for the keyboard. It comprises a rubberised surface on a central pivot so that movement of a foot can drive a cursor up or down, left or right, depending upon which edge is depressed (see Fig. 22.2) . Continued depression produce continuous motion of the cursor.

Fig. 22.2 Sketch of a foot-mouse

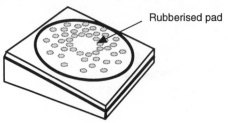

Rubberised pad

The data-glove is a more recent development that has gained popularity with the growth of virtual reality applications. It consists of fibre-optic cables and sensors sandwiched between layers of cloth connected to an interface board near to the wrist, which in turn is connected to the computer. When worn, it provides the user with the illusion of grasping and moving objects as though they were in three-dimensional space. The glove's sensors are wired in such a way that, in conjunction with software, an image is displayed on the screen which mimics the motion of the user's own hand. This permits the user to employ the precision, control and agility of their own hand to point at menus or manipulate displayed objects. It is one of the few three-dimensional input devices available and offers great potential because of its one-to-one relationship between limb motion and pointer movement. However, current designs lack any form of tactile feedback and have to rely on auditory and visual cues.

Eye and head movement activation
The eyes and head are always in constant motion as we view the world around us. When looking at a display screen the eyes move to attain the best possible focus on the sensitive part of the retina (see p. 214), and if eye movement alone is inadequate the head is moved. This motion can be detected and used as input to a computer, perhaps to select options from displayed menus. For users with severe spinal injuries, such movements may be all that is possible.

Eye movement can be detected using either electro-physiological sensors which record the movements of the eye muscles, or photoelectric reflection to detect the light reflected from the eye. Electro-physiological detection requires that electrodes be secured to the skin to detect muscle movement and are therefore subject to the electrical noise generated by general body movement. Photoelectric reflection requires a user to track an object on the screen by moving the eyes to maintain a stable image on the central part of the retina where vision is most acute. This is not easy to achieve, however, since the eyes do not move in a sufficiently smooth fashion.

Both techniques make tracking very small targets difficult because of the number of involuntary movements that occur when the eye is attempting to fix on a point.

Another device that has been developed for people with severe motor impairment is the eye-typer. This device has letters displayed on a panel in the familiar QWERTY keyboard layout with the numerals in a row beneath. Each letter and number has a light embedded in it. A camera in the centre of the display catches the reflection from the user's eye of the particular letter or number that is being viewed. This is converted into a character that appears in a liquid crystal display at the bottom of the panel. Hence the user 'types' by scanning the keyboard and fixing momentarily on each character that is wanted.

Ultrasonic signals have been used for head tracking. The user wears a lightweight headset on which are mounted three signal generators. A detection unit located on the top of the display screen uses the phase difference between the three signals to determine head motion, which is translated into cursor movements. A separate switch operated by the tongue or a suck-puff switch substitutes for the mouse button. Typing is achieved by moving the cursor through a simulated on-screen keyboard and activating the switch at the desired letter. This device can be used even by severely disabled people.

Summary

This chapter has reviewed a number of input devices. Choosing the optimal input device for a task is a complex process that should involve designers, helped by researchers, to analyse a task in detail in relation to the physiological, ergonomic and cognitive characteristics of users.

Many studies have attempted to evaluate various devices in terms of their speed and accuracy for particular tasks and do provide some useful guidelines, particularly for tasks that focus on targeting. The general findings were as follows.

- The touch screen was preferred for applications employing fixed-choice, low-resolution applications (that is, where the area to be selected is large).
- Mice, joysticks, and light pens were preferred for applications requiring quick and accurate selection or manipulation of high-resolution objects (that is, where the object to be selected or manipulated is small).
- There is no clear evidence to support either the mouse, joystick or tracker-ball as being the best high-resolution input device.
- Cursor keys and function keys perform poorly against other input devices.

The tasks used in the experiments and the detailed design of specific input devices have a large effect on the empirical results obtained.

All the devices were compared on either speed, accuracy or subjective preference or a combination of these three measures.

Applications

Electro-mechanical devices still provide the mainstay for human input to information systems and especially computers, be they in the form of keyboards, keypads, or pointing devices. For general-purpose data entry of alphanumeric characters the keyboard remains the most flexible and cost effective option.

Keypads are gaining popularity for specific applications, in particular point-of-sale terminals in retails outlets, where the range of codes that need to be generated is limited by the application. For example, the introduction of bar-code readers in supermarkets has removed the need for all but a numeric keypad with which to enter the item codes that failed the reader. In bars and restaurants the keycaps are labelled with individual drinks or menu items, removing the need for the operator to recall their codes. The current generation of point-of-sale terminals is built around touch-screens and guides the user through the correct sequence of operations for data entry by updating the screen display at each stage.

The growth of GUIs now makes the mouse the second most common input device, providing the user with both continuous entry for cursor motion and discrete entry for option selection. It can be used for all general-purpose applications, such as wordprocessing, spreadsheets and databases, and is especially simple to use for menu and icon selection operations. Perhaps its only disadvantages are the lack of positional accuracy and the additional desk space needed for motion. Some laptop computers employ a small tracker-ball to replace the mouse since it does not require any additional surface area for its operation.

Joysticks and large tracker-balls are preferred for fine detailed applications where precision positioning is important. Dominant applications include CAD, computer animation work, and medical imaging. Other applications take advantage of the fact that neither device requires much working space, for example in aircraft cockpits.

The graphic stylus is another precision input device used for many graphic-intensive applications. However, since the stylus only works in conjunction with its tablet, a large working surface is essential. There is one advantage to this however, and that is the application menus can be located on the tablet, not on the screen, thereby saving scarce display screen for the application.

Light pens used as simple pointers seem to have fallen out of favour with the development of alternative pointing devices. The main reason is that the positional accuracy is determined by the resolution of the display screen, but some concerns have been expressed about the discomfort caused to users. However , pen and pressure-sensitive screen combinations are being developed for other uses. One of these is the pen computer, such as Apple's Newton, which uses a stylus to write directly onto a small liquid crystal display screen. Users interact by writing their instructions which are then converted to the normal ASCII codes. Typical applications include address books, diaries and spreadsheets, although in principle any application could be executed. As with many *natural* input devices, the initial recognition rate of hand-written letters is poor and the user must train the computer to improve performance. Pen and screen combinations have also been applied to user authentication systems. In place of a personal identification number (e.g. the PIN number used with ATMs) these systems record the shape of the signature, the order the strokes are made and the velocity and direction of the pen. The recorded data is then compared to a database of reference signatures and a decision made as to whether access should be permitted or denied.

One of the more interesting input devices is the touch-screen. The majority of users can master control quickly and without prior training, and because it operates over the screen, the display can quickly adapt to show new interactions screens as the dialogue proceeds. The relatively high cost of touch screens and their low resolution has limited their use to those applications intended for casual users. Many public libraries now provide touch-screen based information systems and they are gaining popularity in retail outlets with high staff turnover. The development of touch-screens that can be operated through the security glass of shop fronts has enabled estate and financial agencies to market their wares on the street. For example, the user can be guided through option menus to view properties of interest in selected areas.

23 Visual systems

Introduction

Visual systems play a crucial role in any form of human-computer interaction since a major portion of all output is visual. A typical user of an IT system can spend many hours each day operating with a display screen and as more organisations adopt electronic communications systems (e.g. e-mail and EDI) this type of interaction can only increase.

The display terminal presents a visual user interface, which needs to provide various cues to the interaction dialogue, grab attention when necessary and provide confirmation of the actions initiated.

At the same time the display screen must provide a facsimile of the representation of the information being processed. This is essential for applications such as desktop publishing and graphics design, where the user must be able to preview the printed page. Many word processors now support 'what you see is what you get' (WYSIWYG) screen displays, which again places considerable demands on the user and the technology.

In considering the role of the visual system in the design of the user interface, it is important to have some appreciation of the human visual system and the visual perception mechanisms.

Visual perception

The human visual system is quite remarkable. It is capable of perceiving objects in the brightest of sunlight and in the darkest of night. It can also perceive and follow rapidly moving objects (e.g. flying insects) and rapidly decaying events (e.g. lightning). At the same time there are many things it cannot perceive, such as a bullet in flight, a plant growing, and ultra-violet light. So humans are capable of obtaining information from images varying considerably in quality, size and other characteristics but cannot do so with uniform efficiency across the whole spectrum and at all speeds.

Seeing is an active process in which our view of the world is constructed from both current and historic information. The current information is in front of our eyes and the historic stored in long-term memory. Therefore what we see is not a replica of the world, such as a camera would produce, but rather a construct created by the visual system by transforming, enhancing, distorting and discarding information. The effect is to produce a more constant view of the world than if we were merely to 'see' the images that impinge on our retinas. Hence, when we walk down the street we 'see' buildings as being stationary and people as being approximately the same size and shape, despite the fact that the images that our retinas receive may have radically different positions and shapes. Similarly, the ability to perceive objects on a screen - be they text, graphics, two-dimensional (2-D) or three dimensional (3-D) representations - is as much a result of prior experience as it is fact. Our expectations often transform reality so that we perceive something familiar rather than the unexpected.

Conformance to expectations is something that can be exploited by the user interface designer to both improve the design and avoid the high costs of real-time, real-life displays. For example, in a flight simulator it is less important to deceive pilots into believing that they are flying through real terrain than it is to provide all the necessary information in the right form to allow them to function as if they were in a plane. Furthermore, as you will find in Section 3.3, the visual system can perform certain mental visual tasks such as rotating an imaginary object; this means that realistic real-time image generation is unnecessary for these types of visual task.

Human vision

The visual processing system comprises the eyes and that portion of the brain responsible for the early stages of image processing. The eyes create an inverted image on the retina, a surface of light-sensitive receptors at the back of the eye (see Fig. 23.1) and the brain transposes the image to create our right-way-up world.

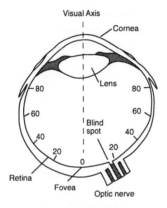

Fig. 23.1 Cross-section through the human eye. The cornea and lens focus light onto the retina. Objects on the visual axis are imaged onto the fovea.

Visible light is the small part of the electromagnetic spectrum to which our eyes are sensitive and is perceived as colours of the rainbow, ranging from short-wavelength blue (400 nanometres (nm)) to long-wavelength red (700 nm). Human perception of brightness and colour depend to a great extent on the intensity and wavelength of the light, but since much of this light is reflected, the properties of the surrounding surfaces also play an important role.

The photoreceptors are of two different types: rods which are very sensitive to light but saturate at high levels of illumination and cones that are less sensitive and so can operate at high luminance levels. Humans have three types of cones, each sensitive to a different range of wavelengths, thereby permitting colour vision.

The majority of the eye's 7 million or so cones are located at the fovea, a small region of the retina (about 0.3 mm in diameter) centred on the visual axis. The high concentration of cones at the fovea means that it is this region of the retina that provides most of the detailed colour information. To see fine detail the eyes, and possibly the head, are moved so that the image is 'fixated' on the fovea.

The 120 million or so rods cover the remaining surface of the retina and provide the peripheral vision. Figure 23.2 shows the density of cones and

Fig. 23.2 The distribution of rods and cones in the retina of a typical left eye

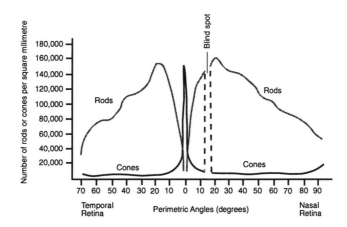

rods on the retina through a cross-section of the eye. The temporal region is that half of the retina closer to the temple, the other half is referred to as the nasal region. The small region of the retina where the optic nerve leaves the eye is devoid of any photoreceptors and so is termed the 'blind-spot'. The retina is also covered by a network of blood vessels, above the photoreceptors, but these do not interfere with imaging since the visual system rapidly ceases to respond to fixed stimuli.

Peripheral vision is almost a hemisphere (about 160 degrees), but the fovea is a mere 1-2 degrees (the angle subtended by a thumbnail at arms length). By comparison the blind spot covers a region of some 5 degrees. The sun and moon subtend angles of about 0.5 degrees.

The visual angle is one measure of determining the image size of different real objects. An object 1 unit high held at a distance of 57 units from the eye produces an image of approximately 1 degree of angle on the retina. Hence the two objects in Fig. 23.3 produce the same size image on the retina.

Fig. 23.3 Retinal image size expressed in terms of visual angle

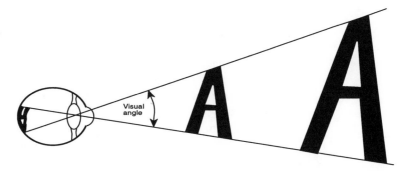

Three-dimensional representations

The real world is three dimensional, a function of stereoscopic vision, so it is not surprising that the growth of computer-generated images should be paralleled with a demand for three-dimensional representations. Flight simulators, CAD systems, virtual reality systems and computer games all demand 3-D images. But as already noted the human visual system does not need a camera-like image, since it can draw from prior experience stored in memory, provided it has the appropriate visual cues.

The most important of these cues relate to depth, and include:

Size: If prior experience suggests that two objects should be the same size (e.g. two adults) then making one deliberately smaller will create the impression that it is further away, as illustrated in Fig. 23.4a. The perception of distance can be enhanced by adding some perspective.

Interposition: If one object partially obscures another then the blocked object is perceived to be behind and beyond the blocking object, as shown in Fig. 23.4b.

Fig. 23.4 Depth cues

a) The objects in the left-hand box are the same size, but displaced vertically to create a sense of depth. Reducing the size of one object, as in the right-hand box, accentuates the sense of depth.

b) Interposition is used in the left-hand box to enhance the sense of depth, compared to the right-hand box which uses vertical displacement

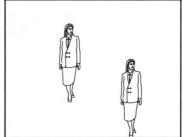

Contrast, clarity and brightness: Sharper and more distinct objects appear to be nearer, and duller objects appear to be further away.

Shadows: Shadows cast by an object provide some cues to the relative position of objects.

Texture: As the apparent distance increases, the texture of a detailed surface becomes less grainy.

Motion parallax: When moving one's head from side to side the objects one sees are displaced at different rates. Objects that are further away appear to move more slowly than objects that are closer. This effect is one of the most important cues that enable us to perceive distances and depth. In screen design, the trick is to move the standpoint of the 'camera' so that the image on the screen moves according to the principles of motion parallax.

The ability to produce apparently 3-D objects on a 2-D screen therefore requires the application of these visual cues. For dynamic representations it is important to ensure that objects on the screen move according to the principles of motion parallax. Sometimes problems arise when using depth cues while trying to make an object appear as real as possible. For example, as the complexity of the displayed image increases, the effectiveness of using brightness as a depth cue decreases. It may therefore be necessary to make compromises depending on the level of realism required.

Colour perception   Colour is all around us. Everywhere we look we see a multitude of natural and artificial colours. The countryside, flowers, hoardings, buildings, decorations, our homes, all have colour which can have powerful effects on and evoke strong emotions in the individual. For the artist the challenge is to capture this in a form that creates mood and atmosphere. For the system designer the challenge is to use colour as a form of coding to display information in the most efficient way.

Unfortunately, many designers new to colour graphics have tried to become artists with disastrous results to the user interface. There is often a tendency to use as many of the available colours as possible and to use highly saturated colours, on the assumption that 'the brighter the better'.

Colour perception is provided by the conical photoreceptors. Some cones are most sensitive to blue light, some to red light and others to green light, but all cones respond to a broad range of wavelengths.

Human perception of colour from a display screen arises from the addition of different wavelengths rather than the subtractive process that occurs with reflected light from painted surfaces. Hence red and green lights stimulate two types of cones and so add to produce the colour we term yellow. Red and green paint reflect red and green light, but filter (i.e. subtract) all the other colours, to produce some shade of brown.

The high density of cones over the fovea provides the best colour vision, whereas their sparcity at the periphery of the retina means that there is almost no colour vision in this region.

Sitting some 50 cm in front of a visual display terminal means that the fovea would encompass a circle of about 9 mm diameter on the surface of the screen. However, assuming good colour vision extends to 10 degrees either side of the visual axis, the circle would increase to about 17.5 cm diameter.

Colour measurement

The three cones of the human eye permit any colour to be specified by a mixture of what are known as primary colours. In the case of television and visual display terminals these primaries (the phosphors) are red, green and blue and are specified by the Commission Internationale l'Eclairage (C.I.E.) Chromaticity diagram shown in Fig. 23.5. This diagram plots the proportion of the red primary against the proportion of green primary. The bottom left-hand corner corresponds to dominance of the blue primary. The points plotted along the curve correspond to discrete wavelengths.

The points R, G, and B correspond to primaries used for the UK PAL colour system and the triangle shows the limits of the colours that can be represented. It can be seen that the PAL system (and hence most visual display terminals) is incapable of displaying much more than 50% of the area of visible colours.

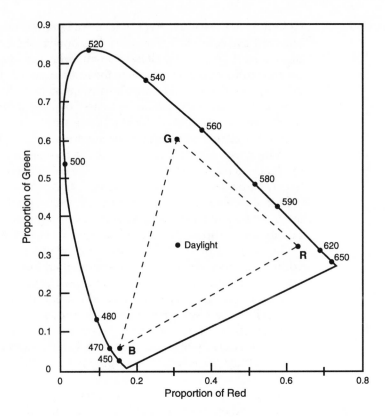

Fig. 23.5 The Commission Internationale l'Eclairage chromaticity chart of 1931

Applications

There are a number of important lessons that can be learnt about the design of user interfaces from an appreciation of the human visual system. A major issue is the quality of the characters and graphics displayed on a screen and how this affects the physical aspects (e.g. brightness and colour), the way the information is displayed (e.g. the composition of icons and size of text) and the need for the display to be safe and not a health hazard.

Physical aspects
Brightness is a subjective description of the illumination that enters the eye from an object: its luminance. The contrast between the luminance of the characters and the background upon which they are displayed is important: if contrast is too high a user will suffer from glare and if it is too low there will be a problem distinguishing characters from one another. Suitable contrast between characters and their background is important. Research suggests that dark characters on a light background produce the optimum contrast. Furthermore, having a light background reduces the possibility of glaring reflections on a screen. Resolution and flicker are other important factors that are determined by the technical design of the display.

Information display
One very important factor is the limitation imposed by the size of the display. Various methods have been developed to overcome this problem,

most notably the use of windowing techniques. They are used to display data or interactions from different applications, different files in the same application or different views of the same file. Windows often include their own menus, dialogue boxes and message boxes.

One of the main advantages of windows is that they provide the user with a means to switch between tasks or to compare data from different sources. Modern software has been designed for windowing environments that permit individual windows to be opened or closed, enlarged or shrunk and moved around with the aid of a pointing device.

Whilst research has shown that users can spend a lot of time manipulating windows (varying sizes to permit as much information to be displayed as possible), it has been found that, once the windows have been set-up on a screen, users complete the job in hand with fewer errors and at least as quickly as in non-windowing environments.

Benefits of colour

There have been some attempts to provide guidelines concerning the use of colours to enhance user-machine interaction. The main findings are summarised below:

Segmentation: Colour is a very powerful way of dividing a display into separate regions. Hence segmentation of a display for detection and search tasks is very useful. In particular, areas that need to be seen as belonging together should have the same colour.

Amount of colour: Too many colours will increase search times, so they should always be used conservatively.

Task demands: Colour is most powerful for search tasks and of little use in tasks requiring identification, categorisation and memorisation of objects.

Experience of user: In comparison with achromatic (black and white) coding, colour has been shown to be of more use in search tasks for inexperienced than for experienced users.

A number of studies have shown that colour has no advantage over a monochromatic display and that alphanumeric coding was superior to colour coding for identification tasks. Other studies have also shown that there is no difference in response time or accuracy for the identification of simple black and white line drawings compared with fully coloured photographic images of the same objects. The implication is that using black and white - particularly for alphanumerics - may be sufficient for the purpose of many tasks. However, colour can be effective as a form of redundant coding. For example, it can provide a further means of alerting the user to a message on a screen which has already been designed to blink when it needs attention. Combining colour with other coding methods, therefore, may facilitate recognition of an object on a screen. It can also be used as a way of cueing the user to look at certain parts of a textual display that are important (similar to the way highlight felt pens are used). It should also be remembered that about eight per cent of the European male population is colour-blind, that is, unable to distinguish between various colours. In addition, therefore, other forms of redundancy such as brightness contrast should be used.

Visual feedback

Visual feedback is important in any screen-based user interface. Users need confirmation of the computer's progress. In particular, a system needs to provide high-quality, timely responses to keep the user informed and feeling in control. This includes providing both information about normal processes and warnings if there is a problem. If feedback is not current, correct or clearly expressed a user may think or do the wrong thing. Moreover, if there is no feedback the user will be left wondering what is happening and may feel control has been lost.

Visual feedback can take many forms such as textual error messages, error windows, or just an icon. It may also employ colours or graphical symbols. The form of feedback should be related to the application domain, so one might reasonably expect the feedback from a control system to differ from that of a word processor.

Dialogue and confirmation boxes may be used to ask users if they are sure they want to quit files without saving them or if they really want to delete files. Icons can be used to provide dynamic feedback (e.g. the hourglass icon used in Microsoft's Windows) informing the user of the current state of the object that the icon represents.

24 Speech systems

Introduction

The idea of speaking to a computer holds strong appeal to many information system users. It is a 'normal' means of communication and something humans are very adept at understanding and it has been shown that when two people co-operate on solving a problem they are about twice as efficient when they talk to each other as when they use other means of communication, such as handwriting, typing or visual signalling. It could relieve people from having to use a keyboard or concentrate on a visual display for long periods of time. It also frees an operator's hands (in, say, sorting or inspection operations) from having to set switches, etc. Instead, users can issue spoken instructions to the machine whilst continuing with other tasks without overloading their cognitive processors.

Another advantage of speech is that it allows us to be freer and more natural in our communication of ideas and information. Users can employ various linguistic cues such as voice tone, rhythm, the rise and fall of pitch, pauses and volume to impart different information. The same words can appear dominating, friendly, submissive, questioning, or bored, simply by varying some of these cues. However, they can cause problems when communicating with computer systems.

Speech also offers the opportunity for a physically disabled users to communicate with computer systems easily and quickly. However the natural conversations portrayed in numerous science-fiction films is a long way from the reality of present systems.

Speech communication does though presuppose an ability to accept spoken information (*speech input*) and to produce comprehensible audible information (*speech output*). A number of techniques have been developed to enable people to use speech as direct input to computer-based systems, such as expert systems (see p. 165) or industrial automata. Computer-generated speech is already a feature of many commercially available information technology products. Eventually, both voice input and output are likely to be provided in information systems.

Speech input and output present a different set of problems to the information technologist. Therefore, we shall take them separately, looking at the less difficult task of voice output first.

Human speech

Extensive research has shown that at the simplest level the human vocal system can be modelled as a series of acoustic resonators excited by a variable frequency sound source. The vocal chords provide the source, vibrating rhythmically to produces puffs of air which travel up the larynx. The frequency of vibration determines the pitch of the voice The resonators are the upper part of the larynx and the mouth and nasal cavities. The resonant frequencies of these cavities filter the source's spectrum by variable attentuation of the harmonics. The resulting peaks are termed the *formants*. Sounds produced by the vocal chords are referred to as *voiced* sounds.

The shape and size of the cavities can be modified by the position of the tongue, jawbone and lips. This is illustrated in Fig. 24.1, which shows a section through the vocal tract for three vowel sounds, together with the corresponding fundamental and formant frequency peaks.

Fig. 24.1 Vocal tract positions and transfer functions for three english vowels

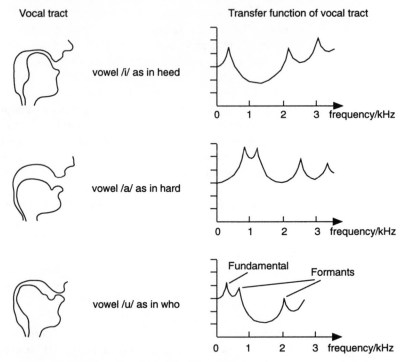

Some sounds to not utilise the vocal chords, for example the 'sh' sound at the beginning of ship, and the 'p' sound at the end. These are produced by turbulent air-flow over the teeth or by explosive release of air through the lips, and are referred to as *unvoiced* sounds.

The variable filter model formed the basis for many of the early developments of speech synthesisers, and even modern systems work on the basis of calculating pitch and pitch amplitude (or for unvoiced sounds the noise and noise amplitude), and the centre frequencies and bandwidths of the first four formants. These parameters are typically updated at about 10 ms intervals.

Human hearing

The auditory system is a remarkable device, able to cope with an enormous dynamic range (some 120 dB) and a bandwidth stretching from 20 Hz to 20 kHz for a young person. The ear is most sensitive to frequencies in the range 1 - 2 kHz.

At the simplest level the ear behaves as a bank of overlapping quarter octave band-pass filters with tunable centre frequencies to maximise the extraction of information from the audible signal. The quarter-octave bandwidth ensures good resolution at low frequencies and yet adequate temporal resolution at higher frequencies. This provides the basis of a good speech processor, since the vocal system output is coded by a combination of spectrum envelope and short-term temporal co-ordination.

Speech output

For speech output to be successful it is important to understand the various aspects of natural speech production, such as grammatical structure, context and its effect on tone and intonation, and how a listener is able to understand a speaker's intentions by interpreting clues such as changes in tone. There are two main techniques of computer-controlled speech generation in current use: synthesis by *concatenation* and synthesis by *rule*.

Concatenation simply means the linking together and replay of previously recorded complete words and phrases. Segments of human speech are recorded digitally and later reassembled and played back to produce the desired words and sentences. In other words, the computer has recordings of basic words and sentences in its (limited) vocabulary and it can manipulate these recordings to produce desired results. A well-known example is the speaking clock service offered on many large telephone systems: there the 'message' is made up of a limited number of stored phrases, put together automatically to form complete sentences.

The main problem with this technique is its unwieldiness for general applications where the number of words and sentences may approach the contents of a full-size dictionary. Also, since usually only one version of a word or phrase is stored, this precludes the variations of stress and intonation normally expected in natural speech. The method has, however, been used successfully in cases where few phrases are used to produce many similar messages. Examples include the speaking clock and British Telecom's star services, which provide routine information such as details about changed telephone numbers and call diversions. The method has also been used with various warning systems. Concatenation tends to be limited to applications requiring small vocabularies of fewer than 200 words.

Synthesis by rule overcomes these problems, but at the expense of complexity. Synthesis here refers to the assembly of words from their constituent elements, the *phonemes*. (There are about 45 of these in the English language, but other languages have a different number of different phonemes.)

In synthesis by rule, the computer stores a large number of empirical rules: to convert text to phonemes, phonemes to parameters of a model of the human vocal tract, and finally the parameters to voice. The parameters determine features like pitch and loudness of the elementary components of speech, and ensure the smooth transition from one to another. The method has the potential of producing a much larger range of responses than speech produced by concatenation. It also allows for pitch and tone to be varied. Even so, the speech produced can sound somewhat synthetic. Systems employing synthesis by rule may offer up to 64 phonemes on a single integrated circuit.

The acceptability of computer-generated speech is greatly influenced by the quality of voice used. It is important, therefore, that the right amount of assertiveness, agreeableness, warmth and so on appears in the output.

Speech input

The development of speech input systems can be regarded as a continuum, with devices that have a limited vocabulary and recognise only single words at one end of the spectrum and systems that attempt to understand natural speech at the other. All speech input systems start with the conversion of speech to computer-compatible form. This is a difficult enough problem because speech is represented by a complex, rapidly varying electronic signal, which gives rise to a vast amount of data to process. The task does not stop here. The challenging part comes in matching the spoken utterance to one of a wide range of possible, pre-stored words, phrases or sentences. This problem is made more difficult by the signals corresponding to a particular utterance being different from speaker to speaker, or even changing for the same speaker, when he or she is suffering from a cold, when in a highly emotional state, when very tired, etc. Moreover, an utterance does not necessarily correspond to one word or one sentence. Some people tend to run the words of a sentence together. So, the majority of speech recognition systems require the speaker to pronounce words with definite pauses between them, and are referred to as *isolated word recognition systems.*

Continuous speech recognition systems are capable of recognising single words within strings of words by segmenting the speech on the basis of its acoustical features (see Fig. 24.2).

As with the processing of visual images, there are two main techniques in use for the processing of digitized speech signals: template matching and feature identification.

In the first case, words can be identified by the 'brute force' method of matching their complete acoustic signal against a stored set of these. The stored set, which can comprise tens of thousands of signal patterns, can be generalised for a wide range of speakers. Better performance, however, is obtained when the set is small and when it is 'tuned' to a particular speaker. This is achieved by the speaker recording all the possible words which the computer will later be called upon to recognise. Even so, speech input systems employing this technique are often better at identifying a speaker, than the words pronounced by that speaker. This becomes a useful facility in applications such as the verification of bank account holders inquiring about the details of their account over the telephone. To set up the system, the account holder must first pronounce some words over the telephone, which are then stored and used later for identification on the basis of the voice pattern. This facility has been demonstrated by Bell Laboratories in the United States.

Alternatively, acoustical features can be extracted from the voice signal and these matched, by the computer, against stored sets of statistical characteristics of human speech, such as the transition between phonemes. Here the emphasis is on the identification of sequences of sounds, rather than of individual phonemes. Systems employing this approach have been able to recognise correctly 96% of words, selected from a 1000-word vocabulary, even though these were spoken by different persons.

The improvement of the 'speaker-independence' of the recognition process is still one of the main objectives of research, together with the increase of the size of the vocabulary, the recognition of fluently spoken words in a realistic environment, that may include background noise and

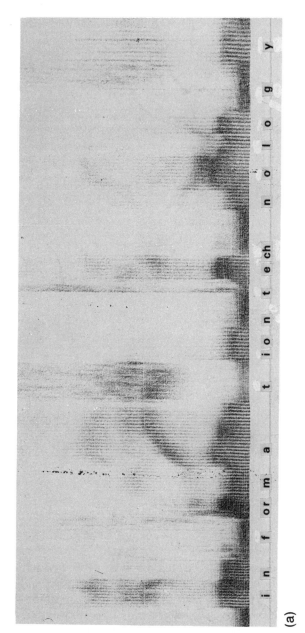

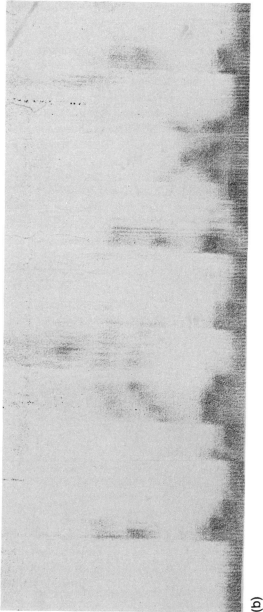

Fig. 24.2 Sonagrams of (a) a male and (b) a female voice uttering the phrase 'information technology'. The opening and closing of the vocal chords are visible as vertical striations for the male voice but, because the pitch is higher, not for the female voice. The formants (concentrations of energy at a particular frequency corresponding to the resonances of the vocal tract) are at a higher frequency for the female voice because the vocal tract is shorter. The frequency scale (vertical) is 0–6 kHz, and the time scale (horizontal) is 2.4 s. (Dr W.A. Ainsworth, University of Keele)

'co-articulation'. More recently, researchers have placed a greater emphasis on 'speech understanding' systems, as opposed to the earlier 'speech recognition' systems. The distinction lies in the type of information that is used to aid the processing of speech signals.

As Fig. 24.3 shows, the 'speech understanding' approach brings to bear many more levels of knowledge about language on the interpretation of utterances. Speech recognition systems usually rely on the bottom two – phonetics and phonology, or the characteristics of speech sounds, and their variability between individuals.

Prosodics is concerned with the stress and intonation patterns of speech. Lexical knowledge operates at the word level, and includes vocabularies and the rules of formation of structures like plurals, tenses, etc.

Fig. 24.3 Kinds of knowledge employed in speech understanding

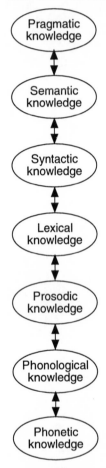

The size of vocabulary is an important characteristic of a speech processing system: most commercial systems are currently restricted to a few hundred words; research systems to a few thousand. In contrast, 'The Times' uses about 27,000 words, and an educated person is estimated to have an 80,000-word vocabulary.

Syntactic knowledge supplies the grammatical structure of a language, including the rules for the correct combination of words into phrases and sentences. At the next level, semantics is concerned with the meaning of words and sentences, while pragmatics provides information on subject context at the conversation level. At its broadest, it incorporates a knowledge of the world.

The power of human speech understanding probably relies on bringing in as much of this vast array of information as is necessary to identify utterances. The difficulty facing artificial speech recognition and understanding systems is how to collect, codify and then exploit all this knowledge in a reliable, fast and low-cost system.

Sound output
Closely associated with speech systems are the growing number of so-called *sound cards* developed for multi-media personal computers. The features offered typically include stereo recording and playback and a multi-voice digital synthesiser. Recording and playback can be performed with 8 or 16 bit samples at rates up to 44.1 kHz, the sampling rate of CD-Audio. A low-level input is provided for dynamic microphone together with a standard line-input (1 volt) for other signal sources. Many cards also feature a connector for external synthesisers that employ the music industry digital interface (MIDI), a serial transmission protocol for controlling the channels of the synthesiser.

Sound cards are generally used for digital speech and music recording and playback, for example, to support voice-mail applications, or speech and music accompaniment to multi-media presentations and computer-assisted learning. However, a number of cards are now sold with speech recognition and synthesis software.

In general the software provides for isolated utterance recognition for a trained voice, since the software makes no distinction between words, phrases or very short sentences. One such product enables the user to train the system to recognise all the commands needed to interact with a menu, including those needed to control the position of the cursor.

The speech synthesis option uses the synthesis-by-rule technique to convert text to phonemes and phonemes to digital codes that can be output via the sound card. This provides the flexibility to convert any text to speech, but with a somewhat synthetic quality. The greatest difficulty when used in conjunction with GUIs is knowing where to locate the text to be spoken. One solution is to use the same mechanism employed for exchanging data between windows, so that any data arriving in the exchange buffer is automatically spoken.

In addition to their role of speech recognition and synthesis, sound cards can also be used to provide the user with audible feedback on their interaction with the computer. Pre-recorded voice messages or synthetic sounds can be used for alarms and beeps for attracting attention or giving guidance on what action to initiate.

Designers of video games have also realised that sound can be used to good effect. Successful moves are often acknowledged by bell-like sounds, whereas failing to score or make a correct move may result in loud noises with low tones. An interesting use of sound is the auditory icon, a way of providing information about system objects. These are essentially sound caricatures of an object. For example, when an electronic message arrives at a user's electronic mailbox an auditory icon that sounds like a letter coming through a letterbox can be produced by the system to inform the user of the presence of a new message. Moreover, the loudness of the sound can indicate to the user how large the message is.

Applications

The potential applications for speech input are enormous, especially those which free the user's hands to execute other tasks. The examples described here are simply indicative of those already marketed, but new ones appear every day.

Automated materials handling using speech input has been in use for some time. Generally, only one operator is involved and the vocabulary is limited, which allows for more accuracy. An advantage of using speech input for handling materials is that it speeds up the process, since one operator can simultaneously do the jobs of identifying the material and directing it. With manual input an operator has to identify an item's location and key in its destination using a keypad while passing along the materials. In the past this has often required two operators working together.

In most *quality control* tasks an operator's eyes or hands or both are occupied in the task itself; the operator handles materials and selects faulty ones as they pass along a conveyor belt. Speech input could be used to instruct the system to remove a faulty item that has been identified.

Speech input for *security* purposes generally takes the form of a person speaking some pre-arranged phrase which the system then verifies by comparing the newly input phrase with previously stored information about the required message and that person's individual vocal characteristics.

In communication, the *retrieval of information* from computerised data-bases over the telephone would be aided by voice-communication equipment. This would both accept spoken inquiries and answer in natural language.

Speech input for *direct computer control* has several potential uses. Among other things, it has been used for programming tasks, for providing instructions on the factory floor, and by pilots to choose among a limited number of entry paths. For example, in mail sorting, the sorter simply tells the computer the destination of an item on a conveyor belt, and that item is automatically directed into the appropriate slot. In car assembly, the list of faults on a particular car can be produced by verbal identification as the inspector examines the car at the end of the production line. In office, commercial and financial applications, voice communication can be a means of data entry to other, computerised equipment – such as ordering and despatch of goods in a remote-sales operation (e.g. mail-order).

There have been a number of specialised speech input devices developed for people with disabilities. One example is a control device that responds to vocalised requests made anywhere within a house (e.g. using voice commands to dim the lights or raise the temperature) and also to commands made over a precoded telephone line.

Another interesting development is the Voice-Operated Database Inquiry System (VODIS), which is a joint research project carried out by British Telecom, Logica (Cambridge) Ltd and the University of Cambridge. The objective of the project was to design a prototype that could eventually be used by ordinary telephone users to obtain train timetable information about the departure and arrival times of specific trains suitable for their personal travel requirements. VODIS uses a continuous speech recogniser that accepts naturally spoken words and phrases and passes them to a dialogue controller which interprets the received speech using knowledge of the application domain. Erroneous matches have occurred when users respond with more than one word at a time. To overcome this problem the questioning was worded so that people were constrained to respond in a restricted way from the outset.

IBM has launched a new speech recognition product, referred to as the Personal Dictation System. The combined hardware and software package runs under OS/2 and is intended to support everyday applications such as wordprocessing and spreadsheets. Like most recognition systems the user must work through a lengthy training sequence, but sentences are used rather than individual words. This permits the software to learn much more about the user's pronounciation style and build up a more comprehensive recognition database. Operating at the sentence level also enables the system to use the context of the words, and hence improve the accuracy when similar sounding words occur (e.g. bear or bare). Although the product name implies limited functionality, the product will in fact permit interaction with OS/2 and any other application.

Speech output is of growing importance in automatic announcement systems, for example, the next generation of digital telephone exchanges will employ it to inform users about the facilities available and to supplement existing information services. In some makes of cars, concatenation techniques have been used to replace warning indicators with 'talking' equivalents (e.g. for low fuel level, or when the statutory speed limit is exceeded).

Similar hazard warning functions can be found on the shop floor or as part of a security system, or in civil aircraft. For example, pilots flying on international routes sometimes have problems in understanding weather reports spoken in heavily accented English. A speech-output system has been used to convert weather data into a consistent English accent.

In health care, voice output has an important role to play in reading devices for the blind, and as an aid for those with speech-production difficulties. Voice input and output would help blind people to interact with any computer-based equipment having these facilities.

In education, voice input and output can perform a useful role in language learning and translation. Devices are already available for checking spelling and for speaking a limited set of sentences in a variety of languages (intended primarily for people who travel to foreign countries). In domestic and consumer applications, there is already a range of electronic games, appliances and personal computer systems equipped with voice output. The applications, often not more than gimmicks, fulfil roles like announcements, operating instructions, audible warnings, etc. Voice input has also started to make an appearance in simple control operations for domestic electronic equipment. The mass market for such relatively trivial uses stimulates and supports work for other applications.

An example of the use of synthesised speech is the Carin navigation system produced by Philips, which is being developed as a driving aid.

Before starting a journey, while the car is stationary a driver is provided with a route map on which his specified destination is shown. As soon as the car starts to move, the map disappears so that the driver is not distracted and speech output is used to instruct the driver where to go. For example, on approaching a roundabout the driver might be told to 'take the second exit, which is marked Eindhoven'.

Much further into the future are 'multi-lingual systems' which act as combined 'voice input to machine translation to voice output' computers. A caller in England, for example, could speak in English, yet a counterpart in Japan would hear the message spoken in Japanese, and vice versa. (Trial versions of such a system have already been built.) Much nearer in the future are voice-activated automatic diallers for car telephones.

25 Health and safety

Introduction

The growth of information systems has changed many peoples daily work patterns. More than 45% of the population is involved to some degree in information processing and much of this will involve interaction with keyboards, screens and other input and output devices. Electronic mail systems have replaced chats in the corridor or telephone calls, so the average information worker of today is much more sedentary than his counterpart of ten years ago. The result appears to be a growth in the number of work-related health problems, especially those linked to eyesight, back pain and wrist injuries. Trade unions have expressed concerns about this trend for many years, but it is only recently that national governments have responded. In some cases the response was a direct reaction to fears about specific equipment, such as the potential risk of miscarriage associated with visual display users.

Europe has led the world for formulating policy towards alleviating the stresses and strains of the information worker. European Directive 270/89/EEC is intended to improve the design of new computer products and the offices in which they will be used, whereas Directive 89/391/EEC covers broader issues of health and safety at work. National and international standards are also emerging, such as BS 7179 and ISO 9241.

In the UK the Health and Safety Executive is repsonsible for enforcing health and safety at work legislation and that most pertinent to human-computer interaction is the Health and Safety (Display Screen Equipment) Regulations 1992. The regulations came in to force on 1st January 1993 and are the UK's implementation of European Directive 89/270/EEC.

Aspects of work covered include: analysis of a user's needs; eyesight testing and the provision of corrective glasses; work planning to permit breaks from the screen and keyboard; and the provision of health and safety training.

There has been considerable debate as to the reality of injuries arising from DSE work, especially the so-called repetitive strain injury (RSI). However, this year (1994) a legal secretary was awarded £40,000 in a claim for compensation and damages arising from RSI by the Mayor's and City of London Court.

Analysis of needs

Employers have a legal responsibility to analyse the working environment relating to display screen equipment for all employees covered by the DES regulations. This covers all employees who habitually use a display screen as part of their normal daily work. Employers must also ensure that new equipment complies with the regulations immediately and that older equipment is upgraded by 1996.

In addition to the equipment requirements, the analysis must consider the suitability of the furniture for the work undertaken, the lighting conditions, the noise levels and the actual work pattern. If any of these are found to be deficient, the employer must remedy the situation by supplying suitable furniture or take remedial action to improve the work environment.

Employees may request eyesight screening, and if necessary an eyesight test, with costs reimbursed by the employer. Employers must also bear the costs of any corrective devices recommended by these tests.

Daily work routines

An important element of the regulations is to ensure that the work undertaken by all DSE users is planned in such a way as to permit breaks or changes of activity. Whilst the number and duration of these breaks is not specified, it is stated that short, frequent ones are better than longer, less frequent ones. The rationale behind this recommendation is to prevent the onset of fatigue.

Many jobs have natural breaks or pauses and whenever possible DSE work should be planned to take advantage of these breaks. Secretaries, for example, may break-off DSE work to answer the phone or respond to some other query. Other staff might combine their DSE work with meetings or on-site visits to clients. This will help to prevent fatigue and vary the visual and mental demands of the employee.

Those jobs requiring only data or text entry and sustained attention and concentration must have deliberate breaks or pauses introduced.

Any activity that would demand broadly similar use of the arms or hands should be avoided during breaks. Similarly, if the display screen work is visually demanding, any activities during breaks should be of a different visual character. Breaks should also allow users to vary their posture. Exercise routines which include blinking, stretching and focusing eyes on distant objects can be helpful.

Since breaks and activity changes are intended to prevent fatigue it is important that they are taken during performance peaks rather than during quiet intervals. Furthermore, the breaks are to be regarded as part of working time, not part of the employees' contracted refreshment time.

The main hazards

The introduction of computer terminals and personal computers has been associated with a number of problems related to the visual system and working posture and are often reflected in various types of bodily fatigue. Most can be readily prevented by applying simple ergonomic principles to the design, selection and installation of equipment, the design of the working environment, and the organisation of the task.

Upper limb pains and discomfort

A range of conditions of the hand, wrist, arm, shoulder and neck have been linked to display screen work activities and are now described as *work related upper limb disorders* (WRULD). These range from temporary fatigue and soreness of part of the upper limb girdle to chronic soft tissue disorders such as:

Peritendonitis or tenosynovitis this is inflammation of the lining of the tendons or tendon sheaths.

Carpal tunnel syndrome this is a condition where the median nerve

	gets squashed by soft tissue swelling in the carpal tunnel as it runs across the wrist into the hand. The symptoms are often felt as pins and needles and a shooting pain of an electric shock quality in some of the fingers.
Tennis or Golfer's elbow	this is severe pain at one or other of the bony points on the inside (golfer's) or outside (tennis) of the elbow. This is where the muscles that turn the forearm inwards and outwards are inserted. The area affected is very tender.
Ulnar neuritis	the ulnar nerve passes in a groove behind the inside bony point at the elbow and sometimes it can get irritated and inflamed at this point, causing pain and pins and needles down the arm and into some of the fingers.

The triggers to the upper limb symptoms can be difficult to evaluate. Studies suggest that the frequency and repetitiveness of keying rates is not always a factor. Quite often a combination of factors is probably associated with the onset of symptoms. Keeping the limbs, back, neck and shoulders in one position for long periods of time (static posture) is associated with musculo-skeletal problems. Awkward positioning of the hands and wrists are further likely triggering factors. For example, poor working techniques or an inappropriate work height may cause the wrists to be bent at an angle which, over a period of time, causes symptoms. Poor positioning of the hand and fingers on a mouse may cause discomfort after a period of time. Quite often the outbreak of soft tissue disorders in the upper limb among keyboard workers is associated with high workloads combined with tight deadlines. In addition to repetition and long periods of static posture required in these circumstances there is the overall stress of getting the job completed and this stress on its own increases muscle tension.

Eye and eyesight effects
There is no medical evidence to suggest that using display screen equipment damages eyes or eyesight; nor that it make existing defects worse. A few users with existing vision defects may become more aware of their problem and a few may need adjustments to their prescription lenses. The focusing muscles of the eye can also suffer from static posture effects if the eye is held focused at one distance for long periods of time. Prolonged focusing on a screen can also reduce the blinking rate of a user and this can lead to a drying of the front of the eye leaving them sore and feeling prickly. Reduced eye and head movement may also lead to headaches and pains in the limbs and back.

Uncorrected visual defects can make work with display screen equipment more tiring or stressful than should otherwise be the case and that is why it is important to have regular eye checks.

Fatigue and stress

Many symptoms described by display screen users reflect stresses arising from their work. They may be secondary to upper limb, back or visual problems, but they are more likely to be caused by poor work planning, lack of sufficient self-control of the work by the user, under-utilisation of skills, high-speed repetitive working or social isolation. The risks of DSE users experiencing physical fatigue and stress can be minimised, however, by careful design, selection and disposition of display screen equipment; good design of the user's workplace, environment and tasks; and training, consultation and involvement of the user.

Other health concerns

Epilepsy

Display screen equipment has not been known to induce epileptic seizures. People suffering from the very rare (1 in 10,000 population) photosensitive epilepsy who react adversely to flickering lights and patterns find they can work safely with display screens. People with epilepsy who are concerned about display screen work should seek further advice from their medical adviser.

Facial dermatitis

Some DSE users have reported facial skin complaints such as occasional itching or reddened skin on the face and/or neck. These complaints are relatively rare and the limited evidence available suggests they may be associated with environmental factors, such as low relative humidity or static electricity near the DSE.

Electro-magnetic radiation

Anxiety about radiation emissions from display screen equipment and possible effects on pregnant women has been widespread. However, there is substantial evidence that these concerns are unfounded.

The levels of ionising and non-ionising electromagnetic radiation which are likely to be generated by display screen equipment are well below those set out in recommendations for limiting risk to human health.

Effects on pregnant women

There has been considerable public concern about reports of higher levels of miscarriage and birth defects among some groups of DSE users, in particular due to electromagnetic radiation. Many scientific studies have been carried out, but taken as a whole their results do not show any link between miscarriages or birth defects and working with DSE.

Preventative actions

Many of the health and safety concerns of DSE users can be eliminated by taking simple precautions before and during work intervals, in particular ensuring that equipment and furniture are properly positioned and comfortable. Fig. 25.1 illustrates the relative positioning of the user, the DSE, and other furniture for typical office tasks. The best general guidelines for DSE users are:

Seating	a chair providing height adjustment and variable position backrest is recommended to ensure a proper viewing height and good support to the lumbar region of the lower back.

Arms	should be roughly horizontal and the desk surface have sufficient space to rest the wrists when not keying.
Legs	space under the desk should be adequate to permit free movement of the legs and chair height adjusted to prevent undue pressure on the backs of the legs and knees.
Screen position	the eyeline should be approximately level with the top of the screen and the screen tilted so as to provide an *angle of gaze* of about 15 degrees.
Reading position	items to be read whilst viewing the screen should be held at the same height as the screen, to avoid awkward movement of the neck.

Fig. 25.1 Seating and posture for typical office tasks

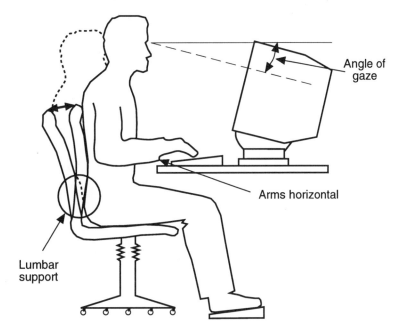

Poor lighting and glare from natural or artificial lighting can also lead to eye fatigue and so screens should be positioned to minimise the problem. Special anti-glare screens are available to attach to the front of display screens. Glare from windows should be eliminated by the use of curtains or blinds, or by adjusting the orientation of the DSE.

"Lighting should be appropriate for all the tasks performed at the workstation, e.g. reading from the screen, keyboard work, reading printed text, writing on paper etc. General lighting, by artificial or natural light, or a combination, should illuminate the entire room to an adequate standard. Any supplementary individual lighting provided to cater for personal needs or a particular task should not adversely affect visual conditions at nearby workstations." (Extract from Health and Safety (Display Screen Equipment) Regulations 1992)

General reading on information technology

Books

Antonelli, C. (1992) *The Economics of Information Networks*, North Holland.

Black, U. (1994) *Emerging Communications Technologies*, Prentice Hall.

Carter, R. (1989). *Students' Guide to Information Technology*, Heinemann Newnes.

Cawkell, A.E. (ed.) (1987). *Evolution of an Information Society*, Aslib.

Chester, M. (1993) *Neural Networks*, Prentice Hall.

Clifton, H.D. and Sutcliffe, A.G. (1994) *Business Information Systems*, 5th edition, Prentice Hall.

Dordick, H.S. (1993). *The Information Society*, Sage.

Eberts, R.E. (1993) *User Interface Design*, Prentice Hall.

Ford, W. (1994) *Computer Communications Security*, Prentice Hall.

Fulk, J.and Steinfield, C. (1990) *Organizations and Communication Technology*, Sage.

Gagliardi, R.M. (1990) *Satellite Communications*, Van Nostrand Reinhold.

Heap, N. (1993) *An Introduction to OSI*, Blackwell Scientific.

Holtham, C. (1992) *Executive Information Systems and Decision Support*, Chapman Hall.

Jeffcote, J. (1994) *Multimedia in Practice*, Prentice Hall.

Kehoe, B.P. (1994) *Zen and the Art of the Internet*, 3rd edition, Prentice Hall.

Longley, D. and Shain, M. (1989). *Dictionary of Information Technology*, third edition, Macmillan.

Mansell, R. (1993). *A Political Economy of Network Evolution*, Sage.

Martin, J., Chapman, K.K. and Leben, J. (1994) *Local Area Networks*, 2nd edition, Prentice Hall.

Mickelson, A.R. (1992) *Guided Wave Optics*, Van Nostrand Reinhold.

Ostram, C. (1994) *Video Compression*, Van Nostrand Reinhold.

Shute, J. (1994) *Parallel Computer Architecture*, Prentice Hall.

Steinfield, C., Bauer, J. and Caby, L. (1993). *Telecommunications in Transition*, Sage.

Periodicals

European journal of information systems. Macmillan.

Information economics and policy. North-Holland.

Information society. Crane Russak.

Information technology and public policy. Longman.

Information technology for development. Oxford University Press.

Information technology: research and development. Butterworths.

Information technology training. Longmans.

Information technology yearbook. Century.

Journal of information technology. Chapman Hall.

Telematics and informatics. Pergamon.

Glossary

amplitude	The maximum value of a signal above its mid-point is called its amplitude. For a sine-wave signal, the amplitude is equal to the maximum deviation of the wave from 0.
amplitude modulation	A method of transmitting a message by varying the amplitude of a carrier signal in response to the amplitude of the message signal.
analogue	(signal) A signal that is continuously variable over its full range of values. For example, the electrical output of a telephone microphone is an analogue voltage signal.
article number	A unique numeric code allocated to an item to be sold. It can be reproduced in a form which can be read automatically, e.g. as a bar code. In Europe, numbers are allocated by the European Article Numbering Association.
artificial intelligence	The formalization of procedures in a computer program to carry out tasks which, if they were done by a human, would be regarded as intelligent.
ASCII	American Standard Code for Information Interchange. An internationally accepted binary code for representing alphabetic, numerical and special control characters.
asynchronous transmission	A transmission protocol in which each character is transmitted in its own timeframe, independent of all other characters that are transmitted. The receiver detects the start and end of each individual character by means of additional bits, known as the start and stop bits.
attenuation	A reduction in amplitude or power of a signal in the process of its transmission.
audio-conferencing	More than two people, in different locations, communicating by voice via the telephone system.
automated teller machines (ATM)	Machines at banks and building societies which provide for cash withdrawals, deposits, payment of bills, transfer of funds between accounts and account balance enquiries.
band	In telecommunications a band is the range of frequencies between two defined limits, e.g. the human ear can hear frequencies in the range 20 Hz to 20 kHz, and this is described as the audible band of frequencies.
bandwidth	The bandwidth of a telecommunications system is the maximum range of frequencies transmitted by the system without significant loss of signal amplitude.

bar code	A code in the form of a series of parallel lines of varying widths printed on paper which is used to enter data into a computer in conjunction with a bar code reader.
base-band	Transmission of signals without modulation.
baud rate	This is a measure of the signalling speed of a digital telecommunications system. In the special case of a binary system, one bit of data is transmitted during each signalling period, hence the baud rate is numerically equal to the bit rate. In the case of a non-binary system, the bit rate is given by the product of the number of bits per signal interval and the number of signalling intervals per second.
binary digital signal	A signal having only two possible values.
binary words/codes	A group or combination of bits used within a computer or telecommunications system to represent the various types of data. The number of bits in the word, or code, determines the number of unique items that can be coded. For example, a 2-bit code can represent four items using the binary patterns 00, 01, 10, 11. The general rule is that an n-bit code can generate 2^n unique patterns.
bit	An abbreviation for binary digit, of which there are two, 0 and 1.
broadband signalling	A signal transmission method in which a data signal is used to modulate a high-frequency carrier, which requires that the transmission channel has a wide bandwidth (i.e. broadband).
broadcasting	1 In communications, the simultaneous transmission of data to several different receivers. 2 In radio communications, the transmission of sound and vision programmes via radio waves for general reception.
bus	One or a group of conductors which serves as a common connection between related devices.
byte	A binary code comprising 8 bits. The byte is commonly used as the unit of measurement for data storage capacity (e.g. for memory and disk storage).
CAD	Computer-Aided Design. Two- and three-dimensional designs are produced on a computer screen where they can be quickly and easily modified.
capacity	1 In a telecommunications system the capacity of a transmission channel (e.g. a telephone trunk) is a measure of the number of individual messages or calls that can be carried by the system simultaneously. 2 In a computer system it is the measure of the quantity of information that can be processed per unit of time or stored on disc or tape.
carrier	In communications, a continuous frequency signal capable of being modulated or impressed with a second signal carrying information.
CCITT	Comité Consultatif International Téléphonique et Télégraphique is an international organisation of national telecommunications authorities responsible for standardising telecommunications.

CD-ROM	Compact discs used for read-only data storage.
cellular radio	A means of providing a mobile radio telephone service in which an open channel for a call is found automatically by computer. Low-power transmitters mean that the same frequency can be used by different calls a short distance apart.
channel	A path along which signals may be sent, either in a computer or in a telecommunications system.
channel capacity	In telecommunications, channel capacity is the maximum volume at which information can be transmitted over a particular channel.
character	Any letter, number, punctuation mark or special graphic symbol used in text or processed by a computer.
chip	In microelectronics, a chip is an integrated circuit on a wafer of silicon, or other semiconductor, together with its protective packaging and circuit connections.
CIM	Computer Integrated Manufacture. The use of computing and communications hardware and software to plan, co-ordinate, monitor and control the totality of manufacturing activities within a firm.
circuit switched	In telecommunications, a circuit-switched link is one made between two terminals by way of a series of switching centres, trunk links and local links.
client-server architecture	A design for distributed information systems that focuses upon the user as a client of a server process or system.
CNC	Computer Numerical Control. Enhanced NC machines which have a programmable computer built into them giving them greater flexibility.
coaxial cable	A cable consisting of a conductor surrounded by, and protected from, a tube of braided copper. They are used in long-distance telephone lines and to connect LANs and WANs.
codec	Coder-decoder. Converts analogue data into a digital signal for transmission and re-converts after reception.
cognitive psychology	The study of how information is processed and represented in the mind.
collision	A condition when, in a packet-switched network, two packets are being transmitted at the same time rendering both of them unintelligible.
command	A string of characters input to a system that causes an action to be performed.
communication network	A collection of interconnected items of equipment which provides a telecommunication service among the terminals connected to it.
compact disc/CD	A disc storing data in digital form which is read by a laser and reproduced either as music, video pictures or data for a computer.
computer conferencing	The equivalent of a telephone conference, but one that uses a computer network. The input is written rather than spoken. Response can be immediate or delayed, as the material remains stored in the network.

computer-mediated communication	Systems which allow people to communicate with one another easily using local area and wide area networks.
computer network	A network of interconnected computer systems that allows data to be transferred between them.
contention	In networking, a contention occurs when two nodes attempt to use the same communication channel at the same time.
CSMA/CD	Carrier Sense Multiple Access with Collision Detection. When networks operate using a carrier sense multiple access method, two or more nodes can start to transmit simultaneously thereby causing collisions. With the addition of collision detection each node continues to listen as it transmits and, if it detects a collision, it ceases to transmit.
data	Facts, concepts or instructions presented in a formalized way which can be communicated, interpreted or processed by human or automatic means.
data multiplexer	A data multiplexer uses time-division multiplexing to enable several terminals, operating at a low data rate, to share the same telecommunications channel, thereby utilizing the full capacity of the channel.
data network	A network designed to transfer data between different computer systems.
data protection	The protection of personal data, in particular, which is stored in computer systems. Data protection legislation aims to ensure that any personal data held on computer is accurate, up to date and open to inspection by the subject of the data.
data subject	The person about whom data is held on a computer.
data user	Someone who processes information about individuals, usually automatically.
data-base	A collection of interrelated data which is stored so that it is available for recall to authorized users. Its structure is independent of the programs which use the data.
DBS	Direct Broadcasting by Satellite. A geostationary satellite is used to retransmit broadcast television and radio services. Its signals can either be received by a master antenna and fed into a cable network or be received by individual domestic dish antennae, over a wide area.
decision-support system	A computer program which is designed to assist decision-making.
decryption	The conversion of a coded signal to a clear text form. (The opposite action to encryption.)
dialogue	Interchange of information between a user and a computer system.
digital	The representation of data or physical quantities by means of digits (discrete elements).

digital signal	An electronic signal that is defined in terms of a set of discrete and discontinuous values, and whose various states are at discrete intervals apart. Computers use data in digital form.
digitization	Conversion of an analogue signal to a digital one.
disc	1 The common name for a flat circular disc coated with a magnetic recording material and used by computer systems for storing digital data. 2 Video disc/compact disc – an optical device for storing the digital representation of audio and video signals.
download	The process of obtaining a computer-held file from a distant location by means of a communications channel, such as a telephone line. Commonly used as a verb and as a communications program command.
duplex systems	1 Full duplex system: A telecommunications system which allows data or messages to travel in both directions simultaneously. 2 Half duplex system: A telecommunications system which allows information to travel in both directions but only in one direction at a time. It requires a special procedure to change the direction of information flow.
EFTPOS	Electronic Funds Transfer at the Point Of Sale. Any payment by a customer to a retailer which is processed electronically rather than by a paper voucher. The payment is initiated by a financial transaction card.
electronic cottage	A term coined by Alvin Toffler to refer to a shift of work from large centralized units to smaller units and ultimately to the home, this being made possible by improvements in telecommunications and computing.
electronic data interchange	The use of computer networks for tasks such as ordering and invoicing in order to save money and improve efficiency.
electronic funds transfer (EFT)	Any message for the transfer of funds which is delivered electronically either by a telecommunications network or by magnetic tape or disk.
electronic mail	A means of sending text messages to individuals or groups of individuals using a computer network. The sender inputs a message to the computer via a terminal, and the receiver uses his own terminal to check whether there are any messages for him and to read or respond to the messages.
encryption	The conversion of a normal text signal to a coded form for security reasons.
ergonomics	The study of human beings in relationship to their environment and the engineering of that environment for comfort, efficiency and safety.
facsimile (fax)	A technique for transmitting text and black and white pictures over the telephone network using synchronized scanning at the transmitter and receiver. The image to be transmitted is broken down into lines of pixels, each of which can be represented by a single bit. To minimize the transmission time, the transmitter uses special codes to represent long sequences of black or white pixels.
fax	See facsimile.

fibre optic	A number of very fine fibres of glass or plastic through which light can be transmitted by total internal reflection, a special type of refraction. In telecommunications, electrical signals are converted to pulses of light for transmission and then converted back into electrical signals at the end of the cable. These fibres have a very large bandwidth, so many more items of information can be transmitted down a fibre optic cable than down a conventional copper telecommunications cable.
fixed service	A telecommunications service between a single transmitter and receiver, e.g. ground station to satellite, or microwave telephone link.
FMC	Flexible Manufacturing Cells. In which a group of machines is combined with automatic feeding, loading and unloading facilities.
FMS	Flexible Manufacturing System. A number of flexible manufacturing cells (FMCs) combined under the automatic control of a supervisory program.
frequency	The frequency of a periodic or repetitive waveform is the number of times the cycle of the waveform is repeated in a second. Frequency = 1/period, and is measured in hertz.
frequency division multiplexing	A process whereby two or more signals are transmitted over a common transmission channel by using different parts of the frequency range for each signal.
frequency-shift keying	A modulation method, employed e.g. in modems, in which a binary signal is represented by two different frequencies near the carrier frequency.
gateway	A device which enables two systems using different network protocols to communicate with one another.
geostationary orbit	A satellite orbit, about 35,780 km above the Earth in the plane of the equator, in which the satellite rotates at the same rate as the Earth and therefore stays fixed relative to a single point on the Earth's surface.
graphical kernel system (GKS)	An international standard (ISO 7942, 1985) for vector-drawing applications.
guard band	The narrow band of frequencies left on each side of a radio-frequency or television channel to prevent interference between channels.
hardware	The electrical and mechanical components of an IT system. For example, the hardware of the home computer comprises the keyboard, monitor, printer, disc drive, etc.
harmonics	The higher-order frequencies making up a repetitive signal. The frequencies of the harmonics are always integer multiples of the fundamental.
high-definition television (HDTV)	A television set in which finer details can be displayed on the screen. This is achieved by: 1 increasing the number of scan lines (>1000); 2 increasing the luminance and chrominance bandwidths; and 3 decreasing the colour dot size on the colour TV display tube.

hosts	The computers in a networking system that execute a user's program.
IBCN	Integrated Broadband Communications Network.
icon	A graphical representation of an object (e.g. file or document).
integrated circuit	A complete electronic circuit comprising transistors, resistors, diodes etc. which is constructed on a single piece of semiconductor material. Simple integrated circuits may contain the equivalent of a few tens of transistors, whilst the very large scale integrated devices contain several hundred thousand transistors.
interactive video/IV	A form of computer-based learning in which a video disc or cassette is controlled by a computer, enabling film, stills and sound to be incorporated into the teaching or training program.
interactive videotex	A videotex service, such as Prestel or Teletel, which provides a two-way communication link via telephone and/or packet-switched systems for consulting and receiving text and graphics stored in computer data-bases, and for inputting messages and instructions. Videotex systems are designed to be simple to operate, low-cost and able to cater for large numbers of users. In the UK, the term viewdata is sometimes used as a synonym for videotex.
ISDN	Integrated Services Digital Network. An integrated digital network used for more than one service, e.g. telephony and data transfer, ultimately for all services (including text and graphics).
ISO-OSI	The International Standardization Organization Open Systems Interconnection. A basic reference model in which the problem of interconnectivity of IT systems is simplified by dividing the communications system into seven layers, each with its own function and relationship to the other layers. The layers are application, presentation, session, transport, network, data link and the physical layer.
Laservision	The proprietary name for the video disc system developed by Philips.
local area network (LAN)	An electronic data network implemented with direct links between devices within a restricted geographical area.
menu	A set of options that a user may choose from - typically displayed as a list on the screen with options selected by a pointing device (e.g. a mouse)
memory	The memory of a computer is its main storage facility, primarily used to store the software needed to operate the computer.
mesh structure	A data-base structure in which there is more than one path from a parent node to some of the nodes in the data-base. Also known as complex structure or network structure.
message	An arbitrary amount of information whose beginning and end are defined or implied.
message switching	A communication technique in which each message is headed by a destination address and is passed from source to destination along a network.

MICR	Magnetic Ink Character Recognition. Used in banks to read details printed on cheques.
minitel	A generic term for the range of terminals provided by the French PTT to telephone subscribers to access the Teletel videotex services.
mobile services	A telecommunications service designed for use by mobile receivers, e.g. ship-to-shore radio and radio navigation.
modem	Modulator-Demodulator. A device that modulates a transmitted signal and demodulates a received signal at a data station; e.g. a digital signal from a computer is converted to an analogue signal for transmission over the telephone system and then back to digital form at the receiving end.
modulation	The variation of some characteristic (such as frequency or amplitude) of a signal (the carrier) in accordance with the instantaneous value of another signal (the message) to make the message signal more suitable for processing, storage or transmission.
mouse	A desktop pointing device used to move a cursor on a display screen and input positional signals to a computer system.
multiplexing	In telecommunications, the process of combining a number of signals so that they can share a single transmission channel. There are two main types, frequency division multiplexing and time division multiplexing.
multiprocessor	A computer system which has a number of separate processing units, commonly one main processor and a number of subordinate processors to handle input and output. This improves efficiency and also enables the system to be easily expanded to cope with more users.
multiprogramming	A means of allowing several programs to be run on the same computer apparently at the same time. This is often achieved by allotting each program a small fraction of the available processor time.
multi-user system	A system in which several users are connected to the main system via terminals and can run their programs at the same time. They can also share access to information stored in the main system.
natural language	The language which is used for normal human communication rather than the more restricted language used to communicate with computers.
noise	In electronics or telecommunications any disturbance or addition to the signal which tends to interfere with the transmission of information.
NUA	Network User Address. In packet-switched networks, the means of identifying a PAD by a unique 12-digit code including country, network, area and location.
optical fibre	A filament of glass or plastic through which a signal-modulated light beam may be transmitted to serve as a telecommunication medium.
optical publishing	Publication in the form of laser discs readable by computers, e.g. using CD-ROM or videodisc.
packet	A block of data with a defined format containing control and data fields.

packet-switched network	A digital telecommunications network in which the messages are broken into a series of discrete chunks or packets which are transmitted independently. Every packet contains additional bytes to define the destination address, so that the route for each packet can be selected dynamically. At the receiving end the packets are collected and reassembled into the correct sequence to regenerate the original message.
PAD	Packet Assembler/Disassembler. Equipment that prepares information for transmission by packet switching and assembles it again on receipt.
PBX/PBAX	Private Branch (Automatic) Exchange, as used by large companies requiring many telephones. It is connected to the public network by the equivalent of a trunk.
period	The time taken to complete one cycle of a repetitive wave. The reciprocal of the frequency.

Period = 1/frequency. |
picture element/pixel	In computer graphics a pixel is the smallest element of display space which can be altered independently.
PIN	Personal Identification Number. A number which must be entered by a user before a terminal can be used to make a transaction or transfer information, e.g. users of ATMs need to use a PIN number as well as a card.
portability	The ability to transfer programs and data between computer systems of different manufacturers.
program	A sequence of instructions which enable a computer to accomplish a particular task.
protocol	A set of rules that govern the orderly interaction between communicating entities.
PSDN	Packet Switched Digital (Data) Network. A network of devices which communicate with each other by transmitting packets addressed to particular destinations.
PTT	Post, Telephone and Telegraph Companies responsible for services such as telemetry, facsimile, television and data messages, e.g. British Telecom.
quantization	A process in which analogue signals, such as sound and light intensity, are sampled and coded into a set of numbers (a digital signal) which can be processed and stored by computers.
quantization error	This occurs when an analogue signal is converted to digital form. It is not always possible to give each signal sample exactly the same amplitude in binary terms as it had originally. The difference between the analogue and digital values is called quantization error.
RAM	Random Access Memory. A memory chip that can have data added to it and read from it, but the contents are lost when the power is switched off.

relational data-base	A data-base composed of a collection of two-dimensional tables of data. Its construction is complex, but, once constructed, finding the required data is easy and fast.
ring network	A local area network topology in which the transmission medium forms a continuous ring with peripheral devices connected to it via transceivers.
robot	A device which can accept an input signal, process the data provided, and activate a mechanical device to perform a desired action. Robots are used on some car assembly lines to perform repetitive tasks which are monotonous for human workers.
ROM	Read Only Memory. A particular type of memory chip used to store programs. The stored codes can be read, but not altered, by the processor. Often used for the start-up program of a microcomputer.
semantics	The study of signs and symbols and the meaning they represent (cf syntax).
sequential structure	A data-base structure which views the file as a sequence of records which are stored and accessed in a linear fashion. It is difficult to amend this data-base and access to the data is slow. It is also called a linear structure.
software	The programs used in a data processing or information system.
speech synthesis	The production of a sound corresponding to spoken words according to stored text or commands.
standard query language (SQL)	An international standard for specifying operations on a database.
standard generalised mark-up language (SGML)	An international standard for describing the formatted features of a document.
statistical multiplexer	Many channels are connected to a system, but only gain access when they become active. This enables active channels to gain access more often than if they were assigned a fixed set of times.
store-and-forward service	Conventional or electronic mail services in which mail is received at a 'sorting office' and then forwarded when transport is available.
SWIFT	Society for Worldwide Interbank Financial Telecommunications. An international financial transaction network.
switched network	A communication network which includes intermediate switching nodes between source and destination terminals.
switching centre	In telecommunications, a switching centre receives traffic from a local terminal or other switching centre and routes it either direct to its destination or via a trunk to another switching centre.
switching node	A node that routes messages or packets within a network.
synchronous transmission	A method of transmission used in data communications in which each bit is transmitted according to a given time sequence. The receiver and transmitter must maintain exact synchronization, but it can provide a higher bit rate than asynchronous transmission.

system	Any set of one or more computers, the associated software, peripherals, terminals, human operators, physical processes, information transfer means etc. that forms an autonomous whole capable of performing information processing and/or information transfer.
syntax	Rules concerning the arrangement or format of objects, especially words or commands.
Teletel	1 The French public videotex system.
	2 The network which connects individual telephone subscribers to service providers. It is made up of: (a) a PSTN telephone link to a videotex access point which connects through to the Transpac packet-switched network; (b) the Transpac packet-switched network; (c) the computers which host the services available.
teletex	A text communication service which includes message preparation facilities.
teletext	An information service which is broadcast by television. It is available on special television sets and specific pages of information may be requested by the user by means of a special keypad. It is a one-way service.
time division multiplexing	A means of using a high-capacity channel for several messages. Each message is allocated time intervals in the channel and the separate parts of each message are reconstructed at the end. It can only be used for digital messages.
token	A special message passing round the nodes in a network, its only function being to grant permission to use the transmission medium.
token bus	An access control technique for tree- or bus-structured local area networks, in which the stations are arranged in a logical ring (see token ring).
token passing	A network protocol in which each node in turn is passed a token giving it permission to transmit data around the network.
token ring	An access control technique for ring-structured local area networks in which a token message circulates around the ring. A terminal may transmit a message by seizing the token, launching the message and then releasing the token.
transmission	In telecommunications, transmission is the action of sending information, unchanged, from one place to another.
transponders	In telecommunications, devices which receive and retransmit signals. In satellite communications, the signal is amplified and retransmitted at a different frequency.
tree	1 A local area network structure in which terminals are attached to a shared transmission medium (usually a cable). The medium may have branches but no closed circuits.
	2 A method of organizing data in a data-base.
twisted pair	A signal transmission medium of two insulated cables arranged in a regular spiral pattern.

usability	A measure of the ease with which a system can be learnt and used effectively.
user interface	All aspects of a computer system which a user may have to interact with.
value added network (VAN)	A network that offers customers a service over and above the simple transfer of data, for example electronic mailbox facilities.
video-conferencing	A method of holding conferences via a telecommunications network, in which both vision and sound are used so that participants can both see and hear each other.
videotex	A two-way information service with a specified protocol and a page-oriented display.
VLSI	Very Large Scale Integration. Used in micro-electronics to describe a fabrication technology producing more than 1000 gates per chip.
wide area network (WAN)	An electronic data communications network usually spread over a wide geographical area and using public or intermediate carriers to effect transmission.
window	A subset of a display screen used for presentation and dialogue with a user.
WORM	Write-Once-Read-Many, the name for devices that allow users to store their own information on optical disc. Once created, the data cannot be modified.
X.25 protocol	CCITT recoomendation for packet-switched networks.
X.400	A series of CCITT recommendations for electronic mail and message handling systems.
X.500	A series of CCITT recommendations for services which provide the logical structures, and means for accesing them, for a global (or private) electronic directory.

Index